16⁰¹

THE FLOGGING OF PHINEHAS MCINTOSH

The Flogging of Phinehas McIntosh

A TALE OF COLONIAL FOLLY AND
INJUSTICE, BECHUANALAND 1933

Michael Crowder

Yale University Press
New Haven and London

Published with assistance from the Kingsley Trust Association
Publication Fund established by the Scroll and Key Society of
Yale College

Designed by Nancy Ovedovitz and set in Times Roman with Gill
Sans type by The Composing Room of Michigan. Printed in the
United States of America by Edwards Brothers, Ann Arbor,
Michigan.

Library of Congress Cataloging-in-Publication Data
Crowder, Michael, 1934–
The flogging of Phinehas McIntosh: a tale of colonial folly and
injustice: Bechuanaland 1933/Michael Crowder.
p.   cm.
Bibliography: p. 236
Includes index.
ISBN 0–300–04098–9
1. Botswana—History—To 1966. 2. McIntosh, Phinehas.
3. Khama, Tshekedi, 1905–1959. 4. Botswana—Race relations.
I. Title.
DT791.C76 1988   968'.1103—dc19
87–17632 CIP

The paper in this book meets the guidelines for permanence and
durability of the Committee on Production Guidelines for Book
Longevity of the Council on Library Resources.

10   9   8   7   6   5   4   3   2   1

For Margaret Black

CONTENTS

ILLUSTRATIONS

DRAMATIS PERSONAE

PRINCIPAL ACTORS IN THE SEROWE DRAMA, IN ALPHABETICAL ORDER

BATHOEN II	ruler of the Bangwaketse, close friend and distant relative of Tshekedi Khama
THE HON. LESLIE BLACKWELL	member of Parliament in Cape Town and legal adviser to the British High Commissioner in South Africa
T. ELLIOTT BOOKER	dispenser at the Serowe Hospital
DOUGLAS BUCHANAN	Tshekedi Khama's lawyer from Cape Town
THE REV. J. H. L. BURNS	resident missionary of the London Missionary Society in Serowe
THE REV. A. E. CHIRGWIN	Foreign Secretary of the London Missionary Society
SHIRLEY EALES	Administrative Secretary in the Office of the British High Commissioner in South Africa
VICE ADMIRAL E. R. G. R. EVANS	Acting British High Commissioner in South Africa and Commander-in-Chief of the Africa Station of the British Navy
J. D. A. GERMOND	Clerk to the Resident Magistrate at Serowe
SIR JOHN HARRIS	Secretary of the Anti-Slavery and Aborigines Protection Society

THE REV. ALBERT JENNINGS	'Tshekedi's missionary' and Secretary of the South Africa District Committee of the London Missionary Society
TSHEKEDI KHAMA	Regent of the Bangwato for his nephew, Seretse
J. B. KIESER	Tshekedi's lawyer in Mafeking
PERCIVALE LIESCHING	Political Secretary in the Office of the British High Commissioner in South Africa
PHINEHAS MCINTOSH	a young wagon builder in Serowe
HENRY MCNAMEE	a young motor mechanic in Serowe
DR. MORGAN	the Government Medical Officer in Serowe
K. T. MOTSETE	first Mongwato graduate, critic of Tshekedi
PHETHU MPHOENG	Tshekedi's cousin and erstwhile close adviser
CAPTAIN H. B. NEALE	Assistant Resident Commissioner of the Bechuanaland Protectorate
CAPTAIN G. E. NETTELTON	long-standing Resident Magistrate in Serowe
OSWALD PIROW	South African Minister of Railways and Defence
CAPTAIN J. W. POTTS	Nettelton's replacement as Resident Magistrate in Serowe
LIEUTENANT COLONEL CHARLES REY	Resident Commissioner of the Bechuanaland Protectorate
HEADMAN DISANG RADITLADI	Tshekedi's cousin
SIMON RATSHOSA	Tshekedi's nephew and long-standing opponent
HEADMAN PETER SEBINA	Tshekedi's secretary and close confidant
QUEEN SEMANE	widow of Khama III and mother of Tshekedi
HEADMAN SEROGOLA SERETSE	sometime Acting Chief for Tshekedi
SIR HERBERT STANLEY	British High Commissioner in South Africa (on leave in London)
T. W. SHAW	a trader in Palapye Road and close friend of Tshekedi
J. H. THOMAS	Secretary of State for the Dominions
MAJOR [?] WEBBER	in charge of the marine detachment

From the *Rand Daily Mail*, Johannesburg,
Tuesday, 12 September 1933

CENSORSHIP AT SEROWE

Official Reticence as to
Trouble in Bechuanaland

PEOPLE SURPRISED BY DEVELOPMENTS

Naval Force Passes
Through Kimberley

Evidently a strict official supervision is being exercised over all news from Bechuanaland, for the telegram from our Special Correspondent, which we print below, conveys in a postscript the information that the message has been "approved by Captain Neale, Government Secretary, Bechuanaland."

No further information as to the real nature of the trouble at Serowe has been allowed to leak out, but the name is given of the European who was tried and sentenced by the native court.

At Lobatsi our correspondent learned of a disturbance that occurred in that vicinity recently, as a result of which a 90-year-old headman of one of the tribes is serving a sentence of imprisonment. It seems that a show of force had to be made before he could be arrested.

Meanwhile the force of bluejackets and marines from the warships of the Africa Squadron passed through Kimberley by special train last night and are due at Palapye Road, the nearest station to Serowe, this afternoon.

OFFICIAL INQUIRY TO
BEGIN TO-DAY

Tense Expectancy in Territory

FROM OUR SPECIAL CORRESPONDENT

Mahalapye, Monday.

Although official reticence and the difficulty of rapid communication in Bechuanaland make it quite impossible as yet to determine with any measure of certainty the full seriousness of the troubles that have arisen in Serowe as a result of the alleged infliction of corporal punishment upon a European resident, Mr. McIntosh, by a native tribunal, it is quite apparent that the authorities take a more serious view of the incident than was at first realised.

At the moment fuller details of the affair cannot be made public, as an administrative inquiry into the incident will open at Palapye to-morrow morning. The inquiry, which will be of a public nature, will concern itself purely with the merits of the case, and the findings of the Commissioners will be submitted to the High Commissioner for whatever further action may be considered necessary.

The inquiry is to be conducted by Captain Neale, Government Secretary for the Protectorate, and Captain Nettelton, magistrate of Gaberones.

The commissioners are spending the night at Mahalapye, and in a statement to me this evening Captain Neale made it clear that until the inquiry is held nothing more can be said about the incident than has already been officially disclosed in the Press.

'The inquiry,' he said, 'will be concerned with the facts of the case, and will be of a purely administrative character.'

IN THE DARK

The civilian community in these parts of this vast territory decline to be drawn in regard to the delicate situation that has arisen farther north, and most of them are obviously in the dark as to what is really taking place. Rumour, however, is furiously active, and the news that a Naval force is on the way to the seat of the disturbance has created a profound sensation throughout the territory.

To-morrow's inquiry is being awaited with tense expectancy, and until then it is not permissible to say more about the case or the nature of the trouble.

PROLOGUE

Rey Versus Tshekedi

In the large village of Serowe on the eastern edge of the Kalahari Desert a series of affrays took place one Sunday afternoon in 1933 whose far-reaching consequences none of the antagonists, black or white, could at the time have foreseen. On that 13 August, two young white men went to the hut of a black villager, Rasetompi, where beer was being brewed illegally. They demanded that Rasetompi give them some, but he would not open the door. So Phinehas McIntosh, son of one of the four licensed white blacksmiths in Serowe, and his friend Henry McNamee smashed it down and seized some beer. Though Rasetompi was by his own admission afraid to tackle them, his wife and a friend tried to stop them from taking the beer. For their pains they were both hit by Phinehas and Henry, who were armed with a knife and a bicycle chain between them.[1]

Around sunset that same day Phinehas, Henry and a Coloured friend, Attie Klink, engaged in another fight in the usually peaceful capital of the Bangwato, the largest of the eight Tswana Tribes that comprised the British-ruled Bechuanaland Protectorate. They were standing outside a small thatched hut which belonged to Phinehas, talking with two white friends, Aleck Jamieson and his sister, Annie. With them was Baikgantshi Dikgobo, a young Mongwato girl with whom Phinehas was currently living. When a Mongwato youth called Ramananeng passed by the hut, Baikgantshi asked him why he had shouted to her friend Sekgabe that morning: 'Good-bye, you girls who carry on indecent intercourse with white boys.' On hearing what his girlfriend was saying to Ramananeng, Phinehas, who spoke Setswana fluently, rushed out of his hut and knocked him down. According to Phinehas, this was not before Ramananeng had hit Baikgantshi.[2] Both Henry and Attie joined in the attack on Ramananeng, until the two Jamiesons stopped the fight.

Ramananeng made his way home bleeding and badly wounded. Shortly afterwards he decided to report the matter to the young ruler of the Bangwato, Tshekedi Khama. In the account given by Phinehas, he himself also planned to report the matter to the Chief but was dissuaded from doing so by some headmen who assured him that Ramananeng was sorry for what he had done.[3] When Phinehas saw Ramananeng on his way to the Chief, he gave chase and caught up with him just after he had entered a hut belonging to an old man called Mokwati, in which a woman was in confinement. Arriving at the hut, Phinehas and his friends asked for Ramananeng but were told he was not there and had not been allowed to enter because of the woman's condition. The young men were convinced their quarry was inside, and so they smashed the door down. On finding Ramananeng inside, they pulled him out and knocked him about some more, only stopping when Aleck Jamieson once again intervened. Despite being hit on the chin by Attie Klink, Aleck succeeded in putting an end to the fight—but not before old Mokwati had been knocked down. Ramananeng had been so badly bruised that he was unable to defend himself, and his condition was such that Aleck Jamieson said 'his blood almost went up'.[4]

Later that evening Henry McNamee had a fight with another Mongwato called Katse, and he and Phinehas also jointly attacked yet one more Mongwato, named Kelebetse.[5]

Only one of the incidents was in the end reported to Chief Tshekedi. Rasetompi was afraid to lay a complaint because he would risk punishment by the Chief if it became known that beer had been brewed in his hut, since consumption of alcohol had long since been outlawed in Gamangwato by Tshekedi's father, Khama III, and Tshekedi himself was a strong advocate of temperance. Kelebetse, for his part, was frightened to bring a case before the Chief because his parents had warned him that he should never be found in the company of Phinehas. Thus it was only the attack on Ramananeng that was brought to the attention of Tshekedi.[6]

The immediate upshot of these assaults was that Chief Tshekedi ordered McIntosh to be flogged—a judgement that the British Resident Commissioner, Lieutenant Colonel Charles Rey, considered outrageous: Tshekedi had overstepped one of the sacred rules of British imperialism by sentencing a white man in a 'native' court, and the incident was soon to be fiercely debated in London by press, Parliament and public. At the same time, Rey was delighted, as he felt he now had an opportunity to depose the young Chief with whom he had clashed ever since assuming command of the territory three years earlier. He looked on the strong-willed Tshekedi as an obstacle to the development of the Bechuanaland Protectorate, which he viewed as being in disarray. Shortly after his arrival in Mafeking in

October 1929 to take over the administration of the region, he had written: 'I have formed the most serious opinion as to the state of affairs in the Protectorate. The white settlers are seething with discontent at the ineptitude and apathy of the administration. The natives are utterly out of hand; the old chiefs like Khama (who was a great King) have died, their successors are incompetent or drunkards and have no control over their peoples; respect for white men is diminishing, seditious propaganda is starting; progress is nil; and the Dutch in Cape Colony look on and grin.'[7]

Rey's response to the state of affairs in what is now the Republic of Botswana differed little from that of Leopold Amery who, as Secretary of State for the Dominions, had appointed him to be the next Resident Commissioner of the Protectorate. In 1927 Amery had toured the Bechuanaland Protectorate and neighbouring Basutoland and Swaziland. He had been shocked that the British, 'instead of spending money and thought on developing their resources and, still more important, raising the general standard of their peoples', had been content 'to protect them from outside interference, leaving them to carry on under a very unprogressive form of indirect tribal rule as museum pieces, human Whipsnades, in an Africa that was being transformed at a breathless pace.'[8]

In the late 1920s, the Bechuanaland Protectorate was one of the most backward territories in Britain's colonial empire. Covering a vast area, it consisted mostly of the Kalahari Desert. The main income of its sparse population of two hundred thousand came from the export of cattle and labour to the neighbouring Union of South Africa. Then only those living below the twenty-two degrees south line of latitude, which bisected the Protectorate, could sell their labour in the mines or on the farms of the Union, since men recruited from further north were considered to be too prone to diseases brought on by the cold winters of South Africa. At the same time, weight restrictions were placed on cattle imported from the Bechuanaland Protectorate, which effectively excluded the bulk of livestock raised by blacks because the majority of their beasts were too light. The food supplies of the black population were jeopardised by regular droughts. A small number of white settlers, concentrated on farms on the banks of Limpopo, cultivated maize and fattened cattle for export, but by and large the main foreign earnings of the Protectorate came from the remittances of its migrant labourers working in the Union.[9]

The basic problem of the Bechuanaland Protectorate was not so much its poverty as its uncertain political future. When the Union of South Africa was established in 1910 under the terms of the British South Africa Act of 1909, provision was made by Parliament for the eventual incorporation into it of the three neighbouring British territories of Basutoland, the Bechuanaland Protectorate and Swaziland. But under Article 151 of the Act this could not take place unless

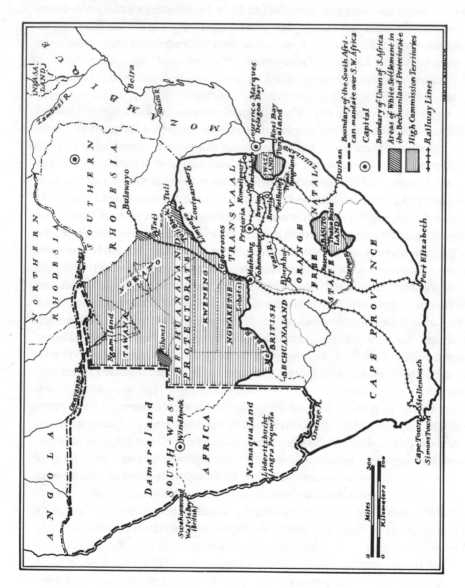

Map 1. Southern Africa c. 1933.

Parliament was satisfied that black interests would be safeguarded, and in any case not before the black inhabitants of the three territories had been consulted and their opinion 'most carefully considered'.[10] In 1925 Amery affirmed that no decision about transfer would be taken 'until all sections of the population have had an opportunity of expressing their views and until such representations have been considered by His Majesty's Government'.[11]

Pending transfer, the three territories were administered by the Governor-General of the Union in his capacity as their High Commissioner. Hence they were known collectively as the High Commission Territories. As High Commissioner, the Governor-General was represented in each territory by a Resident Commissioner, who was responsible for its day-to-day administration but had to refer all matters of policy to him. At the time of Rey's appointment as Resident Commissioner, the Governor-General and High Commissioner was the Earl of Athlone, brother of Queen Mary. He was the last to hold both offices simultaneously. As High Commissioner he reported not to the Colonial Office but the Dominions Office, which had been established in 1925. He had been made responsible for the High Commission Territories on the grounds that their destiny was to become part of the dominion of South Africa. Although the High Commission Territories had been administered by the Colonial Office before the creation of the Dominions Office, they were staffed not by members of the Colonial Service but rather, in the case of the Bechuanaland Protectorate, by former police officers. The dominant role of the police in the administration of the Protectorate was epitomised in the courtesy title of Lieutenant Colonel given to, and used by, each Resident Commissioner in his capacity as Officer Commanding the Bechuanaland Protectorate Police.

To be fair to the Protectorate officials, they had little incentive to improve conditions in a territory which was due to be handed over to another master and whose present master was not prepared to supply them with any funds for development. Indeed, the taxes they imposed on the black population barely paid for their salaries. They themselves were thinly spread on the ground and as a result were largely bound to their desks, answering queries from Protectorate Headquarters which, bizarrely, were located outside the territory in what was known as the Imperial Reserve in Mafeking, fifteen miles across the border with the Union. The Resident Magistrates, as the local British administrators were called (because they had judicial as well as administrative functions), had little time, let alone the resources, to tour the vast stretches of territory which came under their authority. This they left largely to the eight Chiefs of the Tswana states that had been placed under British Protection in 1885 and had collectively given their name to the new British Territory: Bechuana was the British orthography for Batswana, meaning the Tswana people.

The Tswana Chiefs exercised considerable individual autonomy, both because the British administration was so sparse and because the Batswana were one of the few African peoples who had not been conquered by the Europeans but had more or less voluntarily accepted their Protection. Threatened with takeover in 1885 either by the Boers of the Transvaal or the Germans of South West Africa, they had opted for British Protection as the lesser of the evils then confronting them. Their acceptance of British Protection was reinforced ten years later during a trip to London by three of the leading Tswana Chiefs—Khama III, ruler of the Bangwato, the largest state enclosed by the Protectorate, Sebele I of the Bakwena, the senior of the Tswana states in the Protectorate, and Bathoen I of the Bangwaketse, its southernmost state. The Chiefs had gone to London to protest against the impending transfer of their territory to the British South Africa Company, which then ruled the neighbouring British colony of Rhodesia. In securing promises from Joseph Chamberlain, as Colonial Secretary, that they would remain under British Protection, they also gained a commitment that as far as their internal affairs were concerned they would continue to rule their people 'much as at present'.[12] This they subsequently did, with relatively little interference from the British. It was this situation that so distressed Amery on his visit in 1927.

While Amery wanted the administration of the Protectorate to be reformed and its resources developed, it was not with an eye to a future independent of the Union but rather with regard to the early transfer of its peoples, both black and white, to South African administration. Amery's goal was that the three High Commission Territories, efficiently managed and with well-established white farming communities in Swaziland and the Bechuanaland Protectorate, would provide a counterbalance to the Afrikaners in the Union.[13] To achieve this task in the Bechuanaland Protectorate, Amery appointed Charles Rey to be the 'new broom to sweep out the cobwebs of administrative neglect'.[14]

Rey's appointment as Resident Commissioner was by any criterion an unusual one. His career had been largely that of a Home civil servant in Britain who had worked as assistant to William Beveridge, helping him to set up the labour exchanges in 1909 and effectively acting as their 'general manager'. As Beveridge's biographer, José Harris, has written, Rey was 'a bluff, energetic, extrovert character with considerable experience in industrial arbitration. He had little of Beveridge's intellectual power, but he proved to be an extremely forceful departmental negotiator and . . . was particularly skilful at resisting Treasury control.'[15] In 1912 he helped establish a national insurance scheme but within a year had managed to quarrel not only with the Treasury but also with the Finance and Establishment Departments of the Board of Trade, which accused the Insurance Office of 'heading straight for complete independence'.[16] During the First World

1. Lieutenant Colonel Charles Fernand Rey, Resident Commissioner of the Bechuanaland Protectorate, seated behind his desk at Protectorate Government House, Mafeking (Rey Collection, Botswana Society).

War he served in various government departments, rising to the position of Director-General of National Labour Supply in 1918 at the age of forty-one.

Rey's only administrative experience in Africa was in its one truly independent state, Ethiopia, to which he was sent on secondment as General Manager of the Abyssinian Corporation in 1919. This had been established the year before to advance British commercial interests in the country. Though he spent just a year in Ethiopia, it left a lasting impression on him. It also brought him deep personal tragedy: his two sons died there within a month of each other from dysentery.[17] In June 1920 Rey returned to London to take over the administration of the head office of the Corporation. In this capacity he paid four more visits to Ethiopia, where he became a friend of Ras Tafari, the future Emperor Haile Selassie. His travels in the country were recorded in two books: *Unconquered Abyssinia as It Is To-day,* which he wrote in 1923,[18] and *In the Country of the Blue Nile,* published four years later.[19] In both he captures the spirit of a land and people that continued to fascinate him even when he was immersed in the problems of the Bechuanaland Protectorate.[20] Such was his enthusiasm for the country that he also ventured into its history with *The Romance of the Portuguese in Abyssinia,* published in 1929.[21]

His friendship with and admiration of Ras Tafari resulted in his appointment as Commander of the Order of the Star of Ethiopia, an honour of which he was extremely proud. He wrote sympathetically of the future Emperor's problems: 'A Regent—however capable and hard-working he may be—who is hampered and obstructed at every turn by powerful and hostile reactionary elements, and forced to deal with every detail personally, owing to lack of competent assistance, cannot be expected to cope with the modern requirements of the State whose destinies he is striving to direct.'[22] Rey might have been writing prophetically of the way he came to see his own plight as Resident Commissioner of the Bechuanaland Protectorate.

Rey's experience in Ethiopia was hardly one that made him the obvious choice to run a British colonial territory in Africa. In the first place, Ethiopia was an independent state; in the second, it was vastly different in character from the Bechuanaland Protectorate. But what Amery was looking for was really good new men, 'keen both on making the most of the native, and on development generally', to work in the High Commission Territories.[23] He chose Rey to lead the Bechuanaland Protectorate Administration as a man who would go 'all out to put the Bechuana on their feet economically'.[24] And certainly Rey was determined not to disappoint him. As he wrote a month after his arrival in the Protectorate, 'Unless things are dealt with drastically and promptly, I foresee an upheaval in the next few years. And so I am going out with both hands to reform, develope, discipline and organise. It will be a tough job, and a long one. For example there has never been any legal definition of the Chiefs' powers—they practically do as they like—punish, fine, tax and generally play hell. Of course their subjects hate them but daren't complain to us; if they did their lives would be made impossible.'[25]

For the time being, Rey was only Assistant Resident Commissioner, waiting for the departure of the substantive Resident Commissioner, Lieutenant Colonel R. M. Daniel—'the damnedest old fool I have ever struck, the most incompetent bungler, and the most pig-headed ass'.[26] So, as he noted, 'until I am really in charge I can't do as much as I want—or indeed anything really drastic and sweeping.'[27] But he had no doubt that as soon as he took over he would set about codifying and limiting the powers of the Chiefs. In this he was to be bitterly opposed by Tshekedi Khama, the twenty-three-year-old Regent of the Bangwato, who was the first of the Protectorate Chiefs he met, and on whom he commented, 'He is a cunning slippery devil I fancy'.[28] That day, though he did not realise it, Rey had met his nemesis.

Tshekedi Khama was only twenty years old when he became Regent of the Bangwato, who constituted nearly half the population of the Protectorate. He was called to take office in November 1925 on the death of his half-brother, Sekgoma II, whose heir, Seretse, was a minor aged four. Tshekedi was the second son of

Khama III, often known to Europeans as 'the Great'. Khama had died only two years before, when he was well into his nineties. Tshekedi was his second son by his fourth wife, Semane, whom he had wed in 1900 after a series of marriages that had ended in death or divorce. Under the rule of succession by male primogeniture observed by the Tswana states, Tshekedi was the adult male closest in line to the throne and as such was the first choice as Regent for the young Chief Seretse (see Genealogy).

Tshekedi's father had presided over the affairs of the Bangwato for nearly fifty years. He did so first as an independent ruler, or *kgosi,* for a year in 1872–73 and continuously from 1875–85, and then as a protected Chief under the British until his death in 1923. He had become a Christian in 1860, and when he succeeded to the Kingship in 1875 he made Christianity the official religion of his state. Much admired by the missionaries and deeply respected by the British Administration, he did much to hasten the incorporation of his state into the expanding economy of South Africa. In the early days of his rule he and his headmen profited by servicing the wagoners from South Africa on their way through Bangwato territory to the north and by selling hunting products from the Kalahari, in particular ivory, ostrich feathers and skins, to the Cape for export to Europe and America. Khama introduced the notion of private property into his state, dividing up the national herd among members of the royal family and commoner headmen, and by the time of his death he had a large personal fortune, mainly held in cattle. But the early prosperity of his reign did not survive into colonial times. The great rinderpest epizootic of 1895–96 all but annihilated the Bangwato herds, while the British South Africa Company's railway from South Africa to Rhodesia, which passed along the eastern border of Gamangwato, brought an end to the northbound wagon trade and marginalised Serowe, the capital of the Bangwato. Cattle which had sold at £25 in 1900 now fetched only £1.[29]

When Khama died he left to his elder son and heir, Sekgoma II, a well-administered state, many members of whose royal family and rich commoner-headman élite had obtained education in South Africa for themselves (or at least for their sons), and where Christianity was the official religion. The resident Christian missionary rather than the Mongwato priest-doctor (*ngaka*) offered up prayers on all major state occasions. Initiation rites and circumcision had been abolished and polygamy effectively discouraged. In Serowe, the capital, and in the larger towns and villages, some three hundred white traders and artisans and their families lived under the Chief's protection. He gave them plots of land on which to erect their stores or workshops and build their living quarters. (In Serowe whites and blacks lived in close proximity to each other; only the white administrative officials lived in a segregated area known as the Camp, some way outside the centre of the town—see map 2.) He it was who issued them permits to trade or

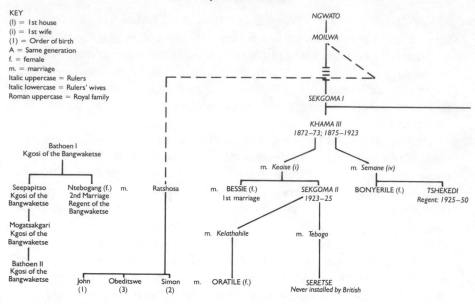

KEY
(I) = 1st house
(i) = 1st wife
(1) = Order of birth
A = Same generation
f. = female
m. = marriage
Italic uppercase = Rulers
Italic lowercase = Rulers' wives
Roman uppercase = Royal family

practice their professions. In all matters other than the administration of the law, the white community of Gamangwato looked to the Bangwato ruler rather than the British administrator as their Chief, sometimes even taking their disputes to him for settlement. Indeed, the white traders seemed to prefer the speedy justice offered by Khama to that of the colonial courts.[30] Traders and artisans depended on the Chief for their livelihood, since if they offended him he could oppose renewal of their permits or even direct his people to do business with rival traders.

The missionaries, too, were deeply dependent on his favour, for Khama had insisted that only one mission proselytise in his state, in this case the London Missionary Society (of Congregationalist persuasion). This gave him a peculiar hold over the missionaries. Because only he could give permission for missionaries to reside within his borders, if the LMS offended him, it was within his power to allow Methodists or Anglicans to establish their churches, an eventuality the LMS missionaries would not risk. Even the Resident Magistrate was beholden to him. Technically the superior of the Chief, the Resident Magistrate was obliged to co-operate with Khama rather than give him orders, since he did not have the staff to administer directly the huge Bangwato state, or Bamangwato Reserve as it was known in colonial parlance. With only a few black police at his disposal, and assisted usually by one white clerk and a black interpreter, the British administrator had to rely on the co-operation of Khama and his successor, Sekgoma II, to administer the Reserve.

These two Chiefs, thus, dominated the lives of the European and Bangwato

The Bangwato Royal Family

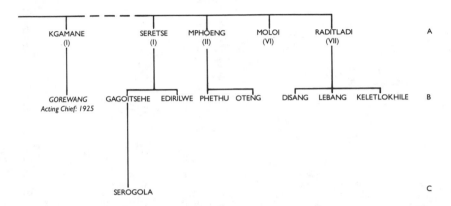

residents of their dusty and sprawling capital. Serowe had only been founded in 1902, but within a few years it had become the largest African, as distinct from European, town south of the equator, with a population of nearly thirty thousand. Its focal point was the *kgotla,* or forum, where the Chief presided over an assembly of adult males and administered justice or discussed administrative decisions. A flat open ground of trampled earth, it was flanked on one side by a hill, on whose lower slopes stood the Chief's house and offices, and on the other by his cattle kraal.

Spreading out in all directions from the *kgotla* were the houses of the Europeans and Bangwato, all located within specific wards, each of which was presided over by a headman. The Europeans and a few rich Bangwato lived in European-style houses. But the majority of the inhabitants dwelt in huts whose thatches glistened in the sun. European-style compounds, like those of the Bangwato, were demarcated by hedges or by fences of thick wooden poles. Between them ran wide roads with surfaces turned to sand by ox-wagons and the few cars and lorries owned mainly by Europeans.

In the context of relations between black and white in southern Africa a spirit of formal cordiality existed between Europeans and Bangwato, though there was little social intercourse between the two groups: the whites, for instance, had their own church. But everyone, including the British Administration, treated the Chiefs—whether Khama III or Sekgoma—with courtesy and a modicum of deference.

The attitude of the Administration to the ruler of the Bangwato underwent a

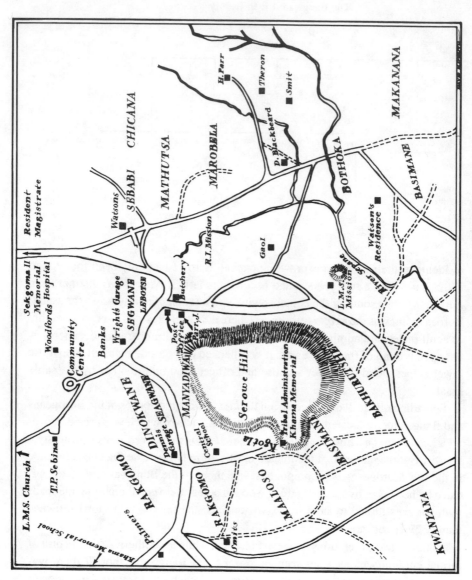

Map 2. Map of Central Serowe, after Neil Parsons.

categorical if subtle change when Tshekedi took over rule of the Bangwato. In the first place, British officials seem to have construed the fact that he was a Regent as somehow making him a second-class Chief. Thus, much to his irritation, they referred to him as Acting Chief, a term the Batswana would use only for one who acted for a *Kgosi* (whether King, Chief or Regent) while he was absent or temporarily incapacitated. In Tswana custom, the Regent had 'all the powers, rights, privileges and duties of the Chief'[31] until such time as the minor for whom he was acting was ready to assume office. In the second place, the British administration found it difficult to deal with the slender youth, straight from studying for his matriculation at Fort Hare College in South Africa, on the same basis as the revered Khama or the respected Sekgoma, who was in his mid-fifties when he died. They tended to treat Tshekedi as the schoolboy he had been up until the day he took on the Regency at the age of twenty. Tshekedi, who despite the rather willowy look of his youth had a strong, almost obstinate, character and was as determined as Rey ever was to get his own way, resented bitterly the condescension of the British officials. He was after all ruler of the largest of the Tswana states, and although he had little direct experience of government, he was very conscious that he was the son of Khama and expected the British Administration to consult with him rather than give him direct orders. 'I want to be taught how to govern my Country, not to be taught how to be governed', he was to write plaintively to them four years after he came to the throne.[32]

In the first years of his regency Tshekedi had to use all his considerable resources of determination, political skill and intellect to assert his authority not only with the British but also with his own people. While there was no question that he was the 'correct person' to hold the office of Regent, he took over control of the Bangwato state amid a bitter faction fight within the royal family as to which set of advisers would have his ear.

Since the turn of the century the powerful Ratshosa family, commoner by status but with royal ancestry, had acted as chief advisers, first to Khama and then to Sekgoma II. They had consolidated their hold on state affairs by judicious marriages into the royal family. Many members of the royal family were resentful of the hold the Ratshosas had over their Chief, none more than Phethu Mphoeng, Tshekedi's cousin (see Genealogy). He had married a daughter of Khama and was his representative in the important district of Mmadinare, thus enjoying a degree of protection from his monarch. But this ceased with Khama's death in 1923. Almost immediately on the accession of Sekgoma II the Ratshosas set about the destruction of Phethu. They succeeded in convincing Sekgoma that he and some other members of the royal family were plotting to assassinate him. So Phethu and his leading supporters were sent on 'the road to Rhodesia', as exile was euphemistically described by the Bangwato.[33]

2. Tshekedi Khama, Regent of the Bangwato, photographed on his visit to London when he was aged twenty-four (*Illustrated London News*).

Shortly before Sekgoma II died he became reconciled with Phethu, who returned to Gamangwato determined to avenge himself on the Ratshosas. Phethu was able to gain the young Regent's confidence and support almost from the day he returned to Serowe from Fort Hare. No doubt Tshekedi allied himself with Phethu because he feared the considerable power that had accrued over the past twenty years to the three Ratshosa brothers, each of whom, though his nephew, was old enough to be his father. He must also have quickly perceived that the Ratshosas were extremely unpopular with the people. By supporting his cousin, Phethu Mphoeng, against his nephews, Tshekedi not merely rid himself of an irksome control, but established his popularity with the people, who resented the Ratshosas' arrogant ways.

Tshekedi also demonstrated that ruthless streak in his character that was to prove the downfall of many an opponent in the years to come. Thus he deprived the senior Ratshosa brother, Johnnie, of his position as Tribal Secretary, which was equivalent to being Chief Executive of the Bamangwato Tribal Administration, and excluded the two younger brothers, Simon and Obeditse, from his counsels. When in pique at their fall from power they openly flaunted Tshekedi's office, he summoned them from a wedding they were attending to his *kgotla,* the forum in which all judicial, political and administrative decisions were made. When they refused to come, he called them again and then sentenced them to a flogging for disrespect. They protested that as royal headmen they could not be so punished. Furious, Bangwato attending the *kgotla* thereupon seized Johnnie and thrashed him, while Simon and Obeditse escaped to their house, returned with guns, and shot at Tshekedi. They wounded him slightly before they fled for safety to the Resident Magistrate's compound. In the meantime Tshekedi organised a party of men, led by the Ratshosas' old enemy, Phethu Mphoeng, to burn down their not inconsiderable property, the traditional punishment for traitors. As he said later, in pre-colonial times they would have been killed for their crime. The British courts imprisoned the two younger brothers for attempted murder, while the eldest brother and several other dissident members of the royal family, including Simon's wife, were sent into exile.[34]

Within three months of his appointment as Regent, Tshekedi had shown that he could be a ruthless opponent, and demonstrated this clearly. Indeed, he clashed on so many occasions with the British Administration in his first years as Regent that in 1927 Resident Commissioner Ellenberger wrote sadly before his departure, 'It is not without sorrow that after 37 years of service among the natives of the Bechuanaland Protectorate and having earned the respect of previous chiefs and enjoyed their friendship and confidence I see myself treated in this way on the eve of my retirement by a young and inexperienced Regent, who two years ago, was still at school.'[35]

Some of the matters over which Tshekedi took issue with the British seem on the surface quite trivial, such as the siting of a borehole in his capital during a period of intense drought, or the effects of a Circular concerning firearms or a new Marriage Proclamation. Others were more obviously of major import, such as the religious and personal freedoms of his subjects.[36]

Whatever the rights or wrongs of Tshekedi's stand on all his disputes with the Administration, he very early on learnt how to deal with the British bureaucracy. He quickly came to appreciate that in the right circumstances the pen could be mightier than the sword. Thus when he was sent a letter requesting him to do something he did not like, he would at first fail to reply to it. After several requests for an answer or report on action taken, he would send in a lengthy letter that had been vetted by his lawyer in Mafeking. This ensured further delay as it was referred to headquarters in Mafeking. From the start Tshekedi had the measure of the bluff policemen who were appointed to supervise the affairs of his Reserve. As he told the High Commissioner several years later, 'We have still to learn that our present Magistrates possess any better and superior qualifications over chiefs so as to entitle them to exercise control over native tribes.'[37] Tshekedi was as well educated as most (and better than some) of the administrators overseeing him, and what is more he was at constant pains to improve himself. Thus after a harrowing cross-examination by the counsel for the Ratshosa brothers who had been put on trial for his attempted murder by the British Administration, he sent off to Juta the Cape Town bookseller for three volumes on the Law of Evidence.[38]

If at times the administration felt that Tshekedi was merely being cussed in his opposition, it was because they did not appreciate the very delicate political position of a Regent in Batswana politics. Although as Regent he had all the powers of a Chief, if he abused these or exercised them incompetently, he could be replaced.[39] Furthermore, he was determined to hand over Seretse's patrimony to him intact. He knew that the most serious charge that could be made against him would be that he was squandering his nephew's inheritance. Again, what the Administration saw as desirable for his people often seemed impolitic to his own eyes.

The lack of understanding by the British Administration of the position of the Tswana Chief was brought out clearly when the Ratshosa brothers took out a civil action against Tshekedi in 1927 for compensation for the destruction of their houses and property in the aftermath of their attempted assassination of him. The Resident Magistrate accepted that Tshekedi had the right under customary law to burn the houses of subjects who had committed treason against him. But the Ratshosas were not prepared to let the matter rest there, and from their prison cells lodged an appeal with the Special Court of the Protectorate, presided over by Patrick Duncan, the future Governor-General of South Africa. Duncan gave judgement in favour of the Ratshosas. Tshekedi was furious at the ruling on two counts: in the first place, it was against custom for a subject to take his ruler to court; in the second place, if the obligation of the British to respect the right of the Tswana rulers to administer customary law meant anything, then he had the right to deal with treacherous members of the community in the way he had. He therefore determined to appeal against Duncan's judgement to the Judicial Committee of the Privy Council.

Both the Resident Commissioner of the day, Jules Ellenberger, and the High Commissioner, Lord Athlone, strongly advised him against this course, fearing that he would lose a case which was bound to be expensive and that, even if he won it, he would not be able to recoup the costs from the now impoverished Ratshosas. Tshekedi rejected Athlone's advice and was proved right in his course of action: in its judgement handed down in 1931, the Privy Council held that he did have the right to inflict the punishment he did on the Ratshosas but expressed the hope that this aspect of Bangwato customary law would be altered in future.[40] From Tshekedi's point of view his stand had been vindicated, and his deep faith in the British judicial system reinforced.

Again, the lack of mutual comprehension between Administration and traditional ruler was demonstrated by the clash between the two over the status of the Basarwa, or 'Bushmen', living in the Bangwato Reserve. Simon Ratshosa had captured the headlines of the South African and British press during his trial in 1926 by declaring that the Basarwa living in the Bamangwato Reserve were little better than slaves. An embarrassed Administration, whose home government had recently agreed to sign the League of Nations' Anti-Slavery Convention, reacted by issuing what came to be known as the Athlone Declaration. This was read out by the royal Earl on a visit to Serowe in August 1926. While Athlone did not accept that the Basarwa were slaves, they 'were a backward people who serve the Mangwato in return for the food and shelter they receive.' Though he agreed that many Basarwa were contented with their lot, 'the Government will not allow any tribe to demand compulsory service from any other and wants to encourage the Masarwa to support themselves.' Athlone then put the onus on the Chief and his headmen 'to help these people to stand on their feet.'[41] Tshekedi was incensed by the declaration, both because it was issued on what he had understood to be a purely ceremonial visit by the High Commissioner, without any prior consultation, and because he considered the Administration to have completely misunderstood the relationship between the Bangwato 'masters' and their Basarwa 'servants'. The issue was one that was to preoccupy Tshekedi and the Administration for the next ten years, and bring him into conflict with Colonel Rey on numerous occasions.[42]

But the most dramatic clash, and the one on which Rey first really became aware of Tshekedi's stubbornness and skill as an opponent, was over the attempts by the Administration to introduce mining into his Reserve.

The British Administration saw mining as the one way to realise Amery's ambitions of raising revenue for the development of the Bechuanaland Protectorate. To this end the High Commission and the British South Africa Company had arranged to implement the Concession the Company had negotiated with Khama III in 1893. As a douceur to Tshekedi the High Commission had persuaded the Company to improve the terms of the Concession. In January 1929 Tshekedi was handed the revised agreement while paying a visit to Captain the Hon. Bede Clifford, the Imperial Secretary in Cape Town, who was responsible for the overall administration of the High Commission Territories on behalf of the Governor-General. Instead of signing it immediately, as Clifford had expected, Tshekedi took the revised Concession away to read. For the next four years he did everything in his power to prevent the implementation of the agreement. It was not that he was opposed to mining in his territory in principle. He believed that at this stage in the development of his people improvement of their agriculture and dairy farming should be given priority. He had seen what mining could do to black people on his visit to Johannesburg. He believed that once mining by a South African company was begun in his territory, the day would soon come when it would be incorporated into South Africa and his people would be dispossessed of their land as so many of the Tswana peoples in the Union had been.

In his struggle with the British Administration, Tshekedi was assisted by the London Missionary Society, in particular by the Secretary of its South African District Committee, the Rev. Alfred Jennings, who had spent many years as resident missionary in Serowe, and by Douglas Buchanan, a King's Counsel based in Cape Town. Together they forged an alliance that Tshekedi relied on in his battles with the British Administration over the next twenty years.

The British Administration were at first bewildered by Tshekedi's opposition, since they believed that mining would bring internal prosperity to the Batswana and provide them with an alternative to seeking employment abroad on the farms and mines of South Africa. Furthermore, the mining companies would buy up the cattle that the Batswana could not sell in South Africa because of the weight restrictions and veterinary regulations imposed by that country. When Charles Rey arrived in Mafeking to take up his duties he gave his support to the stand taken by Lord Athlone and his Imperial Secretary, Clifford, and was to prove, if anything, even more assiduous than they in his attempts to force Tshekedi to accept mining. As far as the atheistic Rey was concerned, Tshekedi was being 'egged on by two poisonous members of the London Missionary Society. These damned missionaries need hanging—they butt into politics and are an intolerable nuisance—I am looking forward to giving them hell when I take over.'[43]

The British insisted that Tshekedi had to sign the agreement even though they were aware that he was under no legal obligation to do so. Indeed, they gave him the impression throughout that if he did not sign he would be taken to court by the Company, even though their own lawyers had advised them that the Company would have no case. Thus Tshekedi was not apprised of the opinion given by the Law Officers to the Secretary of State as far back as November 1927 that the 'Paramount Chief of the Bamangwato, for the time being, is entitled to determine the Concession by giving a year's notice'.[44] Even at the time Athlone and the Imperial Secretary were trying to force mining on Tshekedi, they were fully aware of how weak were the legal grounds on which they stood. As Athlone wrote to the Secretary of State in March 1929: 'It seems evident from the legal opinions submitted by Messrs. Feetham, Blackwell, and Buchanan, and supported by Professor Lee, that the existing concession held by the British South Africa Company is hardly worth the paper it is written on.' Nevertheless, taking the view that 'His Majesty's Government is morally bound to use its influence with the Chief to secure a new concession for the Company'[45], Athlone proceeded to put pressure on Tshekedi to sign the agreement.

Tshekedi was never one to be bullied. Since the Administration could not be moved, he decided to appeal above their heads, by going to London to see the Secretary of State for the Dominions himself. He therefore made a formal request for permission to sail to England. This was not a course favoured by Athlone (nor indeed by Secretary Amery and his successor, Sidney Webb, who had been elevated to the peerage as Lord Passfield). They did everything to prevent Tshekedi from travelling. But as G. E. Nettelton, Tshekedi's Resident Magistrate of the day, was to put it: 'So far as I can see, he will go to England even if he has to swim.'[46] Finally Passfield agreed to see him, after a rancorous meeting in Cape Town in January at which Tshekedi virtually accused Lord Athlone of forcing him to accept mining in his territory, and after intensive lobbying in London on Tshekedi's behalf by the London Missionary Society and the Anti-Slavery and Aborigines Protection Society.

In March 1930 Tshekedi set sail for London, still only twenty-four years of age. There he had two interviews with Passfield, mainly concerned with the Mining Concession, but ranging over a number of other grievances he had against the British Administration. He also sought assurances that the British Government were not planning to hand over the Bechuanaland Protectorate to South Africa, a prospect whose realisation he and the other chiefs of the Protectorate were to campaign against over the next twenty years.

In the two long interviews Tshekedi more than held his own with the overbearing Lord Passfield, and from the first spoke with passion about the consequences for his people if mining were to be imposed on them. 'I have been told that when mining begins in my country my people will find employment. I agree and I also agree that our cattle will find a market in their own country, but there is nothing that would convince me that these two considerations will compensate me for the harm which will be done.' If, he continued, 'any minerals in great quantity are found, towns like Johannesburg will spring up just as Kimberley has sprung up. If towns like Johannesburg spring up it means that we have lost the country.' As far as the young men going to the Transvaal to work were concerned, 'there is not one who ever returns from the mines with anything. The money that they earn at the mines they spend in food. So far as I can see their wages are inadequate; otherwise they would be able to bring a portion of their wages back with them. . . . If mining begins it is not to say we will be enriched by it. The larger proportion of the wealth obtained from the mines will go to other people, the Europeans. What we are asking is that we should also be protected in this matter and be given an opportunity of benefiting by the riches of our own country.'

Tshekedi, true to his strict missionary upbringing, also expressed concern about the impact of mining on the morals of his people. If 'mines spring up in my country, I am concerned about the women of my Tribe. I know what happens if Europeans of the mining class enter into a native country. Another thing which springs from mining is intoxicating drink', an eventuality which to Tshekedi was anathema. The only place in the Bamangwato Reserve where intoxicating liquour could be sold was to whites in the hotel at Palapye Road and bars at one or two other stations within the hundred-yard-wide strip Khama had conceded to the British South Africa Company for their railway from South Africa to Rhodesia. 'I am even now finding myself obliged to deal with cases with my own natives obtaining European intoxicating drink', Tshekedi told Passfield, 'and, if mining begins in my country, I am quite aware of the fact that I shall be quite unable to control it.'[47]

Passfield was unmoved by Tshekedi's arguments and at the second interview told him that he had to implement the Concession since it was legally valid, even though Passfield had been advised only six weeks before that it was open to doubt whether legal proceedings by the British South Africa Company to enforce the Concession would succeed, 'in view of opinions expressed by legal authorities both here and in South Africa.'[48] He also instructed Tshekedi to return to his people at the earliest possible opportunity. But Tshekedi refused to commit himself to this, telling Passfield that he planned to stay a few weeks in Britain seeing friends his father had made during his own visit thirty-five years before. In the four weeks Tshekedi spent in Britain he forged alliances with the Anti-Slavery and Aborigines Protection Society, with the officers of the London headquarters of the LMS, with Parliamentarians of both Houses, and above all the press. During that month he learnt a great deal about the working of the British political system that was to be crucial in his later battles with the Administration of the Bechuanaland Protectorate. In addition, he had organised a wide-based lobby in the imperial capital on which he could call if one day the need should arise.

Tshekedi returned to Serowe at the end of May to be 'welcomed by the biggest meeting of the Bamangwato Tribe which has assembled in Serowe for a considerable number of years.'[49] But he also returned to a Protectorate which was now under the control of Charles Fernand Rey, who had assumed office in Tshekedi's absence. For the next two years Tshekedi and Rey did battle over the Mining Concession. From the start Tshekedi had prepared for the contingency that the Concession might be forced on him, and to this end—at the same time as he tried to prevent mining taking place in his territory—he covered himself by simultaneously negotiating for an improved Concession. In December 1930, dissatisfied with the 'improved terms' offered by the Administration and the Company, Tshekedi served notice that he was cancelling the Concession. The British South Africa Company responded by denying his right to do so and indicating that the matter would have to be settled by the courts. As it was, both Tshekedi and the Company were anxious to avoid the expenses of a long-drawn-out court case, as indeed were the British Administration. It was in a spirit of compromise that the three parties hammered out an improved Concession. Even so Tshekedi haggled over each detail to ensure the best terms possible for his people. He finally signed the revised Concession in March 1932, but not before he had exasperated Rey by a last-minute wrangle over the amount of Crown Land the government had agreed to give him in compensation for the land that would be required by the mining company. 'That young man ought to come to a bad end soon,' Rey confided to his diary after an interview in which Tshekedi has raised no fewer than eight other problems, and Rey had had to read the Riot Act to him about two of them.[50]

The mining dispute emphasized just how different was the approach of the two protagonists to the administration of African peoples. For Rey, mining would not bring the social problems Tshekedi so feared. Rey had visited a mine on the Rand and had been highly impressed by the quality of food, medical services, and general conditions for the miners. 'So when people talk damned nonsense about the "poor wage slaves" in the mines, and their dreadful conditions, and the awful lives they lead you can point to some of these figures and facts, and compare it with the *really* awful life they lead in their native villages—filthy huts full of vermin, no medical attendance, irregular food and not enough of it, ill-treatment by their own chiefs, not even enough water to drink sometimes.'[51] Tshekedi had also visited mines on the Rand at the invitation of the Johannesburg Chamber of Mines 'to see there how the natives were treated. I went there, and on my return I also sent other people to go and see, as they wanted to see for themselves. What we saw did not cause us to desire to go there to work, and it did not raise in us a desire to have mines in our own country; in fact when I visited the Johnannesburg mines, I felt more afraid than ever of having mines in my own country'.[52] Tshekedi of course knew the miners personally and was aware of their own reactions to the conditions they found in the mines. For him the first priority was to improve the conditions in the huts of his people, not export their inhabitants to mining camps, whether in South Africa or Gamangwato. The only way this could be done was by improving their agricultural base.

Tshekedi's vigorous stand against mining even earned him a barely disguised fictional role in the South African novelist Ethelreda Lewis's *Wild Deer,* which tells of the visit of a Paul Robeson figure to Africa in search of his roots. There he meets a 'native' chief on his way to London 'to beg—no, proudly to demand—of his government that no mining concessions should be given in his territory. The young chief', wrote Lewis in her novel published in 1933, 'had seen the life in Goldburg. He had no wish to bring such horrors upon his peaceful country. No, never must it look like this terrible town. But now the time of temptation had come. His people starved. They looked at him dumbly. Many children had died. Their bellies had become swollen and they died. Old people, too, had died hungry. Like Pharaoh he hardened his heart against the will of his people, but it was because he loved them, wanted to save them. Better that a few children and old people should die now, and then of starvation, than that the young men perish of white men's diseases—the young women sell themselves to white men.'[53]

Nowhere were the philosophical differences between Rey and Tshekedi more dramatically exposed than in their clash over the administrative reforms Rey introduced without warning to the Chiefs at the Native Advisory Council in their meeting at Protectorate Headquarters in Mafeking in March 1932. The reforms came in the guise of two draft proclamations, the first concerning Native Administration, the second Native Justice. Tshekedi had been warned by Lord Passfield that 'reforms' were being planned, but he had not anticipated that they would be drafted without consultation or be as radical as they were.

The central institution of the Tswana state was not the Chief but the *kgotla,* the assembly which made all administrative, political and judicial decisions. All adult males had the right of participation in discussions in the *kgotla,* which was presided over by the Chief at the level of the state or by headmen in the wards of the capital city and the outlying villages. Technically all voices in the *kgotla* had equal weight, and the Chief had to listen to anyone who wished to speak before he came to a decision. In fact members of the royal family and headmen had great influence on decisions, many of which were agreed in advance with the Chief. While a Chief was born to his position, as indeed was a headman, he was also responsible to the people. The Tswana have a saying, 'A Chief is a Chief by the people', which means that he has to take account of their views—for in the old days a Chief who alienated his subjects would be assassinated, driven into exile or be deserted by his people, who would vote with their feet by removing themselves from his jurisdiction and establishing a new state. It was thus that the Ngwato state itself had been founded. The Tswana *kgosi* was a presidential monarch, and though Rey saw in him an autocrat, he did in reality have to respond carefully to public opinion and ensure majority support not only among his headmen but also among the people.

The Tswana ruler was not responsible to any formal council, although royal uncles and headmen were consulted regularly by him. Which of them he consulted depended very much on the issue at hand. Nor did a ruler judge cases in consultation with a specific set of advisers, learned in Tswana law and custom. When a man or woman had a case in *kgotla,* it was tried by the Chief with the assistance of all adult males present.

Now what Rey's Proclamations did in essence was to change the whole political and judicial structure of Tswana society. In the first place, the *kgotla* was to be replaced for administrative purposes by a formally constituted Council which would, under the Presidency of the Chief, conduct the affairs of the Tribe. Such a device had been tried among the Bakwena when the British judged that their ruler Sebele II was not fit to exercise authority on his own. It had been a disastrous failure and had been bitterly resented by the people, who saw it as nothing less than an attempt by a group of royal uncles to seize power and establish a barrier between themselves and their Chief. In Gamangwato itself the Council established by the Administration to assist Gorewan, Tshekedi's cousin, during the short time he acted as Chief after the death of Sekgoma II was abolished by Tshekedi, with the general support of the people, once he assumed office as Regent. In the second place, as far as the administration of justice was concerned, Rey proposed to replace the *dikgotla* by Tribunals in which the Chief or headman would sit with two assessors. Thus an offender would no longer be tried by his peers or in civil matters have his or her claim settled by them. Furthermore, the number of *dikgotla* would be drastically reduced, so that access to justice would be limited. In addition, Tswana law and custom would be codified.

The net result of these reforms would be that the Chief would lose power as the final arbiter of matters political, administrative and judicial. Instead, he would be joined in this role by Councillors or Tribunal Members depending on whether the matter at hand was political, administrative or judicial. The people—or at least the adult males—would effectively be excluded from the decision-making processes in the Tribe. Even where the people did consider their Chiefs too powerful or autocratic Rey's Proclamations were no solution: they merely replaced what he considered an autocracy by an oligarchy and removed the people from any restraining role. Finally, and a matter that greatly exercised the Chiefs as well as the people, Rey included in his Proclamations a clause that stipulated that before a

Chief could exercise his functions he had to be recognised by the British Government. The Chiefs all argued that they were born, not elected or appointed. Thus
there could be no question of the Administration bestowing recognition on or
withholding it from a Chief. There was only one Chief, and he was the one born to
the position under the system of male primogeniture. Looming in the minds of the
dikgosi when they read this section of the Proclamations was the example of
Sebele II of the Bakwena, whom Rey had recently and summarily deposed,
replacing him by a younger brother who was not even next in line of succession.
Despite the fact that Sebele had not been the best of Chiefs, the people were not
prepared to accept Rey's replacement and continued to acknowledge the exiled
Sebele as their rightful ruler, while they treated his replacement as an usurper, the
Administration's man.[54]

At the Native Advisory Council meeting in Mafeking in March 1932,
Tshekedi, as the most articulate of the Chiefs, naturally assumed leadership in the
attack on the Proclamations. In introducing the Proclamations, Rey had declared
that they were 'educational and developing in nature; they are designed to help you
forward in the path of administering your own affairs, of developing the mentality
of your people, of making it easier for Chief and people respectively to govern and
be governed. . . . This is a great occasion, a great step forward, a great opportunity. It is for you to take full advantage of it, and I rely with confidence on your
doing so.'[55]

This confidence was quite misplaced. Tshekedi delivered a withering reply to
Rey. 'I perceive that these laws are intended to define the powers of the Chiefs, the
functions of the Chiefs and their Tribes, and to reduce the existing rights of the
Tribes and for this reason I find that the time in which the matter is being discussed
is inappropriate. Looking at the men in front of me, who are called Protectorate
Chiefs today, I find mere boys, and if the subject matter will be found of any
benefit to the Tribes, to my mind it should have been discussed with the original
seekers of the Protectorate. I do not suggest the Government deliberately delayed
action until the death of our fathers in order that they may discuss the matter with
their sons, but I feel that if the matter had been discussed in the time of our Fathers,
they probably would have understood it better than we do—so far as we are
concerned, we are unable to understand it.'[56] But of course Tshekedi understood it
only too well. The powers of the Chiefs were to be reduced and the very basis of
pre-colonial Tswana government through the *kgotla* was to be abolished. As far as
he was concerned this was a violation of the agreement made with his father that he
should govern his country much as before. Tshekedi thus staked out the basis on
which he was to conduct a relentless war with Rey to prevent promulgation of his
Proclamations: they violated 'native' law and custom and therefore were contrary
to the 'Treaty' made by his Father with the British. Trying delaying tactics,

Tshekedi concluded his attack by declaring that 'we should have been given at least five years in which to consider the position.'[57]

To this Rey's response was that if he thought it would take five years to understand the Proclamations he would not have wasted his time drafting them.[58] Rey then instructed the Chiefs to take the Draft Proclamations to their people and discuss them with them. They should send in comments to him through their Resident Magistrates. These would then be considered at the following year's meeting of the Council.

In June 1933 Rey visited Serowe after touring parts of the Bamangwato Reserve. At a long interview with Tshekedi, who had just had an operation to remove his appendix, he described his 'experience of the terrible conditions brought about by the shortage of food in some places along the Botletli River' and promised to provide free grain for the people there.[59] The interview went better than most between the two men, and Rey wrote almost affectionately of Tshekedi in his diary afterwards: 'He is a tiresome little devil but I rather like him in some ways.'[60] Even their discussion of the Proclamations went off quite amicably, with Tshekedi apologising for the delay in dealing with them because he had had to consult his lawyer in Cape Town. For his part Rey replied that he did not blame the Chief for his delay in submitting the criticisms. He merely commented that the document in which they were contained 'was lengthy, and it would take him time to read it carefully, but a rough glance at it showed that it contained some useful matter'.[61]

By the time of the meeting of the Native Advisory Council the following month in Mafeking to consider an amended version of the original Draft, Rey had changed his tune. Concluding his presentation of the revised Drafts, he told the Council that in the written observations submitted by Tshekedi, 'purporting to represent the views of the Tribe he sets out at considerable length what he says is native law and custom and makes a certain number of general observations the effect of which would be, if agreed to, either to defeat the object of the proclamations or to delay for a very long time their enactment, although I know this is not his object.'[62] But of course Rey was only too aware that it was just that. Tshekedi resumed his attack on the Proclamations by pointing an accusing finger at the Administration: 'The amendments that have been communicated to us as coming from the Tribes are those which the Government has accepted. Your Honour has not informed us of the amendments which the Government did not accept. And this is why I say that the discussion in this matter is not even. We are discussing only that which has been accepted and nothing which has been rejected. We can only understand it if we can get the reasons of those who have made the accepted amendments.'[63] He then made his own position and that of the Bangwato unmistakably clear: 'For their part they say they will reject the laws as they stand and they ask that this should come before the Government.'[64]

Rey then suggested that the Chiefs should adjourn for a few days so that they could discuss the revisions to the Proclamations with no British officials present. Their deliberations seem merely to have resulted in a hardening of their attitudes, and no doubt under the leadership of Tshekedi they returned to the Council in an obstinate mood. An angry Rey closed the discussion of the Proclamations at the resumed meeting by telling members: 'I have read with disappointment the further amendments now suggested by the Chiefs in addition to those already circulated and explained. . . . They have submitted a series of observations which cut at the very roots of the principles on which the proclamations are based and which, if adopted, would simply mean that the draft proclamations might as well be torn up . . . they have adopted the attitude that Native law and custom should continue in every respect exactly as at present, and there should be no advance and no improvement. . . . The attitude taken up in these observations is this:- To object to everything that conflicts with any existing custom and to object to anything which touches in any way on what you appear to think is the present position and privilege of the Chiefs.'[65]

Having 'ticked them off well', as he put it in his diary, Rey then took the Chiefs through the rest of the Agenda, 'which was not very thrilling, except that they passed a resolution unanimously, objecting strongly to any idea of going into the Union.'[66]

The next morning the Chiefs left Mafeking, while Rey and Ninon entertained for breakfast Admiral Evans of the Broke and his wife, who were on their way to Bulawayo. The Antarctic explorer and First World War hero was Commander-in-Chief of the Africa Station of the Royal Navy, with its headquarters at Simonstown in the Cape. He was shortly to take over as Acting High Commissioner from Sir Herbert Stanley, who was going on leave to England. Rey found Evans and his wife 'perfectly delightful and charming people and we lost our hearts to them.' When his guests had set off on their journey north, Rey prepared to travel south to Cape Town to interview Stanley before he sailed to England.[67]

For the next six weeks Tshekedi makes no appearance in Rey's diaries, which he kept assiduously throughout his seven years in the Bechuanaland Protectorate. Then on September 1933 Rey recorded that although 'it rained after dinner tonight (a good omen) . . . this month ushered in the biggest trouble we have had in the B. P.—the row with Tshekedi. The first rumblings were heard on Friday and Saturday. Tshekedi had sent in a letter about my Proclamations addressed to Sir Herbert Stanley (who is in England) requesting an interview with the Secretary of State, and completely ignoring myself as R. C. and Admiral Evans as (Acting) High Commissioner. He practically refused to take it back or acknowledge his error—of course, a definitely planned piece of insolence and defiance.'[68]

Tshekedi, accompanied by his fellow Chief, friend and relative, Bathoen II of the Bangwaketse, and by 'his missionary' Jennings, had travelled to Cape Town in order to see Buchanan and try to get hold of a copy of the version of the Proclamations that incorporated the revisions made at Mafeking the month before. These Buchanan secured from Shirley Eales, the Administrative Secretary in the High Commissioner's Office, but not before Eales had consulted Rey by telegram. Rey gave permission for a copy to be handed to the two Chiefs, but warned Eales that he must not imagine that 'any amendments to which we could possibly agree would satisfy the Chief or remove his opposition to the proposed legislation which was "fundamental" '.[69] The letter enclosing the revised Proclamations reached Tshekedi in Buchanan's office at 5 o'clock on the afternoon of Wednesday, 23 August. Together Tshekedi, Bathoen, Jennings and Buchanan pored over the revisions in the few hours left to them before the two Chiefs had to board the 9 o'clock train on their way back to the Protectorate. By the time they did so, they had signed a letter to Eales which much to his 'astonishment' was delivered to him the next morning at 10 o'clock.[70]

Their letter asked Eales to send a telegram to Sir Herbert Stanley, who was already on the boat to London. In their telegram they informed Stanley that the revised Proclamations 'raise very serious constitutional issues embracing our treaty rights as self-governing peoples under the suzerainty of Great Britain as negotiated by our Fathers in London in 1895.' The new Proclamations would, they insisted, reduce Chiefs to the status of 'minor officials of the Magistracy' just as they were in the Union of South Africa. The Proclamations would 'retard Native cultural development and the evolution of a Native type of civilisation. Instead of encouraging Native leadership the Proclamations curtail the possibility thereof and transfer Administration from Natives to Europeans. . . .' In view of this they asked Stanley to arrange for the appointment of a Royal Commission 'to take evidence on the Constitutional position of the Crown in relation to the territories of our Fathers, the Chiefs Khama, Bathoen and Sebele.' If that was not acceptable, they asked that Stanley then arrange for them to come to London to discuss the matter with the Secretary of State for the Dominions 'during your Excellency's presence in England and urge that no action be taken for the promulgation of these Proclamations until after such interview.'[71]

As far as Rey was concerned the time had at last come for a showdown with the young Chief. This was by no means the first occasion on which Tshekedi had written direct to the High Commissioner over Rey's head, and he had already been warned several times against this practice.[72] Indeed, as recently as 12 August Rey had complained to Eales about the fact that Jennings, 'of notorious repute', had told him that Tshekedi had asked Buchanan to see Stanley on his behalf about the Proclamations, and Stanley had in fact seen the lawyer the day before he left for England. Further, Tshekedi had just sent a letter direct to Stanley 'without putting it through me or the Magistrate, and as a crowning piece of insolence in this matter gives a copy of the letter to the Magistrate after the original has gone. . . .'[73] But now, with this request that Stanley deal with the Proclamations while he was on leave in England, Tshekedi had gone too far—at least in Rey's book. He had to be dealt with once and for all. Rey had probably hit the mark when he suggested that Tshekedi's action was deliberate, for Tshekedi was well aware how irritated Rey became over such breaches of protocol. Shirley Eales certainly believed this to be the case. As he wrote to H. N. Tait in the Dominions Office: 'I am afraid that there was deliberate intention on Tshekedi's part not to send his communication through Rey.'[74]

Fortunately for Rey, Admiral Evans was passing through Mafeking on his way back from Southern Rhodesia. So Rey joined him on his journey to Pretoria, and together they discussed what to do with the exasperating young Chief, after which the Admiral went on safari in the Kruger Game Park.

Rey did not record in his diary what plans he had made with the Admiral. But he did write to Eales and say that Tshekedi and Bathoen should be dealt with severely for what he considered was their 'deliberately insulting' action. He also urged that the Chiefs' telegram should not be sent to Stanley, whether at their expense or not, since it should first be commented on by the Resident Commissioner and then by the Acting High Commissioner.'[75] To the two Chiefs Rey wrote a coldly polite letter drawing to their attention the proper channels of communication which they should have observed in submitting their telegram for Stanley to Eales. Tshekedi's reply was quite unapologetic; indeed, it was almost rude in its tone.[76] Meanwhile Admiral Evans wrote to Rey that 'it appears that Tshekedi has made a deliberate attempt to ignore the whole Administration; if so, he is deserving of reproof.'[77] But before Rey could take any more dramatic action against Tshekedi, his adversary played right into his hands—or so it seemed to Rey. 'And then on Thursday 7', he wrote in his diary, 'the storm burst, and I got a telegram from Captain Potts, R. M. Serowe, to say that Tshekedi had flogged a European publicly in Kgotla!'[78]

Now it was a cardinal principle of British colonial rule in Africa that black men did not try white men, whatever their offence or whatever their status. Certainly black men did not flog white men. So for Rey it appeared that he had at long last been presented with an opportunity to rid himself of a man who had been a thorn in his flesh from the moment he arrived in the Bechuanaland Protectorate, and above all was leader of the other Chiefs in their opposition to the Proclamations which he saw as being the principal momument to his incumbency as head of the Bechuanaland Protectorate administration. What happened over the next three weeks, its implications for relations between white and black in Tshekedi's territory, and more broadly for his relations with his British overlords, is the subject of the chapters that follow.

The high drama that was to unfold over the next three weeks of September 1933 in Gamangwato did so in a land beset by problems such as it had not experienced since the rinderpest epizootic of 1895–96. Bechuanaland was, as the Johannes-burg *Star* put it, a 'land sucked dry of water', and 'the drought that is stalking through the Protectorate has brought conditions for man and beast unknown to traders who have been here 35 years.'[79] Game and cattle were dying by the thousands, and in some parts of the Protectorate all surface water and water found within a few feet of the surface had been consumed by the people. No rain had fallen since February and, reported the *Star,* 'although there was drought lasting three years about 15 years ago the conditions are described as infinitely worse because the decreased rainfall of the last few years has not replenished superficial water.'[80]

As if the drought were not bad enough, foot-and-mouth disease had broken out in the territory in January, and much of Colonel Rey's energies over the past months had been expended in cordoning off areas where the disease had been notified, so as to prevent its spread. Every available police constable, and many members of the white staff, had been co-opted in the effort to stem this disaster to the Protectorate's principal resource. Thousands of cattle were inoculated. Of course, with foot and mouth in the Protectorate, export of any cattle to the Union was impossible, whether or not weight restrictions were in force. The disastrous state of affairs had recently been the subject of a major Commission of Enquiry by Sir Alan Pim, whose report was presented to Parliament by the Secretary of State for Dominion Affairs in June 1933. Pim was shocked by the lack of development and made a number of proposals for improvement of both economic and political administration in the territory. But, he had concluded, for 'some years to come . . . it will be impossible for the Administration to meet any part of the cost from its own resources', and he therefore recommended that the Imperial Govern-ment assist it with grants-in-aid.[81]

The situation in the Bechuanaland Protectorate was further exacerbated by the effects of the Depression, which had brought the trade of the country practically to a standstill. The local LMS missionary, the Rev. J. H. L. Burns, reported that his mission was 'six months behind with the payment of salaries to ministers and evangelists, as it is. What we are to do I cannot see'.[82] Unfortunately, although South Africa had recently come off the gold standard, the resulting boom was not yet fully underway and certainly had not yet had an impact on the Protectorate. Hardest hit were the white traders and artisans. In Serowe, one of the leading traders, Samuel Blackbeard, had written to Semane, Tshekedi's mother, that 'owing to the Depression I find I am unable to carry on without assistance. I am now appealing to my old friend to help me in my times of stress.' He asked Queen Semane whether she could therefore lend him between £1,200 and £1,500, on which he would pay her 6 percent interest as against the 3½ percent charged by the banks. He promised to pay the interest monthly and give his farm, Sunnyside, as security. If she needed further security he would give her his insurance policies.

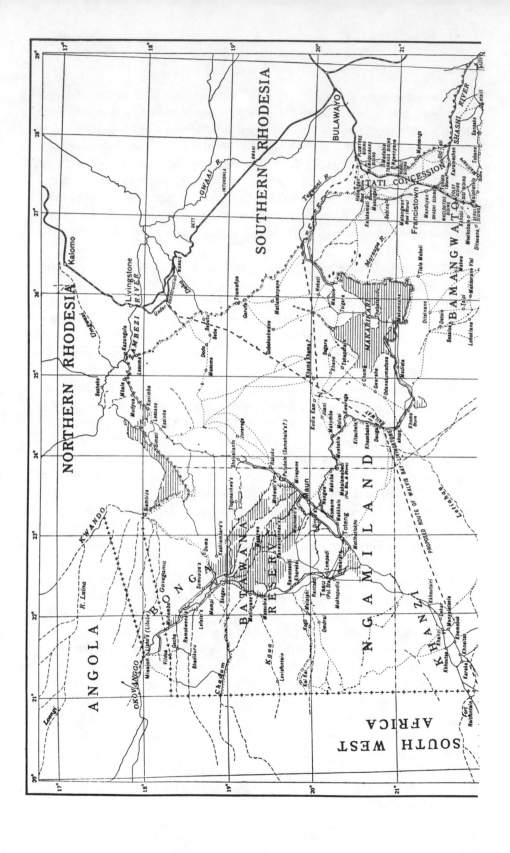

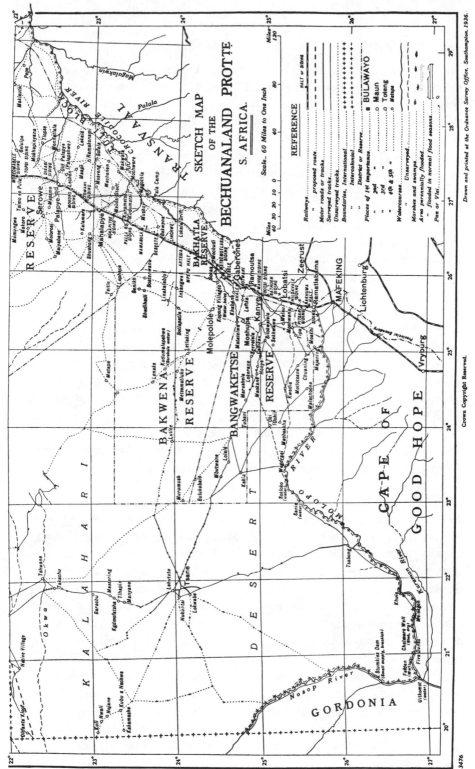

Drawn and printed at the Ordnance Survey Office, Southampton, 1936.

Map 3. The Bechuanaland Protectorate in 1936.

The problem was that he owed the bank £1,250, and because of the foot-and-mouth outbreak 'they were calling in their loans.'[83] Though there is no indication whether Semane did lend Blackbeard the money, Tshekedi himself in early August reduced the rent on the premises Blackbeard Bros. were leasing from him in 'view of hard times'.[84]

 What this exchange of correspondence demonstrated was the close-knit relationship that existed between the white community and their Chief. Tshekedi was on particularly good terms with both missionaries and traders, visiting them when they were sick, condoling with them when death struck their families, and undertaking many small acts of generosity such as lending his car when needed. It was only with the local officials of the Administration that he clashed. Indeed, Nettelton's replacement as Resident Magistrate, Captain J. W. Potts, had become so distressed by his relationship with the Chief that only a few months before the flogging of McIntosh he had asked Rey to transfer him from Serowe 'or to predate the time of my retirement from the service on pension, or to obtain my transfer to another public service.'[85] The immediate cause of Potts's distress was the fact that Tshekedi had gained access to a letter in which his uncle, Mokhutshwane, had made critical remarks about him to Potts. Tshekedi claimed that he had been shown the letter by a member of the Administration. He further suspected that the letter had been written for Mokhutshwane by his nephew, the Rev. Keletlokhile Raditladi, who was the first Mongwato to have been ordained a minister by the LMS. Tshekedi was bitter that Potts had accepted a letter from one of his subjects without informing him. For his part Potts was upset that someone in the Administration had apparently divulged the contents of a letter that had been sent to him in confidence.[86]

But the difficulties between the two went back further than that. In January 1932 Potts had reported that after 'twelve months' association (official) with [Tshekedi], I can say that he is an extreme Mongwato Nationalist, a past master in the art of obstruction when it suits him, grasping in the extreme in negotiations, shrewd and undoubtedly courageous, but lacking in ability to carry the Tribe as a whole with him. . . .'[87] For his part, the Chief disliked Potts, as a member of the Administration who knew Tshekedi well recorded, and he was determined to impress on him as well as Colonel Rey 'that he was a man to be reckoned with and no young schoolboy to be badgered about. Tshekedi resented the dictatorial and patronising attitude of Colonel Rey . . . and rather blunt manner of Potts.'[88]

It is clear from this dispute between Potts and Tshekedi that the latter's relations with his subjects were not always as harmonious as with the traders and missionaries living in his Reserve. His authoritarian ways were resented by members of the educated élite with ideas of their own as to how Gamangwato should be developed. Factions of the royal family still conspired against him, and in 1932 there had been a serious challenge made to his Regency by an illegitimate son of Sekgoma II, who tried to claim the Ngwato throne for himself and thus displace not only Tshekedi but also his young ward, Seretse. In this crisis, the British Administration gave Tshekedi their full support in dealing with the Pretender, whom they jailed. Tshekedi had had considerable trouble, too, from some of his so-called subject peoples, in particular the Bakanswaswi and Bakhurutshe, who resented what they considered his harsh rule.

Several petitions had also been sent to the British Administration complaining about Tshekedi's conduct as chief. The Ratshosa brothers, released from prison but forced to live in exile, stirred up as much trouble as possible for Tshekedi, with Simon being particularly skilful at passing on information about Tshekedi's internal troubles and autocratic ways to visiting journalists. Despite all this, Tshekedi was in firm control of his own country when his conflict with Rey came to a head. As he wrote to Alexander Kerr, the Principal of his old college, Fort Hare, on the eve of the 'flogging': 'So far as the relationship between me and my tribe is concerned despite press publications to the contrary, it is, in my opinion, very satisfactory and I have no uneasiness about it.'[89]

For Colonel Rey, the drought and the outbreak of foot and mouth were an added frustration to his ambitious plans for the development of the Protectorate. Over and above that he had recently been defied by a minor headman, Gobuamang of the Mmanaana-Bakgatla, whom he insisted on calling 'Gobbleman' in his diaries. With only a thousand men at his disposal, Gobuamang had resisted all attempts to subordinate him to the Chief of the Bangwaketse and to pay taxes to him. With his small band of police engaged on foot-and-mouth cordons, Rey determined to deal with him firmly. In April 1933 he planned an invasion of Gobuamang's hill eyrie at Moshupa and even proposed using an aeroplane to bomb the village. The Dominions Office vetoed this course of action but did agree to bring in troops from Southern Rhodesia.

In the end Gobuamang had given up before force was used. But Rey's experience with this petty chief, who had only a thousand men at his disposal, informed his reactions throughout the crisis with Tshekedi. He was convinced of the virtues of exemplary punishment as a means of avoiding greater trouble: the 'destruction of the village of Moshupa is . . . entirely in accord with native law and custom . . . the normal consequence of disobedience to . . . a chief . . . it would be thoroughly understood and seen as just by the natives generally.'[90] Gamangwato, however, had a population nearly a hundred times greater than that of Moshupa and was altogether a tougher nut to crack. And the young and educated Tshekedi was an infinitely more skilful opponent than the aged and illiterate Gobuamang.

CHAPTER I

The Flogging of Phinehas McIntosh

The assaults by Phinehas McIntosh, Henry McNamee and Attie Klink which led to McIntosh's sentence to a flogging were not the first time that Tshekedi Khama had had trouble with young Phinehas McIntosh, a wagon builder by trade, or with his fellow in mayhem, Henry McNamee, a motor mechanic. Both of them had been born in Serowe, and were, as Tshekedi was to put it later, living as natives.[1] The two had been involved in a number of assaults on Bangwato before. But what most concerned Tshekedi was their frequent fornication with young Bangwato girls. Indeed, almost from the time he became Regent of the Bangwato for his four-year-old nephew Seretse in 1925, Tshekedi had been concerned about the way some members of the small white community residing in his territory slept around with local women. Tshekedi had been brought up a strict Christian and was 'determined to live cleanly and to help uplift his people to live cleanly', as Arthur W. Wilkie of the Lovedale Missionary Institution where Tshekedi went to elementary school wrote to Dr J. H. Oldham of the London Missionary Society, which was strongly opposed to inter-racial contacts of a sexual nature. 'It is not without importance', Wilkie added, 'to know that syphilis is one of the curses of that part of the country'.[2]

In 1927 Tshekedi complained to Captain Nettelton, the Resident Magistrate representing the British Administration of the Bechuanaland Protectorate in Serowe, that the amount of sexual intercourse between Europeans and 'native women' was on the increase and that the practice was not confined to bachelors.[3] Captain Nettelton referred Tshekedi's complaint to the Serowe Chamber of Commerce as the only institution in the Bamangwato Reserve that could in any way be

3. Phinehas McIntosh, wagon builder, and Henry McNamee, motor mechanic, photographed in Serowe in 1933 at the time of the crisis arising from Phinehas's 'flogging' by Tshekedi (Associated Press Ltd).

called representative of its white community. At a special meeting of the Chamber held in the Town Hall on Thursday, 13 October, it was pointed out by members that 'this was scarcely a matter for the Chamber to deal with, but it was finally agreed that support should be given to Chief Tshekedi in his efforts to keep the stadt clean.' Mr Harris, the Secretary, seconded by Mr Smith, proposed that a letter be sent to the Resident Magistrate suggesting that the Resident Commissioner, who had overall charge of the administration of the Bechuanaland Protectorate, be asked to issue a proclamation forbidding such intercourse, along the lines of the law obtaining in the Union of South Africa which made sexual relations between black and white a penal offence.[4]

Although the Chamber of Commerce felt that it was not an appropriate body to deal with the problem of inter-racial sex in the Bamangwato Reserve, Captain Nettelton considered that as a result of his bringing attention to the question 'an improvement took place.'[5] But trouble recurred in 1929 in the aftermath of the influx of white workmen employed by the Protectorate Administration on the new hospital and the new premises for the Resident Magistrate. The Chief, for his part, had tried to stop Bangwato women visiting the workmen. A Mongwato labourer called Lukas, who was accused in *kgotla* of acting as a pimp for one woman, was flogged for his trouble and warned never to let her go to the hospital.[6] Two women who were caught disobeying the Chief's orders were flogged in his *kgotla*.

Nettelton, however, had been forced to explain to the Chief that there was nothing he personally could do legally to stop the men seeing the women. Tshekedi's response was that he would in that case have to take action against the women, since they at least were subject to his authority. One thing that particularly concerned Tshekedi over and above the question of 'immorality' was that 'when offspring resulted they were left without maintenance and the number of half-castes were growing up in the country as a section of the people unwanted by anybody.'[7] For this reason Tshekedi asked 'the Government to have a serious look into this matter and like other provinces make legislation for the prevention of practices of this nature.'[8] Optimistically Nettelton envisaged an alleviation of the problem once work was completed on the construction of the new Serowe hospital. But like Tshekedi, he felt that the best long-term solution to the problem was to make intercourse between whites and blacks 'an offence on the part of both persons.'[9]

It was not until 1930 that complaints against Phinehas McIntosh and his friend Henry McNamee were first brought to the attention of the Resident Magistrate by Tshekedi. So concerned had the young Chief become at their wild ways that he asked Captain Nettelton to take the matter up with the Resident Commissioner. According to Nettelton the two lads, as he called them, were given to roaming around the village at night drinking beer and getting intoxicated, seducing women and generally defying the laws of the Chief and his headmen in the Bamangwato Reserve. Henry McNamee, who was then eighteen years old, had already been brought before the Magistrate's Court twice. In August of that year he had been charged under the Police Offences Act and been reprimanded and discharged. Two months later he had been charged with assault and fined £2, with the alternative of one week's imprisonment with hard labour. Alongside McNamee, McIntosh, who was twenty-one years old, had been charged under the Police Offences Act in August and was similarly reprimanded and discharged.[10] But, Nettelton wrote to the Government Secretary, 'they are both very cunning and have managed to avoid serious trouble.'[11] Nettelton proposed to bring the two young men before him and warn them if they did not give up their 'bad habits' they would be evicted from the Reserve.

Meanwhile, at Henry's request, Nettelton was seeing whether he could get him employment as a white labourer on the Railways.[12] His endeavours in this direction were not fruitful. Mr Clark, the District Engineer in Mafeking, capital of the Bechuanaland Protectorate, informed the Government Secretary that there would be little hope of his being employed by South African Railways, which controlled the line through the Bechuanaland Protectorate, as they employed only 'natives' as unskilled labourers. He did, however, suggest that the General Manager of the Rhodesia Railways be approached, since he thought they did give employment to unskilled white labourers. In the meantime the Government Secretary informed Nettelton that the Assistant Resident Commissioner could not understand why the police had not dealt with the young men. In future the police should give their cases special attention. And if they were sentenced to terms of imprisonment they could serve their sentences in a gaol outside Serowe, in Gaberones, Lobatsi or Francistown, all of which were situated in white settler territory. Indeed, a term of gaol might have a good effect on them. It was not possible, however, to deport them from the Bamangwato Reserve as Nettelton had suggested, because they had been born there.[13]

Nettelton did not find the suggestions from Protectorate Headquarters in Mafeking very helpful. There was no question that the Rhodesia Railways would give McNamee employment, as he had already been deported from Southern Rhodesia for stealing a motor car, for which offence he served a month in Bulawayo gaol. 'You rightly observe', Nettelton wrote to the Government Secretary, 'that these two boys were born here and they are our legacy for all time. For this reason I am not working with the object of making them habitual criminals— they are on the way to that state. I desire to make some attempt to turn them into useful citizens and they will only do this in some place other than a Native Reserve. . . . I am aware of the possibilities of prosecution under the Police Offences Act, which has been used already. I will instruct the Police to give special attention to them but I am not in favour of putting these two boys in Gaol if it can be helped.'[14] Nettelton still believed that the only solution to the problem was to remove them from the Bamangwato Reserve. He did not think that an appeal to their parents would serve any purpose, since like all parents they 'believe nothing bad about their children.'[15]

Nettelton was perhaps more concerned about the behaviour of these young men than most Resident Magistrates would have been: his sister, Madge, had married into the Serowe white community as the wife of a prominent trader, Page-Wood.[16] It was therefore with some feeling that he continued his letter to the Government Secretary: 'It is not pleasant to contemplate either of them figuring as co-respondent in a native divorce case or in an action for affiliation. It is bad for European morale in the District and for offences such as seduction and adultery no Police action can be taken.'[17] As to warnings, these were quite useless. The last time he had warned Henry McNamee, he had expressed complete repentance. But that very night he had defied the Chief's laws by telling a crowd of women who were creating a disturbance and who had been told to stop on Tshekedi's orders to take no notice and carry on, which 'they duly did until day dawned.'[18] One Christmas Eve the two young men had celebrated the occasion by setting off sticks of dynamite outside the front entrances of people's compounds. The police had been told to investigate the matter, but there was not sufficient evidence to charge them. Though Nettelton would have liked to have been able to sentence them to 'cuts', he was prevented from doing so under the Police Offences Act. All he could propose was to ask Tshekedi to furnish him with 'definite evidence against them to enable me to call them up and confront them with it.'[19] Among other mischiefs said to have been committed by Phinehas was changing the notice outside Botalaote village, 'Speed limit in Serowe not to exceed 15 miles an hour', to '115 miles an hour'. Ex-Postmaster Quinlan alleged that Phinehas had put sugar in his petrol tank.[20] More serious were the series of allegations made by Bamang-wato Tribal Policeman Matome on oath before a Justice of the Peace at Palapye Road. He related that on many occasions he had tried to break up rowdy and disorderly beer-drinking sessions involving Phinehas, his brother Tom, and their friends, including Henry McNamee and Attie Klink.[21]

The Government Secretary wrote back to Nettelton sympathizing with his dilemma but giving him little comfort except to suggest that if the two youths persisted in their behaviour it 'might in course of time justify the enactment of some other drastic measure to remedy the case.'[22]

At this juncture Captain Nettelton was transferred to the Francistown Magistracy and replaced as Resident Magistrate by Captain Potts. Though nothing was done about the specific cases of McIntosh and McNamee, Colonel Rey, the Resident Commissioner, addressed a Circular Minute to all Magistrates and Medical Officers on 28 September 1931 drawing attention to the proclaimed evil of inter-racial sexual intercourse and instructing them to consult with police officers, missionaries and Chiefs in their districts and to forward their observations to him at an early date.[23] Captain Potts obtained replies from both Chief Tshekedi and the Rev. Sandilands of the London Missionary Society. These he forwarded to the Resident Commissioner on 8 October 1931, suggesting that 'a law should be framed in such a way as to make either promiscuous intercourse or marriage between Europeans and Natives illegal, and provision made for the maintenance of any offspring from such unions. . . . Of course it is even now open to any native woman to sue for maintenance, but I have only one such case in mind and it was brought against a policeman in this place some years ago and failed—the offpsring, on production, being as black as coal!'[24] The Rev. Sandilands's view was that the 'offence' was heinous.[25] Tshekedi's own view was that the matter was not only a difficult but delicate affair to approach and that though he had commented on the subject, a 'very small percentage of many such cases came to the notice of the magistrate.'[26] In Potts's opinion it was quite clear that Tshekedi was 'unwilling to launch a campaign against offending Europeans and probably other chiefs have the same feelings about the subject.[27] Rey also brought the matter up before the European Advisory Council of the Protectorate to which whites living in both the Native Reserves and the so-called European Blocks sent representatives. He told them he was considering possible ways of mitigating the 'evil'.[28]

As far as Tshekedi was concerned the Administration appeared to have let the matter drop. But McIntosh and McNamee continued to plague the town. On 9 December 1931 the two were brought for trial before Sydney L. Forster-Towne in the Serowe Resident Magistrate's Court charged with assaulting Kleinboy, a member of Chief Tshekedi's Special Police, whom they were accused of kicking and striking with a sjambok on the night of 27 November when he tried to disperse a dance at which Bangwato were present contrary to the Chief's law. Both were fined 10 shillings, with the alternative of two weeks' imprisonment with hard labour.[29] Previous to this conviction McNamee had been sentenced to a month in prison with hard labour and no option of a fine for assault and a further concurrent week's imprisonment for malicious injury to property.[30] It was not until April of 1932 that Tshekedi once again asked the Resident Magistrate to take up the case of McIntosh and McNamee with the Resident Commissioner, with a view to having them expelled from his territory. Potts had gone on leave, and once more it was poor Nettelton who had to grasp this thorny problem. Sourly he noted in a private letter to D. W. How, the Government Secretary in Mafeking: 'Those European youths I have written to you about are absolutely beyond anything. I have done all I can in the matter and I give it up. We don't want any more half-castes than necessary in the country. I must say Tshekedi and his people have been long suffering and this owing to their parents being fairly decent.'[31]

Officially, Nettelton wrote to the Government Secretary that since he had last raised the matter there had been 'endless trouble' with the two young men. There was evidence against them that was 'so abundant that it would be tiresome to recapitulate it all. . . . The main complaint against the men is that they are living as natives and co-habiting with natives. They have been responsible for producing several half-caste children and I am informed by the Chief that they live with one native girl and when she becomes pregnant she is cast off and another one taken. . . . They are constantly mixed up in petty assault cases. One of their achievements is assaulting a policeman.'[32] The parents of the two youths were too afraid of their sons to do anything to control them. McIntosh's parents 'are very respectable people who work for their living', while McNamee's though 'not of a good type . . . do not give a great deal of trouble.'[33]

Captain Potts had had similar trouble with the two young men in his brief stint as Resident Magistrate in Serowe, so what Nettelton now proposed was that an enquiry be held into their activities before deciding what to do with them. 'This action might have a very chastening effect upon quite a number of other not very respectable inhabitants of this Reserve.'[34] Nettelton's suggestion was referred to Captain Reilly, the Acting Resident Commissioner, as Colonel Rey was on leave in England. Reilly considered that the enquiry was a good idea.[35] But Nettelton did nothing to set up one before Potts returned from leave to take over again as Resident Magistrate of Serowe in September. When he got back from England, the assiduous Rey, though unaware of the suggestion for an enquiry, pursued the matter of miscegenation in the Protectorate by preparing a Draft Proclamation for consideration by the British High Commissioner in Pretoria who, of course, also had overall control over the other High Commission Territories of Basutoland and Swaziland. This he submitted in October. It was modelled on the Union of South Africa Immorality Act No 5 of 1927.[36] But the proposed Proclamation would have to be promulgated in all three territories over which the High Commissioner had charge, so it became the subject of lengthy discussion and correspondence and in the end it was shelved in February 1933 because of the objections raised to it.[37]

A month later Colonel Rey and the Resident Magistrate could have wished that the Proclamation was in force. Mr T. Elliott Booker, the Dispenser at the recently completed Sekgoma II Memorial Hospital, so named after Tshekedi's late half-brother for whose son, Seretse, he was acting as Regent, laid a complaint against McIntosh and McNamee. Their hut was close to his quarters, and his nights were disturbed by the constant serving of beer and 'the screaming of native women. Their mode of life is disgusting and objectionable, and I would be glad if they could be caused to remove from the neighbourhood of my quarters.'[38] Potts responded by asking Tshekedi, with whom his relations were to say the least antagonistic, to clear the women out of McIntosh's hut and tell the two men that their presence in Serowe was undesirable.[39] Tshekedi pointed out that 'if these men had been natives, I should have dealt with them long before to-day, but I have been unable to do anything beyond reporting to you their disgraceful conduct and their undesirable presence in Serowe. But when I report about these men to the Magistrate, I am asked to collect evidence against them, and this at once makes me disheartened, because as the Magistrate knows, no evidence is wanting against such notorious individuals, and that in all sincerity evidence so obtained would tire even the Magistrate to listen to.

'I think it is up to you, in your capacity as Magistrate, to take immediate definite steps against them: my assistance will, of course, be available, but my removing them from Serowe merely means them settling in the outside villages where their influence will be worse than it is in Serowe, their conduct calls for serious attention and I must say it is getting too late for action to be taken.'[40]

The response of Captain Potts to what was little less than a rebuke from the Chief was to send for McIntosh and in the presence of Mr Germond, his European

Clerk, administer to him 'the severest reprimand that I have ever administered to a European during the whole of my public service.'[41] He further warned him that he would be put out of the Reserve if he did not mend his ways. But Potts further imposed on Tshekedi, writing to him that same day to tell him that as Chief he had the power to order the native women living with the young men to return to their homes, since he took it they were concubines rather than wives. Potts further thought that the Chief should tell both men that 'they are not conducting themselves in a seemly manner' and that 'they should reside with their people. If you do not feel able to do this I will send for them and tell them, but to my mind it is clearly your province to deal with the native women.'[42]

Tshekedi, obviously trying to control his anger, replied three days later, agreeing that he did indeed have powers to order 'native women' to return to their mothers' homes. But, he suggested, 'there are interesting facts to observe before such a step can be taken. The people in question have now got children together, and is the Magistrate going to leave such action unchecked as far as the males are concerned? Sending the girls to their homes is meaningless: there is nothing to stop both Henry and Phean going to these women during the night, as is their habit.

'You will readily see that the matter needs your further consideration.

'I would again repeat that had this been a case between natives and natives, I should long have brought it to a conclusion. The matter calls for your firmer attention.'[43]

In the meantime Booker had reported to Potts that the nuisance had ceased. Thereafter Potts appears to have given the matter no further attention, firm or otherwise, until, when sick in bed, he learnt on 6 September that Tshekedi had ordered Phinehas to be flogged in his *kgotla*.

By the time Tshekedi had come to learn about the assault by Phinehas and the other white youths on Ramananeng two days after it took place, he had clearly come to despair of obtaining any help from Potts. In exasperation he decided to deal with the matter himself and summoned Phinehas to his *kgotla*. But as Ramananeng wanted to call a witness who was not present in the *kgotla*, Tshekedi directed Phinehas to appear again the following day. That night Tshekedi had to travel, so when Phinehas came for his trial the next morning he was told by Acting Chief Serogola Seretse that he would have to wait until the Chief returned. Clearly the matter of trying a white man for assault was one that Serogola felt only the Chief himself could handle; or else, Tshekedi had given instructions that the case should be held over until he got back. It was not until Wednesday, 6 September that Tshekedi was able to take the case. It is not clear why he chose to make an example of Phinehas rather than Henry McNamee, possibly it was because Phinehas was the elder of the two. But Tshekedi was also under pressure from his people to take some action. According to one official, 'Parents had stated with good reason that their daughters were no longer safe.'[44]

Phinehas responded to the summons to the *kgotla* and appeared before the Chief, who was flanked by a number of his senior headmen.[45] The Plaintiff, Ramananeng, and Phinehas both had their say, as did witnesses, including Tribal Policeman Matome, who recounted his many earlier run-ins with Phinehas.[46] Then Tshekedi pronounced his judgement. He did not refer the matter to the full assembly in the *kgotla* for, as his cousin Serogola Seretse, who had acted for him from time to time when he was absent from Serowe, later stated: 'The case was of a slight nature, and it was in accordance with both justice and recognized custom.'[47] Another royal headman, Disang Raditladi, also affirmed that the procedure followed by Tshekedi was correct, since when a case is 'a mere child's play like the case of McIntosh, there is no reason why the Chief should have referred it to the kgotla; it only rested for the Chief to give judgement to McIntosh and those others concerned' in what was 'just a trifling matter where harlots were concerned, and there was nothing important in it.'[48]

As it was, the judgement Tshekedi gave nearly brought about his downfall. He told Phinehas that it gave him 'pain to punish him in the way I was to do, but as he did not live the life of a white man neither that of a Native, some solution to correct his action had to be found.'[49] He then ordered McIntosh to be given lashes. Thereupon Phinehas dashed forward to the Chief—walked, according to Phinehas—in order to beg him to be let off the flogging, which procedure he understood to be the custom. The people around the Chief, mistaking Phinehas' intention and perhaps recalling the fact that soon after Tshekedi became Regent an attempt had been made to assassinate him in *kgotla,* seized McIntosh and threw him to the ground. He was given at least two cuts with a sjambok by one of the Tribal Policemen before Tshekedi intervened and ordered him to be left alone and Serogola drove some of the men off him. His shirt and trousers were torn. Thereafter Phinehas received no further cuts. Phinehas believed that the one who had lashed him was his old antagonist, Matome, since he was the only policeman he saw with a sjambok.

As soon as Potts, who was ill in bed with influenza, heard what had happened in *kgotla* from his European Clerk, Germond, he asked him to deliver the following message to Tshekedi:

1. Magistrate requires confirmation of Chief's action in his Kgotla this morning.
2. That if the alleged facts are correct, he wishes to record his utter disapproval of Chief's action which is in direct conflict with the law obtaining in this Protectorate.
3. That he requires the Chief's report in the matter immediately.
4. That the matter will be referred to His Honour, the Resident Commissioner, for transmission to His Excellency the High Commissioner.

5. That the Chief is well aware of the fact that McIntosh as an European does not fall under the jurisdiction of the Chief's Court; and that if the Chief had a case against McIntosh it was his duty to refer the case to his Magistrate—whose court alone had jurisdiction in matters affecting European subjects.

6. That the Magistrate is grieved and alarmed at the step taken by the Chief and wishes to stress his displeasure at the manner in which the Chief dealt with this matter.[50]

Before delivering the message that afternoon, Germond telephoned Tshekedi to say he was coming to see him. Tshekedi told him he was writing a report on 'the steps I was obliged to take in kgotla this morning.'[51] In this report Tshekedi once more referred to the fact that he had brought the behaviour of Phinehas as well as his younger brother, Tom, and their friend Henry McNamee to the attention of the Magistrate who 'was unable to find an effective solution to an ever-growing and unbecoming conduct of the above mentioned lads. In fact they are entirely at large to act as they please.

'I may have no jurisdiction in cases where white people and Natives are concerned, but my decision was given in the interest of real and substantial justice, and for the good administration of the Tribe, and I think it was only proper for me to do.

'I have always treated all the white people with respect, no matter what their stations in life are, and the action I took this morning was both in the interest of administration and judicial course.'[52]

In conversation with Germond, Tshekedi told him that he felt 'it was his duty to protect his people from the actions of these lads—bearing in mind that the Government had no legal machinery to cope with questions relating to cohabitation between European and Native . . . whether or not he had acted beyond his jurisdiction would no doubt be decided in due course.' Germond made it clear that he considered Tshekedi had been perfectly aware that he had no jurisdiction over a European in a matter of this nature and that in fact his action was illegal. It might be true that the Magistrate's Court did not possess the necessary legal machinery to deal with cases of cohabitation between Europeans and natives, but the case he had just tried was one of common assault. And he surely realised that the Magistrate's Court could have dealt with this. After all, just recently Henry McNamee had been sentenced to one month's hard labour in Serowe Gaol for assault.

Tshekedi's reply to this was that the steps taken by the Government seemed to have had no effect on the young men, and 'he hoped and believed that McIntosh's punishment in the kgotla would have a beneficial moral effect on him and on the likes of him.'[53]

Germond did not accept Tshekedi's argument, but he did agree to place before

Potts his request that the circular letter to the European residents he had prepared be sent out by the Magistrate's office. In fact, the circular was taken round the white community by Headman Peter Sebina, Tshekedi's devoted personal friend and Secretary, and was duly signed by them.[54] The circular informed them: 'You may hear rumours that I had occasion to give corporal punishment to young Phean McIntosh in my Kgotla this morning, and I wish to give you first-hand information on the matter.

'Several times cases have been brought to my Kgotla in which either or all of the following lads—Phean McIntosh, Tom McIntosh and Henry McNamee— were involved. Such were the cases of assault by these lads on Native people, complaints by girls or their parents about young Native girls who have been put in the family way by these lads; these lads openly had Native beer brewed for them in the village. Their actions are too numerous to be numbered, and I think their behaviour in the village is well known and needs no explanation.

'This morning a case was brought before me in which Phean badly assaulted one Native lad who happened to talk to one Native girl with whom Phean is in love. After listening at some length to evidence against Phean McIntosh and also to his defence, I was compelled to give corporal punishment to Phean McIntosh in the interests of justice and administration. However, before such corporal punishment could be given Phean made a dash at me and the people present caught hold of him to stop him, and I do not know whether he was badly handled or not—I stopped the people from doing him harm, and after this nothing was done to Phean in the way of punishment.

'It has always been my principle to treat my white residents with respect, no matter what their stations in life are. The lads in question have persisted in causing disturbances amongst my people and punishment ordered this morning was given with no malice, but with determined effort of giving a check to this endless trouble and unbecoming influence.'[55]

Tshekedi then prepared to go on tour that evening to Nata in the northernmost part of his territory where he had some cattle posts. Before he left he found time to write a much longer explanation of his dramatic action, addressed to the Resident Magistrate.[56] Whether or not it was received by Potts is not clear. It does not appear in the Resident Magistrate's file on the subject of the flogging of Phinehas McIntosh, nor is it included in the exhaustive printed correspondence related to the subsequent events prepared by the Dominions Office.[57] The carbon copy in Tshekedi's file would suggest that it was sent. In it he rehearsed at greater length his earlier arguments but in addition he made the surprising statement, 'I have the painful task to say that it appears to me the predominating aspect of the matter is the racial prejudice irrespective of the facts. . . . Rightly or wrongly I have tried several cases between the white people and the black people in my country, and so far no complaint has been brought to my notice by the white people regarding such cases, and on the other hand they have sometimes expressed their appreciation of my decision even though given against them. Colour should be no limit to the extent a Native judge should give a decision—the merits of the case should be the limit.

'The sentence of corporal punishment has not been abolished in the Magistrate's Courts, and there is no law which says that corporal punishment should only be administered to the Natives. If this punishment was undesirable I have no doubt that it would be abolished for both white and black. I am moved to ask myself why there should be an alarm at the action taken before it had been ascertained that justice had been ill-administered, the reply can only be that because a Native Chief has passed the sentence on a white offender.'[58]

In the meantime a coded telegram was sent on the morning of Thursday, 7 September by Potts to Colonel Rey in Mafeking informing him of the flogging of Phinehas McIntosh. For Rey, whose telegraphic address was somewhat appropriately 'BLASTSTOVE', Tshekedi's action was outrageous, since 'the offence committed by the European, i.e. striking a native was a common, indeed everyday occurrence in South Africa.'[59] But although Rey expressed outrage at Tshekedi's daring to take the law into his own hands and to try to punish a white in his own Court, he was in fact thoroughly pleased. For three years now he had crossed swords with the young and equally headstrong Chief. Indeed, he had more than once contemplated deposing him, just as he had done the Chief of the neighbouring Bakwena in 1931. Yet Tshekedi was careful never to allow Rey quite enough rope to hang him with. This time, however, it seemed to Rey that at last Tshekedi had done just that. As he wrote the next day to the Acting High Commissioner, Admiral Evans of the Broke, 'The climax which I have for a long time feared, and the possibility of which I have ventured to point out before, has now been reached. In view of this latest development it appears, as I have already said, impossible to conceive of retaining Tshekedi as regent.'[60] Or, as he put it more earthily to his Private Secretary, Edwin Arrowsmith, when the telegram from Potts arrived: 'I've got the little bugger now.'[61]

CHAPTER 2

Send in the Marines

Rey was in Mafeking when the telegram from Potts arrived and 'the storm burst'.[1] In the first of a flurry of telegrams that was to keep the lines from Mafeking to Serowe busy for the next ten days, Rey instructed Potts to tell the Chief that he was not to leave Serowe, as he might be needed either at headquarters or in Cape Town. If he had already left for Nata, a messenger should be sent to call him back.[2]

Tshekedi had in fact set off the night before and according to Potts's information was planning to stay at Shashane for two or three days before going on to Nata. Since this was only twenty-four miles away, Potts was confident of getting Rey's instructions to the Chief without difficulty. For even if Tshekedi changed his plans, he would be easy to track down, as he was travelling by mule wagon and his northward progress would be slow. Trooper Lenanile of the Bechuanaland Protectorate Police was therefore sent on horseback to fetch him back to Serowe.[3]

Rey then sent a further telegram to Potts, who was still lying on his sick bed, requesting him to prepare a full report of events surrounding the flogging and put it on the goods train leaving for Mafeking that night from Palapye Road, the station some thirty-five miles due east of Serowe. If he could not get it to the train in time, then he was to telegraph his report.[4]

Happily for the bed-bound Potts he had an indefatigable assistant in his Clerk, Germond. It was Germond who called Phinehas McIntosh into the Magistrate's Office and in his capacity as a Justice of the Peace obtained a sworn statement from him about the events leading up to and surrounding the flogging. As far as the Administration's case against Tshekedi was concerned, Phinehas was a disappointing witness. 'I do not know', he told Germond, 'whether I am subject to the

Chief's jurisdiction or not. I thought the Chief has a legal right to adjudicate in my case, I have never before been flogged by a Native Court, nor have I been tried by the Chief before this for any offence, but I have had a civil matter against me decided by the Chief once before in connection with some work I had done for natives.

'When the Chief passed the judgement under question against me I did not object to the procedure. I did not report the matter to the Magistrate as I was satisfied the procedure was in order. I do not wish to lay a charge against the Chief.'[5]

Potts wrote out a somewhat terse report on the flogging, to which he attached McIntosh's statement with the letter he had received from Tshekedi and a copy of Tshekedi's circular to the white residents of Serowe.[6] Germond managed to get the report on to the goods train which was due to arrive in Mafeking the next day at 1:38 P.M.

On Friday, while waiting for Potts's report, Rey sent off a telegram to Admiral Evans, the Acting High Commissioner, who was still on holiday in the Kruger National Park. To try to ensure that it reached him, Rey sent copies to him at 'various likely places in the Game Reserve'[7] care of the station masters at Sabie and Nelspruit respectively. He informed Evans that 'a further and more serious situation' had arisen with Tshekedi.[8] Presumably the Admiral did not go on safari with his code books, so Rey had to send it *en clair* and risk the perusal of the curious eyes of telegraph clerks and station masters. Divulging as little information as necessary, he asked Evans whether he could meet him in Pretoria as early as possible the following morning. He himself would leave that night for the South African capital, where he would be staying at Polley's, his favourite hotel. Only at the very end of his telegram did he indicate that the crisis concerned the flogging of a white by Tshekedi. He then telephoned Shirley Eales, the Administrative Secretary in the High Commissioner's Office in Cape Town. He briefed him on what had happened and asked him to set off straight away for Pretoria with Leslie Blackwell, Legal Adviser to the High Commissioner. They would hold a conference with the High Commissioner on Sunday morning and decide what to do about Tshekedi.[9]

Eales responded to Rey's telephone call by alerting his masters in the Dominions Office to the situation. Echoing Rey, he informed them that the 'Chief could presumably be tried for assault, but having regard to seriousness of offence and bearing in mind state of public feeling in South Africa in the matter between Europeans and natives strong administrative action may have to be taken. It may be necessary to suspend Tshekedi immediately from exercise of functions of Acting Chief and order him to leave the Bamangwato Reserve'.[10] Eales would be leaving for Pretoria that afternoon at 4:00 P.M., but because of the time the train took from Cape Town it would be impossible for him to get there before Sunday morning. He therefore suggested that any messages for him from the Dominions Office be sent to await his arrival in Pretoria.

When the Dominions Office received Eales's telegram, the Secretary of State, J. H. Thomas, was away in Hove on holiday. He was, however, planning to stop by at the Office on Monday morning, so his officials urged Eales to send in a full report of Sunday's conference by cable so that Thomas could consider it when he came in. He should also send any information available as to the character of the alleged offence of McIntosh as well as any explanation which may have been given by Tshekedi.[11] With remarkable prescience Sir Geoffrey Whiskard, Assistant Under Secretary of State in the Dominions Office, minuted on Eales's telegram: 'This may well lead to trouble.'[12]

Back in Mafeking, Rey, while getting ready to take the train to Pretoria, continued to 'blast off' telegrams to Potts, asking him whether the Chief had yet returned to Serowe and ordering a medical examination of McIntosh if that had not already been organised.[13] Potts arranged for McIntosh to be examined by the Government doctor at Serowe, Dr A. Austin Morgan, who found that he bore two wheals across the shoulders and back. The first extended across the left shoulder and down the left arm; this was raised and at the time it was inflicted had clearly drawn blood. The second extended across the small of the back. There were no other definite marks of injury to be seen. Dr Morgan opined that the two wheals could have been inflicted by a sjambok.[14]

Much later a Mongwato friend of Phinehas was to allege that the Administration had tried to persuade, then suborn, Phinehas into taking out a case against Tshekedi. Ketshuhile of Maboledi ward in Serowe, where Phinehas had his hut, reported that Phinehas had told him that the day after he had been flogged he was called by the Magistrate's Office and advised to make out a case against the Chief. He had been 'very much surprised by this advice because he had not appealed against the Chief's judgement.' He said that when he went to the hospital for his medical examination he had again been advised to bring a case against the Chief but had refused to do so. When Ketshuhile asked why McIntosh was unwilling to lay charges against Tshekedi, he replied that 'the Chief was his Chief in the same way that he is a Chief to me.' Ketshuhile then told him that 'the Chief was my Chief because I am a Native, but McIntosh was a white man. McIntosh said he lived by the Chief, and that the people who were advising him to make a case against the Chief only wanted him to leave the place and have no means of making a living. McIntosh further said that he was told that if he made a case against the Chief, he would probably get Forty pounds as compensation, and McIntosh said that even if they had promised him one hundred pounds he would never agree to make a case against the Chief; his heart . . . revolted against such action, even were he threatened by being sent to gaol. McIntosh said that he would be pleased if the Chief could be told these words.'[15]

Ketshuhile's statement reflects both the suspicion in which the Bangwato held their British overlords at the time and the dilemma that confronted any white then resident in the Bamangwato Reserve. He might not be subject to the Chief's justice, but if he wished to work in the Reserve he had to recognize the fact that he could only do so with the permission of the Chief. But the response by Phinehas to these alleged overtures also fits in with his subsequent unqualified acceptance of Tshekedi's authority.

Before he boarded the overnight train to Pretoria, Rey completed a lengthy report on the McIntosh affair which was to serve as the basis of his deliberations with the High Commissioner the next morning and to provide them with an agenda for action against Tshekedi. Potts's report was now in his hands, and it served as a springboard for his own even more melodramatic effusion. Potts had written: 'Tshekedi's action is intolerable. He has now acted in total disregard of the Administration and in such a way that if this incident finds its way into the Press I would not venture to say where it will end . . . but I must formally ask that the matter be taken further. It is immaterial whether McIntosh is a native clothed in a white skin. A fundamental principle is at stake and Tshekedi should, I venture to say, be put in his place.'[16]

This of course was exactly what Rey intended to do. 'The effrontery and insolence' of Tshekedi's attitude, he wrote, 'as revealed in these documents is such as to need no comment from me—it is complete and barefaced defiance of all authority.' Rey then emphasized that in law it was quite clear that Tshekedi had no right whatsoever to try whites in his court, and an amendment to the Proclamation of June 1891 forbidding this had been made in 1922 by an amending Proclamation to ensure that 'even if a European consented he could not be tried by a Native Court'.[17]

For Rey it was 'impossible to exaggerate the effect in the Protectorate and in South Africa generally of the public flogging of a European by natives in a Native Court. The effect on the native mind in the Territory, and on the Chiefs in particular, must be such as to render insecure the position of Europeans in the Territory, to cause the Government at large to be regarded with contempt, and to make it impossible any longer to carry on the administration of the Territory, unless immediate and drastic action is taken.

'The effect on public opinion in South Africa—of all parts of the world—of an action of this kind is too serious to contemplate without the gravest misgivings. The Union Government could not, with its six million inhabitants, contemplate acts of this kind in a neighbouring territory being tolerated, and there is little doubt that they would feel compelled to take action of a nature which may well be guessed.' Tshekedi, he continued, had acted in cold blood and with his eyes open. 'It is not even as if the Acting Chief were a man addicted to alcoholic excess and that in a moment of drunken excitement he had allowed his feelings to run away with him. . . . His action is therefore . . . alike amazing and inexplicable.'

Rey proposed that as a preliminary step there should be an Enquiry into the Chief's conduct. 'I am, of course,' he volunteered with characteristic lack of reticence, 'fully prepared to conduct the enquiry myself assisted by the Magistrate, and my experience of this sort of work might be valuable. On the other hand as I shall have to deal with the matter administratively and shall be responsible for the carrying out of Your Excellency's ultimate decision in the matter, I think it would be preferable for the enquiry to be carried out by Captain Neale', Rey's second-in-command.

Rey's conclusion was that if the facts as known were confirmed by the enquiry, 'the only possible course would be to remove the Acting Chief from his position and to invite the Tribe to suggest to the Resident Commissioner for consideration by the High Commissioner names for his successor.' Tshekedi himself should be exiled to Ghanzi, a remote settlement in the Kalahari on the western border of the Protectorate, as 'it is unlikely, I fear, that the Union Government would allow him to live in Union Territory.'

Rey was convinced that the Chief would not obey the order to move to Ghanzi, so there would be no option but to arrest him. With the memory of his difficulties with Gobuamang still vivid, he urged Evans that this 'cannot be done without the display of a strong force; I have none available, and in the circumstances it seems necessary to ask that a detachment should proceed to Serowe from the Fleet, or that men should be borrowed from Southern Rhodesia as was agreed by the Dominions Office in a recent case. I am strongly in favour of the former course.' He then went on to speculate about the prospects of criminally prosecuting Tshekedi. 'I feel, however, that the object to be attained is not so much the punishment of the Acting Chief—desirable though this may be—but his removal from his functions which indeed appears essential. In other words, the action to be taken seems to me to be administrative rather than judicial.'[18]

Rey arrived in Pretoria the next morning to find that his attempts to contact Evans had been successful. The High Commissioner had arrived in Pretoria that morning. When the two met, Rey wrote in his diary, he learned 'much to my surprise and rather to my alarm' that Evans had already telegraphed to Cape Town to order up a detachment from the Fleet.[19] Why he should have been alarmed is not clear, since Evans had merely anticipated his own recommendation. Rey and Evans then spent the morning making plans with the Political Secretary to the High Commissioner, Percivale Liesching, who was in Rey's opinion 'an exceedingly able and very delightful young man'.[20] Not waiting for the arrival of Eales and

Blackwell, the three adopted Rey's programme of action. Evans himself would 'proceed to the Protectorate with the least possible delay to settle the matter personally on the spot' as 'it was essential that before giving any decision I should have before me an authoritative account of what had actually taken place as far as the facts could be ascertained.'[21] Evans further informed the Dominions Office that he considered it 'very necessary that there should be an effective demonstration by the Imperial Authority of its determination to maintain order.'[22]

That morning at 12 noon Evans paid what was to have been a courtesy call on his friend Oswald Pirow, the Minister of Defence. The meeting, along with one with the Prime Minister, General Hertzog, which was cancelled at the last minute, had been arranged before news of the 'flogging' of Phinehas McIntosh came through. The courtesy call now developed into a Council of War. Pirow responded enthusiastically to Evans's request for permission to 'move troops across Union territory.' As Liesching later reported to the Dominions Office, Pirow, who combined the portfolio of Railways with that of Defence, 'not only promised every facility for rail transport, but offered to supply any material in the form of bombs and aircraft, and to place a Union Defence Force aeroplane at the disposal of the Admiral for his journey from Pretoria to Palapye Road. Admiral Evans with whom I had previously discussed the undesirability of accepting any assistance in men and material from the Union Defence Force or Police, confined himself to accepting the offer of railway facilities.'[23] After the meeting, Evans wrote formally to Pirow to obtain permission to send an armed escort from Simonstown to Serowe, 'should the occasion arise.'[24] Pirow himself had been so enthusiastic about the expedition that, as Evans later reported, the Minister 'was longing to bomb Serowe.'[25]

Both Evans and Rey exaggerated the necessity of assuaging outrage in the Union over Tshekedi's action in flogging a white man. Their fears in this direction were more anticipated than actual, since news of the flogging did not appear in the press until the next day and was based on a press statement by Evans issued on Sunday morning.[26] And in the event white attitudes were to be much more ambivalent than Rey had predicted. It seems that as far as a hardline approach was concerned Evans was partly guided by Oswald Pirow, whom he much admired.[27] Indeed, the pro-Nazi Pirow, who had studied at Oxford and was notorious for his ruthless repression of the black riots in Durban in 1929, was his closest contact in the Union Government. 'We had a great deal in common,' Evans later wrote. 'He became my greatest friend in the Southern Hemisphere. His company to me was like a glass of champagne after a successful Admiral's inspection.'[28]

Evans's course of action was also much influenced by his own brief experience of Tshekedi, whom he considered 'a difficult, suspicious and temperamental young man of considerable intelligence and education' who 'has made things so difficult that no magistrate in the Protectorate willingly serves in his capital,

Serowe.' Colonel Rey, who was 'himself of a somewhat impulsive and arbitrary temperament', had had 'great difficulty with Tshekedi since his appointment three years ago.'[29] But even more revealing of the attitudes that informed his approach to Tshekedi was his account of his time in South Africa which he gave in his autobiography some fifteen years later. In it he presents himself as an unashamed negrophobe. From the Union leaders he had learnt 'valuable facts concerning the various Negro races, and the dangers confronting the Europeans, which were not made less by the Negrophiles, who fail to gauge the character and inclinations of the various Negro races employed in the mines, on the land and in domestic and commercial service.

'The Negro is a great liar, he is naturally lazy, he loves talking *ad infinitum,* and in *kgotla* he will talk for days on the most paltry matters. He understands rough justice, but petting and pampering are considered by the natives as signs of weakness.' And of all these 'natives', he considered 'the nastiest are the Bechuanas.'[30]

Rey was genuinely fearful that if the Bangwato were to make trouble he would not be able to deal with them, since the bulk of the Bechuanaland Protectorate Police were engaged in monitoring the foot-and-mouth cordon he had just established. Though there was no specific reason to suppose that the Bangwato would use force to oppose the Administration if their Chief were deposed, Rey had the memory of his difficulties with 'Gobbleman' at Moshupa only too clearly in mind.

And so Evans, in his dual capacity as Acting High Commissioner and Commander-in-Chief of the Africa Station, ordered up an armed escort, to consist of a marine detachment of maximum strength, three howitzer guns and crews, one seaman platoon to be selected from HMS *Carlisle* and/or the sloops. Sufficient blank ammunition was to be supplied for saluting purposes, while each man was to be supplied with three hundred rounds of ammunition. If possible the escort, comprising some two hundred men, was to arrive at Palapye Road Station, more than a thousand miles from Simonstown, by Wednesday morning.[31]

While Evans and Rey were conferring in Pretoria, Potts and Germond were concerned that the Chief had still not returned to Serowe. Trooper Lenanile had failed to find him at Shashane and so was pursuing him up the road to Nata. The first instruction to reach Potts as a result of the decisions made by Evans and Rey was to make the necessary arrangements for the Enquiry at Palapye Road for Tuesday, September 12. Tshekedi, his councillors and headmen were all to be there along with any others 'whose testimony might be helpful'.[32] Hotel accommodation should be reserved for Captains Neale and Nettelton, as well as for a shorthand writer. An interpreter should also be provided. Soon after this telegram another arrived which put a further nail in the coffin intended for Tshekedi. This contained an official reprimand to be delivered to him for his audacity in addressing a telegram direct to the substantive High Commissioner, Sir Herbert Stanley, even though he was going on leave, and for failing to pass it along the proper channels of communication of which he was perfectly aware. 'It appears that he has made a deliberate attempt to ignore the whole Administration and if so is deserving of reproof.'[33]

As Evans and Rey prepared to put themselves on a war footing, instructions were given to keep telegraphic communications between Serowe and Mafeking open on the Saturday and Sunday afternoons between 2:00 P.M. and 5:00 P.M., when normally they would be closed.

At last at 2:00 P.M. that Saturday afternoon Tshekedi returned to Serowe. The various messages for him were delivered, including the one instructing him to present himself at the Enquiry at Palapye Road on Tuesday morning. Similar instructions were issued to T. Elliott Booker, Dr Morgan, and to Phinehas McIntosh, who was told that a warrant for him to be conveyed to Palapye Road by the post lorry would be provided and requisitions made for his food during his stay there.[34]

The Administration seemed to be riding high in the first stage of its 'war' with Tshekedi. The only cloud on the horizon was to be found in the reply sent by Captain Potts in answer to a query by Rey as to whether Nettelton had ever held his planned enquiry into the conduct of McIntosh and McNamee. Potts had to report that Nettelton had done nothing at all about it and indeed had not even given him the file on the subject when he returned from leave in September 1932. But there was good news: Potts was now confident that he would be well enough to assume full duties on the Monday.[35]

When Eales and Blackwell arrived in Pretoria on Sunday morning, they were horrified to discover that Evans and Rey had not waited for their advice before taking action. The two proconsuls had already committed themselves to sending in the marines without consulting their Legal Adviser or referring the matter to the Dominions Office. The marines were now getting ready to entrain on the long journey north. In Blackwell's view this 'magnified into a serious crisis what was but a petty incident.' Both he and Eales advised strongly against the proposed expedition and asked that it be sent back. Blackwell told Evans that 'it would be quite sufficient to summon Tshekedi to Pretoria; if he flouted this order, which was most unlikely, then there might be a necessity for strong action.'[36] Eales warned Blackwell to be very discreet in what he said to Evans and Rey, 'as they were both very jumpy and very much on the defensive over their actions'.[37] Blackwell was in a strong position to disagree with Evans. He was only part-time Legal Adviser to the High Commissioner and had his own practice as a silk. Furthermore, he was a member of the Union Parliament. As Evans's Administrative Secretary, Eales was much more precariously placed, but nevertheless he too opposed his temporary master's course of action.[38] The only change Evans did eventually make to his plans was to cancel his original intention of arriving at Palapye Road at the head of his naval escort on the eve of the Enquiry. Both Neale and Nettelton had expressed their opposition to his doing so, since they felt it would prejudge the outcome of the Enquiry,[39] as if this were in fact ever in doubt.

The meeting with Blackwell and Eales changed nothing except that it was now decided to hold the Enquiry on Wednesday rather than Tuesday. This would enable the marines to get to Palapye Road in time and also give Tshekedi an opportunity to consult with his lawyer, for the one concession Blackwell seems to have secured for Tshekedi was that he should have legal representation at the Enquiry.[40]

Evans then sent off a telegram to the Dominions Office informing them for the first time that he was despatching a naval expedition to the Kalahari to deal with Tshekedi.[41] He also informed them that he was setting up a Commission of Enquiry into events surrounding the 'flogging' and was suspending Tshekedi from his functions as Chief pending the outcome of the Enquiry. He considered it absolutely necessary to make a demonstration of force and decided to use British troops from the Royal Navy rather than a force from the Union or Rhodesia. His principal justification for this somewhat drastic course was the affront delivered by the Chief to the racial sensitivities of white South Africans. In 'matters of this kind', he insisted, 'failure on our part to take effective measures would have serious consequences and might lead to public demand that the Union Government should intervene',[42] an eventuality he knew the home Government would not wish to risk.

In Serowe, Tshekedi was quite unaware that the British Administration were mounting an 'invasion' of his territory. So, too, at the time was Potts. Tshekedi, who had an almost blind faith in the British legal system ever since he had won his appeal to the Privy Council in 1930, sent one of his royal headmen, Disang Raditladi, to see Potts and request that the Enquiry be postponed for two weeks in order to prepare his case and obtain legal assistance. He also informed the Magistrate that Tshekedi objected to Officers of the Protectorate Administration conducting the Enquiry. There should be independent commissioners or failing that a Judge of the Supreme Court, 'the reason for this being', Disang informed Potts, 'that at times he (the Chief) does not see eye to eye with the Officers of the Bechuanaland Protectorate Administration, and this sometimes causes misunderstandings between him and the Administration.'[43] The Chief further objected to the Enquiry being held at Palapye Road, since the events in question took place in Serowe and most of the relevant witnesses lived there.

According to Disang, when he had finished delivering the Chief's message Potts became angry, in particular at the Chief's allegation that he was only going to Palapye Road to be arrested. Potts told Disang that he was speaking like a child and that 'the Bechuana said they are killed when they are not actually killed.'[44] He assured Disang that the Chief was not going to be arrested and that the Government would arrange legal representation for the Chief and if necessary fly his chosen lawyer to Serowe. Potts had already been informed an hour earlier that the Administration were willing to arrange for a lawyer for Tshekedi.[45] Disang then told Potts that Tshekedi wanted his legal adviser from Cape Town.

Tshekedi was of course quite correct in his assumption that he would be arrested when he went to Palapye Road for the Enquiry. The very day that Potts was rebuking Disang for supposing this to be the case, Admiral Evans signed an order suspending Tshekedi from the exercise of his functions as Chief,[46] while Rey signed another confining him to Palapye Road Police Camp until the results of the Enquiry were made known.[47] Both orders, however, would come into effect only on the Wednesday morning, when Rey planned to hand them to Tshekedi in person before the Enquiry opened. Failure to obey the order restricting him to Palapye Road would make him liable 'to imprisonment with or without hard labour for a period of not less than a month and not exceeding six months and with or without a fine not exceeding one hundred pounds and in default of payment to a further term of imprisonment for a period not exceeding six months.'[48]

The reason Rey did not want the two orders served on Tshekedi the day they were signed was not the result of some perverse desire to deliver the instrument of his downfall to him in person, but because he did not dare do it without the presence of the naval escort which, he informed Potts by telegram, would be arriving on the same train as himself on Wednesday morning. It is not clear whether this was the first time Potts learnt that an armed escort was arriving, but there is no reference to it in any earlier telegram. It is just possible that he may have heard about it by telephone, since the message sent by Rey announcing its arrival does imply prior knowledge by Potts. In this coded message Rey told Potts 'for his information only' that he would hand Tshekedi the order suspending him from office on Wednesday morning. Potts received this message some three hours after his meeting with Disang Raditladi, and so had not lied to him. Just before the coded telegram arrived Potts was informed that Buchanan would be leaving Cape Town for Serowe on Monday morning. He then sent for Disang and gave him the good news.[49]

There was a second important reason for retaining Tshekedi in office for the next three days. Both Evans and Rey wanted to announce the conclusions of the Enquiry and the punishment to be meted out to the Chief in the largest possible *kgotla* in Serowe. And only the substantive Chief could organize this. And so Tshekedi, unwittingly though not unsuspectingly, was being asked to make the arrangements for his own public humiliation. The Administration depended on him to send the messengers to the outlying districts to bring the people in.

But Potts had his chores, too, in connection with the *kgotla*. In the first place,

Rey anticipated that there would be too many people to fit into the Chief's *kgotla* and so suggested that it be held in a large open space outside it. Eventually the showground was chosen. There Potts was to ensure that a dais was erected for the High Commissioner to stand on and deliver his speech. A flagstaff was to be planted nearby. The Bangwato would be assembled in a semi-circle in front of the dais, at either side of which the naval escort would be positioned.[50]

Tshekedi's suspicions must have been aroused by the timing of the *kgotla*. By calling for it to be held on Thursday morning immediately after the Enquiry which he had now been told was put back from the Tuesday till the Wednesday, Tshekedi was in fact served notice that the Enquiry would be a speedy affair. Tshekedi's own not inconsiderable experience was that the wheels of British justice normally turned exceeding slow. As for McIntosh, he was unaware that he and his friend McNamee were to be deported from the Bamangwato Reserve at the conclusion of the Enquiry.[51]

In Cape Town, Buchanan was in his bath when he first learnt from a guest that the Navy was on its way to the Bechuanaland Protectorate. At first he expressed disbelief, but this was confirmed for him when, according to Buchanan's account written some twenty years later in his draft biography of Tshekedi, Blackwell telephoned him to tell him that his friend Tshekedi was in great trouble. Blackwell told Buchanan that the Administration had offered to get hold of any legal counsel Tshekedi asked for, and he wanted to know whether he could travel to Palapye Road by Monday's train. Tshekedi was adamant that if he could not have Buchanan he would defend himself. 'I felt I had no alternative,' Buchanan wrote, 'but to say that I would come by the said train.'[52]

That night Rey motored over to Johannesburg from Pretoria to meet his wife, Ninon, who had come down from Mafeking in their beloved Armstrong Siddeley, 'Topsy', with the intention of spending a few days there. He stayed the night with her at the Carlton Hotel.[53]

If Sunday had been no day of rest for the sickly Potts, Monday was even worse. The indefatigable Colonel Rey continued to bombard him with telegraphic instructions. He was asked to be at Palapye Road on Tuesday evening, provided he was well enough, and to make sure all the witnesses were there too. Potts confirmed that he would be present and that so would Phinehas McIntosh and his associates Henry McNamee and Attie Klink.

Much of Potts's day was spent in organising lorries to take witnesses to Palapye Road and to then be available for use by the Naval detachment. He had to send to as far away as Francistown to get them. Additional lorries were borrowed by the High Commission from the Rhodesia Railways with the assistance of the Southern Rhodesian Government. Potts also had to occupy himself with booking accommodation in the dusty little railway settlement at Palapye Road, which had only one small hotel, for members of the Commission of Enquiry and the 'lady short-hand writer'. Over and above this he had to arrange suitable accommodation for Chief Tshekedi within the confines of the Police Camp.

When Evans finally accepted that it would not be wise for him to arrive in Gamangwato at the head of his troops, his enthusiasm for railway travel diminished accordingly. He took up the original suggestion made by Oswald Pirow and planned to fly to Serowe. But first he needed assurance that the Serowe aerodrome, as it was rather pretentiously designated, was 'absolutely' safe to land on. Potts personally went over what he more appropriately described as the Serowe landing ground and found no obstacles in the way of either landing or take-off. He did, however, issue a caveat: 'It is difficult for me as a layman to express a definite opinion as to the absolute safety of landing ground but other airmen who have landed here said it was a very good ground.'[54] He then suggested the landmarks that might be useful to the pilot in landing: flying west from Palapye Road he would pick out the Serowe church spire and the *kgotla* hill on his right and the cattle pens in the middle of an open plain. He could also use the platform erected for the Admiral and the flagstaff to help find his bearings.[55]

On the basis of Potts's report the Government Engineer assured the High Commissioner that Serowe airfield was safe for landing. Potts was then instructed to mark the centre of the airstrip with a cross of white cloth in strips five yards long by one yard wide or a similar whitewash one. A smoke fire on the down wind end of the aerodrome was to be maintained throughout the day of the High Commissioner's arrival.[56]

A major headache for Potts was the reception of the Naval contingent and accommodation for the others attending the Enquiry. In the first place, he kept receiving contrary advice as to the time of arrival of the naval escort. In the second place, he did not have all the requisites for the impending influx of visitors to the sleepy railway siding of Palapye Road. So he had to telegraph Mafeking to send up tents, portable baths, towels, soap, camp beds, plates, cups, cutlery and bedding.[57] In addition, he had to find out how much ammunition was stored in the Police Stations at Palapye Road and Mahalapye, the second-largest settlement in Gamangwato, some thirty miles down the railway line from Palapye Road. Furthermore, he was instructed to keep the telegraph line between Serowe and Mafeking open on a twenty-four-hour basis and to do so was forced to arrange with the Postmaster that Germond sleep in the post office that night.[58]

Potts's biggest headache by far was of course Tshekedi himself. The young Chief was losing no time in building up his defences. He sent off telegrams to white supporters both within and outside South Africa. As a matter of priority he contacted Alfred Jennings, that long-standing opponent of Rey and the Bechuanaland Protectorate Administration, who was in Tiger Kloof attending a meeting of the Executive Committee of the Southern Africa District Committee of the London Missionary Society, to whose members he was reporting 'the salient features of the matters at issue between the Chiefs and Government in regard to the Chiefs' powers under the system of Protectorate Government.'[59] Tshekedi asked him to come straight away to Serowe because of the unexpected crisis that had developed. Jennings also received a telegram from his friend Buchanan informing him that he was travelling by the boat train to Palapye Road at Tshekedi's request. Jennings immediately made arrangements to board the boat train at nearby Vryburg with the full support of the Executive Committee, 'who "prayerfully" commended to God their brother and the Chief in the difficult times through which they were passing.'[60] The Rev. J. H. L. Burns, the resident missionary in Serowe, and two others attending the meeting, waited for it at Tiger Kloof.[61] That night from his bed in the Tiger Kloof guest room, the Rev. Burns had seen 'the train with its sailors and marines, compartment lights ablaze, as it rushed past on its way north.' The Rev. Haile, who also saw it, said in the morning that it 'gave me a sickening pain in the tummy to see that train go past.'[62]

Tshekedi also telegraphed his friend Charles Roden Buxton, author of *The Race Problem in Africa* and a leading member of the Anti-Slavery and Aborigines Protection Society in London whom he had met on his visit there in 1930: 'Unexpected crisis reached regarding powers of chiefs and jurisdiction of native courts. Political capital made out of painfully petty case. Friends of the weak peoples please watch developments more closely.'[63]

Tshekedi was equally intent on drumming up support from among his own people. Already he had been able to use Headman Disang Raditladi, whom he had long seen as a source of opposition to his position as Regent, as a go-between with the Resident Magistrate. Now he sent out to district headmen, including the powerful Phethu Mphoeng, alerting them about the developing crisis. In particular he asked that certain girls who were known to have had relations with Phinehas be traced and sent up to Palapye Road for the Enquiry. Mompati of Mahalapye was requested to bring in two witnesses and to obtain an advance for their rail fares from a white trader in the town called Maclean, whom Tshekedi had already asked to advance money if the need arose. A further telegram to Mompati instructed him to get hold of a girl at Mokwoshana. A special runner should be sent for her and she should bring her son, Morgan, with her. Again Mr Maclean would provide her train fare. Tshekedi also cabled his close friend and fellow Chief, Bathoen II of the Bangwaketse, asking him to come to Serowe and 'watch developments personally'.[64] It was common practice in the colonial period for Chiefs to attend the others' *dikgotla* and offer advice or make themselves available for consultation.

That day Tshekedi also learnt from J. B. Kieser, his lawyer in Mafeking, that he would be at Palapye Road for the Enquiry. Kieser asked him to confirm the name of his counsel and the nature of the charge against him.[65] Tshekedi was of course still under the impression that the Enquiry would be a judicial one with himself represented by Buchanan. Desperate for more time to prepare his case and consult with his lawyers, he sent another delegation to Potts's office to reiterate his request for a fourteen-day delay. Led by Tshekedi's cousin, Headman Serogola Seretse, the delegation told Potts that they had been sent by the Bamangwato tribe and that the tribe considered the time allowed for preparations to be too short, especially if the Enquiry were held on the Wednesday at Palapye Road and the *kgotla* the very next day at Serowe. If the two-week extension was not granted, at least let there be a two-day interval between the Enquiry and the *kgotla*. This by implication would allow members of the Tribe to get back from Palapye Road in time for the *kgotla* and also give the opportunity for witnesses to speak at the Enquiry. 'In view of their experience of these Europeans they request that they might be given ample opportunity to speak.'[66]

After consulting Mafeking, Potts informed Tshekedi that he was clearly under a misapprehension as to the nature of the Enquiry. It was 'not a judicial trial but an administrative enquiry to establish the facts of the happenings at Serowe on the 6th September. . . . In these circumstances no prolonged legal consultation is necessary and in view of the gravity of the position caused by your action the High Commissioner is not prepared to consider any further delay nor alter persons appointed to enquire. The enquiry must take place as arranged.'[67] In a further letter to Tshekedi, Potts told him that under no circumstances was the Tribe to go to Palapye Road. It was essential that they should all be at Serowe for the *kgotla* for Admiral Evans. Potts had been considerably disturbed to learn that Tshekedi had given notice in his *kgotla* that morning that there was to be an Enquiry at Palapye Road and that as a result everybody would attend it. In consequence, he warned Rey that 'it will be well to be prepared for an outburst at Palapye.'[68]

On Monday morning, Rey set off once more for Pretoria while his wife, Ninon, returned to Mafeking, driven by their faithful chauffeur, Matsepane, whom Rey insisted on calling Marzipan. Rey spent the day in further conference and then also set off for Mafeking accompanied by Liesching, Political Secretary to the High Commissioner, who had been made a third member of the Commission of Enquiry. They travelled by train in the High Commissioner's personal coach. Before he left, Rey telegraphed Mafeking to instruct the station master to arrange for the train carrying the naval escort to be delayed until he arrived next morning, so that his coach could be attached to it.[69]

All was now ready for the 'invasion' of the Bechuanaland Protectorate. As far as Evans was concerned there might be between two thousand and seven thousand 'natives' at the *kgotla*. They would probably be unarmed, though there might be arms in the vicinity. It was therefore his intention to 'impress the natives with a display of force and to take such action as may be necessary to uphold the prestige of the white population. . . . Although it is unlikely that fire will have to be opened, Vickers and Lewis guns are to be ready for firing and magazines of rifles loaded with ball ammunition, cut offs closed, bayonets fixed.'[70] The ball ammunition was specifically designed to provide a wide spread of shot when fired.

In Cape Town, Buchanan managed to sort out some of his forthcoming legal commitments and get on the Monday morning boat train. He talked on the station with a naval officer who seemed concerned that two hundred marines had been sent north without his knowledge. Buchanan suggested that the problem with Tshekedi could be easily rectified. If Tshekedi had exceeded his authority or done anything wrong, he was certain he would admit it and undertake not to do so again and further reiterate his loyalty to the British Crown. 'On the other hand, if Tshekedi had done nothing wrong, then wild horses would not compel him to say he had, and I, certainly, would not advise him to say so.'[71] In reply the officer concerned said he would 'burn the wires' and see what could be arranged 'to find a quick and amicable settlement of what we both felt was a situation that should never have arisen.'[72] The officer than gave Buchanan a 'chit' to hand to the Admiral's Flag Lieutenant on arrival at Palapye Road.

In his compartment on the train Buchanan was joined by Archie Frew, the young correspondent of the South African Press Association and Reuter, who 'gave me all the dope—not very much—then known to the Press—about the navy going to Bechuanaland.' According to Buchanan, Frew was a 'charming and well-informed young man who knew his job and it was extremely fortunate for Tshekedi that he was "on our side" '.[73] Frew knew Jennings, who was a close friend of his father, and had obtained from him a lot of background information about the Bechuanaland Protectorate. Jennings was later to report that Frew had 'roped in the whole Press of the country [South Africa] by his influence and the righteousness of Tshekedi's cause.'[74]

In London, Evans's telegram, which had arrived at the Dominions Office at 3:35 A.M. on Monday, caused considerable consternation. Before replying to it, Dominions Secretary Thomas wrote to his Prime Minister, Ramsay MacDonald: 'No one knows better than you that very serious political reactions may result, even to the extent ultimately of an enquiry. It looks, on the face of it, as though the Europeans in the case are scoundrels, but equally there is the question of the native position to be considered.'[75] Thomas also wrote to Eyres-Monsell, First Lord of the Admiralty: 'It is hardly necessary for me to remind you that this looks very dangerous. . . . It may be that the Admiral is a good politician, I hope he is.'[76] As far as Thomas was concerned, a 'crisis, or semi-crisis, was precipitated by Admiral Evans', who 'acted with the (shall I say?) traditional British spirit, took the law into his own hands even as Tshekedi had done, and marched up country with a company of bluejackets. It was British in spirit but it wasn't discreet: most certainly it wasn't diplomatic. It was a moment when anything might have happened, and I had to act with despatch in order to prevent anything like a far-spreading reaction.'[77]

Thomas, therefore, gave Evans firm instructions in a telegram sent off at 5:15 P.M., by which time the Navy was well on its way to Mafeking: 'I am seriously disturbed at situation which has arisen and shall await with anxiety your further report. . . . I assume that in its inquiry Commission will include examination of charges made by Tshekedi against Europeans and also alleged failure of Resident Magistrate to take action in the matter, and that if inquiry should show that there is prima facie evidence of criminal offences having been committed by Europeans prompt and adequate measures will be taken to ensure trial and, in the event of conviction, punishment.

'While I fully appreciate considerations relating to feeling among all sections European community in South Africa referred to in your telegram, I cannot too strongly emphasize deplorable effect which might be created here by anything which might be construed as laxity on part of the Administration in dealing with offences against natives committed by Europeans.

'I am glad to note that you have taken the necessary steps to ensure that the Chief shall be adequately advised. . . .

'I note that you have deemed it necessary to arrange for a naval detachment to proceed to Palapye Road. Whilst fully appreciating the considerations urged in your telegram I am sure you will not be unmindful of the paramount importance of avoiding any action which may lead to the use of force.'[78]

Early the next morning, Tuesday, 12 September, the train conveying the naval detachment steamed into an almost deserted Mafeking station. Among the few present to welcome the marines and sailors was a reporter of the *Mafeking Mail,* who learnt that when they received orders to go to Palapye Road they were sailing off the Eastern Cape near Port Elizabeth in a forty-mile-an-hour gale. The reporter found them 'a very business-like crowd'. They were travelling in a train of eight coaches, a dining car, and a double bogie with four howitzers, two Lewis guns and two Maxims. 'They were really a happy lot of boys ready for anything.'[79]

At 7:30 A.M. the train drawing the High Commissioner's coach came into the station. Rey was met by Ninon, who was to travel with him. He sped back to his residence in the Imperial Reserve, which he had renamed Protectorate Government House, to give it a more gubernatorial air. There he collected some clothes and his uniform, and went back to join the train.[80] His coach hitched on to the navy train, Rey steamed north for his confrontation with Tshekedi.

The news of the flogging and the naval expedition was now generally known in South Africa and had reached the newspapers in Britain. As yet there was little editorial comment. Papers concerned themselves with reporting the bizarre turn of events. The *Natal Mercury* did, however, worry as to whether the Union's neutrality had been violated by Admiral Evans's action,[81] while in London the *Daily Mail* informed its readers that 'Tshekedi is said to be one of the most enlightened of African chiefs'.[82] The *Times* assured its readers that the 'Bechuana people are a generally tractable race, and the use of force is not likely to be necessary.'[83] In the *Rand Daily Mail,* Douglas E. Ritchie produced a short biographical sketch of Tshekedi, concentrating on his previous skirmishes with the British Administration, and concluded Cassandra-like that 'the settling of these new problems will require as much patience and understanding of the curious workings of the native mind as did the last.'[84]

Meantime, telegrams continued to flow in to Serowe for Potts about the arrangements for the Enquiry. Tshekedi confirmed that he would be at Palapye Road on Wednesday and, as instructed, would be ready to meet the Resident Commissioner half an hour before the Enquiry started. He sent a second telegram to Charles Roden Buxton to explain further the nature of the crisis that had developed. 'My action,' he assured Buxton, 'truly intended to check this behaviour. To my surprise obviously interpreted as action taking power upon self trying cases between Europeans and natives. Local European sympathies with me. Rumoured aeroplanes and marines coming. Greatly indignant about ruination of tribe at no fault of their own.'[85] Tshekedi in turn received a curious telegram from his old adversary and would-be assassin, Simon Ratshosa, advising him to be 'magnanimous pay respect and obedience to administration. Resistance is useless. Turn to that flag which means purity of government with equal rights and equal duties to all men.'[86]

When Buchanan's train steamed into Mafeking later that day, he was joined by his fellow lawyer, Kieser. On the train they conferred with Jennings as to how best they could help Tshekedi, even though they had little to work on. But the two lawyers were confident that the Enquiry was to be a judicial one, especially as the press had reported, erroneously as it turned out, that the Administration was to be represented by Leslie Blackwell.[87]

For the Administration the request made by Thomas that Tshekedi's allegations against the Resident Magistrates be considered at the Enquiry caused consternation. While they were fully prepared to follow his injunction that unlawful acts by the whites concerned be dealt with by the Commission, Evans told Thomas: 'I should strongly deprecate inclusion within the scope of the Commission inquiry as to the alleged failure of the Magistrate to take action on the Chief's earlier representations. I will, however, ascertain the Resident Commissioner's views as to what steps, if any, should be taken administratively.'[88] Clearly the Administration was not prepared to put itself publicly on trial. Evans did, however, give Thomas a much-needed reassurance: 'I have very much in mind paramount importance of avoiding any action which might lead to the use of force.'[89]

Although Thomas had been assured by Eyres-Monsell of the Admiralty that Evans was a 'man of wide experience and has never shown lack of judgement',[90] he still reiterated his fears about a one-sided Enquiry in his next telegram to Evans: 'If there is any truth in the allegations made by Tshekedi against Europeans it is certain that a decision which dealt solely with Tshekedi's action would create a deplorable effect in this country, and I therefore regard it important that announcement of decision, whenever it is made, should cover not merely case of Tshekedi but also if any ground for action is disclosed case of Europeans as well. . . .'[91] He was prepared that the conduct of the Magistrate should not be included in the Enquiry itself but wanted Evans to give him his recommendations as to the action to be taken regarding Tshekedi's allegations.

Thomas was also relieved to learn from Evans that Buchanan had told him he was going to advise Tshekedi 'to reiterate his unabated allegiance to the King, to apologize to the High Commissioner in whatever way I might desire and to leave it to my discretion what punishment should be inflicted and to abide by my decision. Buchanan had further emphasized that the Chief would accede to my request without the use of force.'[92] Buchanan makes no reference to this conversation which runs contrary both to the advice he did give Tshekedi at the Enquiry and the position he and Tshekedi adopted throughout its proceedings. It is possible that Evans interpreted too optimistically Buchanan's exchange with the naval officer on Cape Town station or that the officer misunderstood the burden of what Buchanan was telling him in reporting it to his superiors.

Unknown to Evans, the man he had replaced temporarily as High Commissioner, Sir Herbert Stanley, was being asked for his advice by the Dominions Office. Whiskard, the Assistant Under Secretary, had contacted Stanley while he was on leave at Windsor and was told that it was necessary that 'these three youths were properly dealt with, and it would also possibly be necessary to take some disciplinary notice of the dilatoriness of the Resident Magistrate. At the same time it was clearly and absolutely essential that Tshekedi should be sharply and publicly brought to book.' As far as the British Government was concerned, no occasion should be afforded the Union Government to intervene because of undue leniency. Yet it was essential that action against Tshekedi should not give rise to violent tribal disturbances and it should also not be the occasion for attacks in Britain on the local Administration. He was disturbed that Admiral Evans had ordered up a naval escort, which he thought unnecessary at this stage.[93]

Evans sent a telegram to Rey in which he communicated Dominions Office thinking about enquiring into Tshekedi's allegations against the Resident Magistrates, addressed to him at Debeeti station, where the naval train was due to stop at 3:52 P.M. A second copy was sent to await him at Palapye Road.[94]

For Evans the expedition he had launched into the Kalahari was a matter of great pride. It had 'established a precedent for Imperial troops to be taken through the Union and made clear to the Dutchmen that we were capable of managing our own affairs in the Protectorates.'[95] As far as the Afrikaans newspaper *Die Vaderland* was concerned, Evans had indeed taken the right action. Its editorial applauded 'the efficient speed with which the High Commissioner acted. A show of power and prompt action were both necessary. If we allow a white man to be whipped by natives, we can expect worse things.'[96] The naval detachment finally pulled into Palapye Road station at 8:30 P.M. At the station to watch the arrival of the train was Tshekedi, dressed in a blue serge suit, a light-grey hat and brown shoes. Together with him were a large number of his people, who watched in awe as the marines unloaded their 'full arsenal of military equipment and their elaborate commissariat capable of holding out for several weeks in the bush' and which 'gave the impression that they had come prepared for any kind of emergency.'[97] Among the crowd was Phinehas McIntosh, 'one of the principal actors in tomorrow's drama.'[98]

CHAPTER 3

Kangaroo Court

Serowe was almost deserted on the eve of the Enquiry. All day long men had streamed along what the correspondent of the *Natal Mercury* called 'the aching road' to Palapye.[1] Some were on foot, some on donkeys or oxen, while others were ferried there by lorries supplied by the Chief. Many of them carried weapons—old rifles, staves or knobkerries—even though Tshekedi had personally given instructions through Headman Disang Raditladi that no arms were to be taken to the Enquiry.[2] He had not, however, followed the Magistrate's instructions that only councillors, headmen and witnesses should travel from Serowe to Palapye Road. Like any Tswana ruler, Tshekedi was well aware that in the last resort 'a Chief is a Chief by the people', and that in a crisis like this it was important not only to have the people behind you but that this should be seen to be the case.

Serowe was thus largely a town of women and children that Tuesday, since neither of these groups was supposed to take part in the political life of the *morafe*. The Bangwato capital bore no signs of tension or excitement.[3] The only sign of the dramatic events about to unfold were the preparations at the showground where the dais for the High Commissioner had been erected, and a broad white line fifty yards long had been painted twenty-five yards in front of it. On Thursday the Bangwato men would be assembled behind this line drawn from east to west as the High Commissioner, facing due south and with no sun in his eyes, informed them of the fate of their young Regent.

One group that did go about its business in Serowe was the small white community. Evans had already reported to Thomas in London as a partial justification for

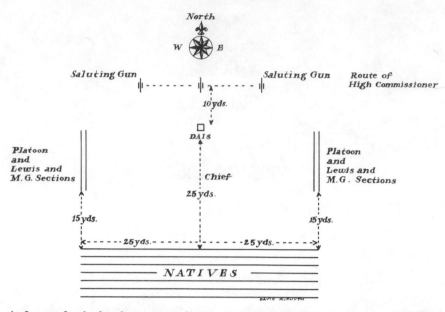

4. Layout for the *kgotla* ceremony for the suspension of Tshekedi at Serowe on 14 September 1933, as specified by Admiral Evans.

the use of force that the Resident Magistrate had received representations from two of the leading white residents in Serowe, Parr and Fodisch, requesting protection for their families.[4] Fodisch had apparently been told by Tshekedi that there was a possibility of his being deposed. He had asked the Chief whether he thought there would be any trouble. Tshekedi had replied, 'No, but of course if I am deposed I cannot then say what will happen.' At this Fodisch and Parr, in the words of a fellow trader, D. G. McLaggan from Mahalapye, got 'windy'.[5] Some whites were reported to have sent their children away from the capital.[6] But the correspondent of the *Natal Mercury* found that the whites in the town did not view the situation with any kind of anxiety. 'They are for the most part curious, as to what will be the outcome of tomorrow's enquiry.'[7] He thus confirmed McLaggan's view that Fodisch had overreacted when he said that the position was really serious. As McLaggan reported later, Blackbeard, the senior trader in Serowe, 'pooh-poohs this idea, so do most people in Serowe.'[8]

The white community in Serowe had about as little access to information as to what was really going on as the Bangwato themselves. Indeed, the *Rand Daily Mail* of that day accused the Administration of imposing censorship on stories coming out of Serowe.[9] When Mr Woods proposed to send a copy of Tshekedi's circular letter to the white residents of Serowe for publication in the Johannesburg

Star, he was asked not to by Potts, who told him he had consulted Captain Neale, the Acting Assistant Resident Commissioner, and 'we are both agreed that it would be advisable to hold the publication of such a document over until after the Enquiry.'[10]

Tshekedi himself had left for Palapye Road in the afternoon and was found that evening in the lounge of the railway hotel sipping a glass of ginger beer by the assiduous representative of the *Mercury*, who thought him 'an engaging young man' who 'is popular not only among his tribesmen, but also among the European community at Serowe.'[11] Although the hotel was technically outside the Bamangwato Reserve, being located within the hundred-yard-wide railway strip controlled by the Rhodesia Railways and therefore able to operate a colour bar, Tshekedi as Chief was given the privileges of an honorary white man.

Palapye Road itself presented a scene of unprecedented activity that evening. There were more cars parked outside the station than at the time of the visit of the Prince of Wales in 1925. Tshekedi's supporters had set up camp around the huts of the small Bangwato population of the town. Among those who had arrived for the Enquiry was the young Chief of the Bangwaketse, Bathoen II,[12] who had responded immediately to the appeal from his friend Tshekedi for moral support.

When Colonel Rey arrived at Palapye Road he was relieved to find that all was quiet, but irritated that despite his orders to the contrary Tshekedi had brought in thousands—some correspondents put the number as high as fifteen thousand—of his supporters from Serowe and other parts of Gamangwato for the Enquiry. This was 'the very thing I had wished to avoid,' he wrote later in his diary, 'as the Enquiry . . . was likely to create trouble and I didn't want to have to deal with a huge crowd; that was why we had the Enquiry at Palapye instead of Serowe.'[13] But Rey was at least consoled by the fact that Tshekedi was 'exhorting his people to keep quiet'.[14] Rey and his wife decided to sleep the night in the High Commissioner's coach, which took some of the pressure off the small railway hotel where every available bed was taken up by government officials, typists, shorthand writers and journalists.

The marines and sailors also slept in the poorly ventilated carriages that had brought them up from Simonstown. None of them was quite sure what to expect the next day. On the way up the commander of the marines, Major Webber, had even asked Edwin Arrowsmith, the young political officer acting as assistant to Rey, whether he thought the 'natives' would throw down missiles on them from their housetops, as had happened in China. Patiently Arrowsmith explained that the huts of the Bangwato were neither high enough for, nor their sloping thatched roofs particularly suited to, such tactics. The Major did not speak to him again throughout the journey.[15]

Half an hour after his arrival, Rey held a conference with Liesching, Neale,

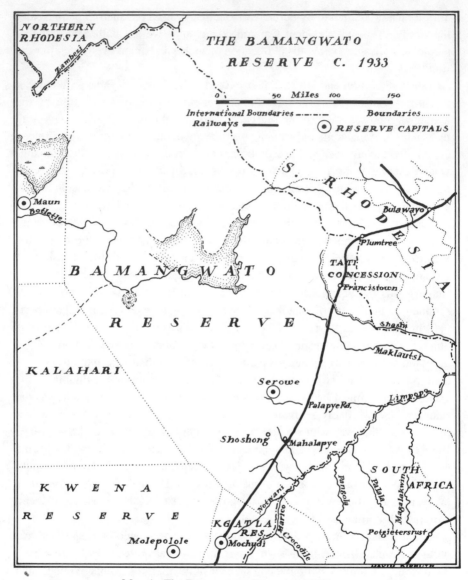

Map 4. The Bamangwato Reserve c. 1933.

Potts and Nettelton during which they discussed procedures for the Enquiry the next day. Immediately afterwards Rey conferred with Major Webber and the other officers of the naval detachment about the disposition of their troops in the morning. At midnight the telegram from Evans, conveying the Secretary of State's concern that some form of investigation of Tshekedi's complaints against the

Magistrates be made, finally arrived. In view of this Nettelton asked permission to excuse himself as a member of the Commission of Enquiry as he was a subject of the allegations made by the Chief, and to this Rey readily agreed. It was then decided that investigations into Tshekedi's allegations would be made by Rey and Liesching after the main Enquiry had completed its business.[16] Rey finally got to bed with a foul cold and a temperature of over a hundred degrees,[17] at the end of one of the hottest days local residents could remember.[18]

The boat train from Cape Town did not arrive until two in the morning, when even the inexhaustible Rey was asleep. Tshekedi, dressed in pink striped pyjamas and an overcoat, was at the station to meet Buchanan and his party.[19] Jennings persuaded Mr John Whiteside, an LMS missionary stationed at Plumtree in Southern Rhodesia, who had been present at the Tiger Kloof meeting, to break his journey at Palapye Road so that he could make a shorthand record of the proceedings of the Enquiry the next day. When the Rev. Burns had greeted Tshekedi, he asked him: 'What do you think of all this?' Tshekedi replied, 'Isn't it ridiculous? We don't need to be convinced of British power. We know it already.'[20] Then lawyers and missionaries followed Tshekedi to the house of Mr Thomas Shaw, a prominent local trader and nephew of Lord Craigmyle, who had put his home at their disposal for the evening. On the way Buchanan tried to trace the Admiral's Flag so that he could give him the chit from the officer he had spoken with at Cape Town station before departing. It was then that he learnt that the Admiral had not come up on the train with the marines.[21]

After a short discussion at the Shaws' house, everybody went to bed with the exception of Burns, who motored on to Serowe. After catching two hours' sleep himself, he sought out two of the leading white residents of the town, Mr Fodisch and Mr Blackbeard, with the intention of persuading them to come to Palapye Road as witnesses for Tshekedi. Mr Blackbeard's son, E. W. Blackbeard, promised to contact Mr H. Parr, another leading light in the European community, and ask him if he would also be a witness. Then at 8:05 P.M. Burns set off for Palapye Road again, leaving behind him a nervous community of blacks and whites, both of whom feared that a naval bombardment of their town was imminent.[22]

The village of Palapye Road had been awakened early that morning by the unfamiliar sound of bugles calling the reveille. The marines and sailors unloaded their guns from the bogies and then began setting up camp. Bangwato who had trekked in from Serowe and other parts of the Reserve for the Enquiry could watch the marines in pith helmets and with fixed bayonets on their rifles practise skirmishing or the signallers at work with their heliographs.[23] Field telephones were laid from the train to various strategic points in the village.[24] One guard of marines was posted outside the Court House and another, comprising only twenty Bechuanaland Protectorate Police—all that Colonel Rey could produce from a force

5. Marines training at the Palapye Road camp before the Enquiry (Rey Collection).

that was extended by its work on the cordons established to control the recent outbreak of foot and mouth—was posted outside the site of the Enquiry itself under Captain Croneen.[25] Rey was determined that the Protectorate should openly demonstrate that it was actively concerned with the control of its own crisis; as it was, the twenty policemen were the only black faces in an otherwise white sea of enforcers of law and order.

At 8:30 A.M. Buchanan went to see Rey to try to get the 'trial' postponed[26] or, in Rey's account, to 'stop the whole thing'.[27] Buchanan, who was accompanied by Kieser, was unsuccessful in his endeavour. Further, he was informed by Rey that he could not represent Tshekedi at the Enquiry, since it was an administrative and not a judicial one.[28] This was in direct contradiction to the earlier instructions Rey had telegraphed to Potts and copied to his Government Secretary on 10 September 1933: 'Inform Chief that if he wishes legal representation we will bring any lawyer he wishes by car from Mafeking and if necessary by plane from Johannesburg. If he wishes Cape Town lawyer we will get in touch with him by telephone. . . . Administration will take every reasonable step to assist him obtain legal assistance at his own expense. . . .'[29] The two lawyers were, however, granted permission to be present beside Tshekedi at the Enquiry.[30] According to Jennings, Buchanan's 'eyes glistened' at the news that he could not represent Tshekedi. 'Thank goodness they refused', Jennings alleged the advocate remarked, presumably because he realised what political capital would be gained thereby.[31]

Buchanan and Kieser had little time to confer with Tshekedi over this new development before he was due to present himself to the Resident Commissioner at 9:30 A.M. Accompanied by Potts, Rey handed Tshekedi the High Commissioner's order suspending him from 'the exercise of all or any of the functions of the Chieftainship of the Bamangwato Tribe'. The order was dated 10 September 1933, and Potts certified on the file copy that the original was served on Tshekedi at 9:30 A.M. and that at Tshekedi's request he had explained its purpose to him in English.[32] Rey then handed Tshekedi his own order, likewise dated 10 September 1933, and addressed to 'Tshekedi Khama, residing in the Bamangwato Reserve'. He was to confine himself 'during His Majesty's pleasure within the limits of the Government Camp at Palapye Road in the Bechuanaland Protectorate and during such period not to enter any other area of the said Protectorate.'[33] According to the correspondent of the *Natal Mercury,* the news that Tshekedi had been placed under open arrest created a profound sensation among the Bangwato when it became known.[34]

Rey was, nevertheless, at pains to make sure that Tshekedi was made comfortable while he was restricted to the Government Camp. The Assistant Resident Magistrate's house there had been prepared for him, and Rey directed that he should be allowed to hold interviews with anyone he wished to see while staying there,[35] which at least meant he could consult with his lawyers and missionaries.

Both Tshekedi and Rey found time to send off telegrams before the Enquiry opened at 10:00 A.M. Tshekedi sent one to Charles Roden Buxton informing him: 'I am under arrest and suspended from exercising Chief's powers. This done before any enquiry made. Have committed no wrong.'[36] For his part, Rey informed the High Commissioner that Tshekedi had defied repeated Government orders to arrange the *kgotla* for Thursday morning and had brought practically all his people into Palapye Road 'with obvious object of defeating Thursday's meeting.'[37] Evans later replied that as the majority of the tribe was at Palapye Road it would suit him if the *kgotla* were held at midday instead of in the early morning as was customary. 'This would give Tshekedi no ground for complaint that he could not get his tribe to Serowe in time for Kgotla as ordered.' He went on to inform Rey that he would be arriving at Palapye at 5:30 P.M. that day.[38]

By the time the Enquiry was formally opened at 10:00 A.M., the heat had intensified in the dusty Government Camp at Palapye Road. In an open space among the tin-pan-roofed offices and residences of the Government officials and police, a canvas awning had been erected under a large shady tree to protect the Commissioners from the sun. Detachments of marines, sweating in their khaki uniforms and helmets, stood guard nearby, seeking what little shade was available. Their howitzers were trained on the huge Bangwato crowd, sitting or squatting sullenly behind a wire fence separating them from the table behind which their Chief sat facing the Commission of Enquiry. He had personally supervised their disarming and seen that all potential weapons were left in the police station. Among the Bangwato was Phinehas McIntosh, sitting on one haunch but smartly dressed in a double-breasted suit, white-and-black tie and broad-brimmed trilby.[39]

The arrival of the Commissioners was marked by a formal salute by the small detachment from the Protectorate Police. The Commissioners were guarded at their table by three marines with fixed bayonets on their rifles. Tshekedi faced them with Buchanan at his right hand.[40] Once the Enquiry had opened, Rey left and sent off a telegram to the High Commissioner to confirm that it was underway and that the two orders had been served on Tshekedi.[41]

Rey now, for once, had nothing much to do. He could only wait until the Enquiry was completed. So he took time off to inspect the naval detachment—'a wonderful body of men—one hundred and sixty five in all. Sailors and marines with four small field guns, fit and hard and jolly, doing their drill and field practice, working their camp kitchens, testing their field telephones, and generally bringing a wonderful atmosphere of Britain into the veld. The officers are a jolly crowd, and by Jove weren't they all efficient and keen. One old quartermaster was priceless. I heard him remark ''My Gawd, fancy me after thirty years in the Navee just goin' on pension and now come up to this Gawd forsaken sand bin to be stuck in the bloomin' stumick by a bleedin' Kaffir.'' '[42]

While Rey was talking with the sailors, Captain Neale began proceedings with the announcement that Captain Nettelton had requested permission to withdraw from the Commission 'on the grounds that he may have been connected directly or indirectly with matters coming within the scope of the inquiry.'[43] Neale then told everyone there, including the large crowd of Bangwato for whom the evidence was interpreted into Setswana: 'I wish to make it clear to you that this is an enquiry and not a judicial trial. It will include an investigation of all the circumstances connected with certain unlawful acts alleged to have been committed by Acting Chief Tshekedi Khama, or any other person who may be concerned.'[44]

The first witness to be called was Phinehas McIntosh, who was given no indication by the Chairman that he, as much as Tshekedi, was on trial. He gave his evidence in a clear and straightforward way, but added nothing new to the statement he had made to Germond the day he was 'flogged'. When the Chairman had finished questioning McIntosh, Douglas Buchanan rose and informed him: 'I am here on behalf of Chief Tshekedi at this enquiry.'[45] Captain Neale, as Chairman, immediately interrupted him: 'I am sorry I cannot allow anyone to appear; I can only acknowledge you, Mr. Buchanan, as the Chief's legal adviser. This is an Administrative Enquiry and we cannot allow anyone to represent anyone else.'

Buchanan then said that he bowed to the Chairman's ruling but reminded him that the Administration had earlier informed the Chief that if he wished legal representation they would bring along any lawyer he requested. He then made formal application to represent Tshekedi, which the Chairman summarily dismissed. Tshekedi was thereupon asked whether he wanted to cross-examine McIntosh in what Buchanan later described as proceedings that were 'a travesty of British Justice.'[46] Buchanan, however, continued to sit at the small table on Tshekedi's right-hand side, practically acting as his 'junior counsel'. Tshekedi 'certainly carried on as ''senior counsel'' in that he quickly absorbed any points I suggested and included in his arguments any written notes I passed him when speaking.' In Buchanan's view, Tshekedi's cross-examination of witnesses was devastating.[47] Tshekedi was further assisted by Kieser, Jennings, and Burns, while Whiteside took down a complete record of the proceedings for his use afterwards.[48]

6. Tshekedi Khama photographed during the Enquiry (Associated Press Ltd.).

In cross-examining witnesses, Tshekedi tried to establish two points. The first was that McIntosh lived as a native rather than as a European and therefore was properly tried and sentenced by him. The second was that the proclamation denying Chiefs the right to try whites did not apply in the case of the rulers of the Bangwato.

It is worth recording in full Tshekedi's cross-examination of McIntosh, not only because it shows that Buchanan was not exaggerating when he wrote admiringly of the Chief's skills as a legal adversary but also because McIntosh himself gave little comfort to the Administration in his replies to Tshekedi's questions. Above all, the exchange between the two raised the central question as to whether a man who lived in most respects like a Mongwato was not one just because he happened to be white.

TSHEKEDI: Where did you stay?
MCINTOSH: In Serowe.

7. Tshekedi cross examining, from a photograph in the *Rand Daily Mail* of 15 September 1933 (Botswana National Archives).

TSHEKEDI: In what village?

CHAIRMAN: This is a cross-examination and must be confined to the evidence that has been given by the witness.

TSHEKEDI: The enquiry is that I had no right to flog witness. The trend of my questions is to show that this man is not a white man but that he is a native and that he lives as a native, in a native stadt and living with native women, not European women.

CHAIRMAN: You contend that because a man lives with native women he ceases then to be a person of European descent?

TSHEKEDI: I want to bring these statements to the enquiry—

CHAIRMAN: That can come very well in your statement. At this stage I would rather you confined yourself to cross-examination.

Tshekedi then continued his interrogation of McIntosh.

TSHEKEDI: What was the complaint brought against you by Ramangeneng[sic]?

MCINTOSH: Assault.

TSHEKEDI: Do you admit you assaulted him?

MCINTOSH: Yes, I do admit it.

TSHEKEDI: For what reason?

MCINTOSH: Hitting the girl I was staying with.

TSHEKEDI: Native or white?

MCINTOSH: Native.

TSHEKEDI: Is this girl your wife?

MCINTOSH: I am staying with her, not married.

TSHEKEDI: Are you living with her as man and wife?

MCINTOSH: Yes.

TSHEKEDI: Where?

MCINTOSH: Serowe.

TSHEKEDI: European house?

MCINTOSH: Native hut.

TSHEKEDI: In a white or native settlement?

MCINTOSH: Native settlement.

TSHEKEDI: Is this the first girl you have lived with in the way you live in this case?

MCINTOSH: No.

TSHEKEDI: How many times have you been tried in the Kgotla?

MCINTOSH: I do not know.

TSHEKEDI: Is it so many you cannot remember?

MCINTOSH: No.

TSHEKEDI: What do you mean?

MCINTOSH: We have not had a real case in the Kgotla yet.

TSHEKEDI: You said that this was not the first time you have been tried in the Kgotla—can you remember what the other occasions were?

MCINTOSH: I cannot just for the moment, it was some time back.

TSHEKEDI: Were they connected with your living with black women?

MCINTOSH: Yes.

TSHEKEDI: Did we force you to come to the Kgotla?

MCINTOSH: Just called me.

TSHEKEDI: Had you any objection?

MCINTOSH: No objection.

TSHEKEDI: Have you any complaint about my judgement?

MCINTOSH: I made no objection.

TSHEKEDI: What I mean is do you think you have been justly dealt with?

MCINTOSH: That is a hard question to answer, but I was satisfied with the judgement.

TSHEKEDI: You say you understand the native customs?

MCINTOSH: Some of them.

TSHEKEDI: And you say you know a custom that when a man is flogged he runs to the Chief?

MCINTOSH: I do not know the custom properly, but this is what I have heard.

TSHEKEDI: You were trying to do that?

MCINTOSH: Yes.

Tshekedi concluded his cross-examination of Phinehas at this point and gave no opinion as to whether or not it was a custom for a person sentenced in *kgotla* to beg the Chief or headman who had sentenced him to let him off his punishment.

McIntosh then withdrew and was not called again. Unknown to himself, he was also 'on trial', for the evidence he gave was later used by the Chairman, Captain Neale, to decide on his fate. Unlike Tshekedi, he had not even been given the benefit of legal advice or the right to cross-examination of witnesses. The proceedings in court and the heat clearly had their effect on him, for later, according to one newspaper, he fainted and had to be given a chair to sit on.[49] The Administration continued to build up its case against both Tshekedi and McIntosh by calling in Germond and Dr Austin Morgan. Neither added information that was not already known, though as a result of Germond's references to the statement he took from McIntosh on the day of the flogging Tshekedi was able to apply successfully for a copy of it.

The only witness, other than McIntosh, who gave Tshekedi support—intentional or otherwise—was Peter Sebina, his secretary and headman of one of the major wards in Serowe. Although he had been called by the Administration, his evidence bolstered Tshekedi's case that McIntosh was effectively living as a native. Sebina told the Commission that Phinehas was 'a quarrelsome man. He goes about swearing at people, and this I do not approve of. Once he even made an attack on my home and attempted to fight me, but I settled him, and he ran to the Chief and reported it. The Chief was very annoyed and instructed me to take him to the doctor and have him attended to but I did not do that. I have got correspondence from his father and himself. . . . In the Tribe generally people did not approve of his conduct. Our difficulty is that he lives like ourselves, but his colour is different to us. If it had not been for this difficulty we would probably have asked for him to be away from us. I once had him warned by the Magistrate—I thought he would listen to the Magistrate. He has been warned of his conduct.'

The Chairman then asked him why Phinehas had been reported to the Magistrate.

'It was on account of his fighting,' Sebina replied, 'and not understanding each other with the natives, he being a white man.'

'You said that McIntosh lived like yourselves,' the Chairman continued, 'but he had a different colour, that was the reason he was not liked?'

'I did not say that,' Sebina immediately responded. 'What I meant to say was that if he had been a native who had given us the trouble he had, he would have been expelled long ago. Our experience is that although he is living with us, he is not of the same colour. He states he is a white man, and how can we deal with a white man?'

What was clear is that Peter Sebina had indeed dealt with Phinehas as a headman would deal with anyone else living in his ward. He told the Enquiry that McIntosh had made one girl in his ward pregnant and that their child was still alive. 'We knew Phean's position, he was a poor man, and he paid with one head of cattle for the damage he had done.' In Tswana custom if a girl had been made pregnant by a man who was not going to marry her, her parents were entitled to compensation in cattle because she had been 'spoiled' (*o sentswe*); that is, her prospects of marriage had been decreased.[50]

Further evidence against McIntosh was given by T. Elliott Booker, who recounted that McIntosh lived in a small 'native' hut near his own house together with Henry McNamee, who was also to find that he was in effect being tried, but in his case in absentia, since neither he nor the more fortunate Attie Klink was summoned to appear before the Enquiry.

When Booker had finished giving his evidence, the Commission adjourned for lunch for an hour, returning at 1:15 P.M. It was pointed out to Buchanan at lunch that 'though we had not observed it, our minds being fully occupied with other matters, there was a Lewis gun fully charged pointed directly at the table where Tshekedi and I were sitting and only about 10 yards from us. This was causing great amusement to the on-lookers though not quite so amusing to us. I went up to the sub-lieutenant in charge, after lunch, and suggested that he should point the gun elsewhere but all he said was that he was under orders and would I please not talk to him on the subject.'[51] Lieutenant Commander Searle, one of the officers present at the Enquiry, said: 'I heard nothing of this machine gun business. No one in his senses would lie down in the dust behind a Lewis gun within a stone's throw of a target.' Captain McKinnon, another eye-witness, also reported years later that he saw no machine-guns so used.[52]

When the Commission resumed its business, Dr Morgan was recalled to give evidence about McIntosh's character. It was now obvious that McIntosh was on trial, but unlike Tshekedi he was not called to defend himself. Dr Morgan, however, confined himself to stating that he knew McIntosh often visited 'native huts' and chiefly had 'native' friends. Thereafter the main focus of the Enquiry turned on whether or not Tshekedi had the right to try whites in his *kgotla*. Tshekedi began by reading a long statement objecting to the present proceedings on the grounds that they concerned matters he wanted investigated by a Royal Commission or discussed with the Secretary of State. Chief among these was the lack of a clear definition of the constitutional relationship between His Majesty's Government of the Bechuanaland Protectorate and what he called the Treaty Chiefs, of whom he was a successor in office. Pending a decision about his request for a Royal Commission or an interview with the Secretary of State, the issue at hand was 'sub judice and the institution of the present proceedings is prejudicial to the interest of the Chief and Tribe.'

Tshekedi went on to argue that he was entitled to take the action he did on four grounds. The first was that his father, Khama III, had exercised civil and criminal jurisdiction over all inhabitants within his territory, including whites with their consent, and that he as his father's successor continued to exercise the same jurisdiction concurrently with the European courts established under the Order in Council of 9 May 1891. Second, that Section 10 of the Proclamation of 1891 as amended by Proclamation No 17 of 1922 did not have application to the Bamangwato Tribe, in that 'at all times Chief Khama and his successor in office have lawfully adjudicated in all civil and criminal cases and/or matters dealing with Europeans, with the consent of all parties concerned, and that the said McIntosh on previous occasions as well as on the occasion which is now at issue, did so consent.' Tshekedi's third argument was that 'McIntosh is living in a native hut in the ordinary acceptance of the term in like manner as a member of the native community of Serowe with a female member of the Bamangwato tribe and by reason of his habits and mode of living is regarded in law as a native and accordingly amenable to the jurisdiction of the Chief's Kgotla.' Fourthly and finally, that 'it was known and represented to the Administration and/or its officials that the said McIntosh was a man of bad and immoral character and a danger or potential danger to the moral welfare of the native community' but that 'no steps were actually taken to remove the said McIntosh from the territory concerned, or to check his misconduct.' In these circumstances he had been forced to try McIntosh, with his consent, in the *kgotla*.

Tshekedi concluded by saying that, 'having acted in a judicial capacity in Kgotla, I am consequently immune from any civil, criminal or other proceedings . . . and furthermore that in as much as these proceedings have been conducted as an enquiry and not as a trial, either criminal or civil, I am prejudiced in not being represented by Counsel as I would have been in such cases and more particularly after I had been informed on the 10th September, 1933, that I could have, if I so wished, legal representation.'

In his arguments, Tshekedi conveniently ignored a fact that must have been only too well known to him. In 1885, when his father had negotiated the Protectorate with the British Representative, Sir Charles Warren, he had stated in writing: 'Further, I give to the Queen to make laws and to change them in the country of the Bamangwato with reference to both black and white.' Captain Neale, too, ignored (or was ignorant of) this key statement. His response to Tshekedi's arguments and objections was simply to overrule them. As far as his allegations that the Magistrate had done nothing about his complaints regarding McIntosh's behaviour, there would be a special enquiry into this conducted by the Resident Commissioner and Mr Liesching immediately afterwards.

Tshekedi then read to the Commission the series of letters he had exchanged with Captain Potts about McIntosh's and McNamee's behaviour to show why he had finally been forced to take the action he had. He then said that what pained him most was the belief among some British officials that he was opposed to the Administration and to the King. Indeed, because he feared that 'one day I would be in the position I find myself today', he had brought his fears to the attention of Sir Herbert Stanley, the substantive High Commissioner, as recently as last July. He had received in reply an assurance from him 'that there is not, nor has there ever been any doubt in my mind, or in that of the Resident Commissioner and others of the Administration as to your loyalty to the King and to His Majesty's Government. I desire also to assure you that if as High Commissioner I should at any time have to make any complaint as to your conduct in the discharge of your duties as Acting Chief of the Bamangwato, I should not fail to communicate to you the grounds of such complaint before taking any action in the matter.'[53]

Tshekedi then told the Chairman: 'And in the position in which I now find myself today I cannot say the High Commissioner has carried out his promises.' Tshekedi asked to bring as witnesses some of the white residents of Serowe, but the Chairman refused him permission. Tshekedi also had waiting in the wings some of the young girls with whom Phinehas was alleged to have slept.[54] One official later reported: 'To my knowledge he had, standing bye [sic], a truck load of Coloured men and women and children whom he proposed to produce as evidence. In the circumstances they were never called—to the great relief of many.'[55] Tshekedi merely had to content himself with cross-examining his Resident Magistrate, Captain Potts, who had in fact to be protected by the Chairman, so searching were some of Tshekedi's questions. Referring to the letter he had received from Potts the day of the flogging informing him that he had no right under Section 10 of the Proclamation of 1891 to try whites, Tshekedi suggested to him that since it referred only to 'appointed chiefs' it did not apply to him as a hereditary chief.

TSHEKEDI: Would you deny that my father, my brother, or myself have not been appointed?

CHAIRMAN: It is not of much moment. I cannot allow that question.

TSHEKEDI: I am putting it to the witness and not to the Chairman.

CHAIRMAN: I know that, and I disallow the question.

TSHEKEDI: I think I am entitled to ask whether I have been appointed under Section 10.

CHAIRMAN: You were appointed as Acting Chief.

TSHEKEDI: I respectfully ask the Court to show me the law.

CHAIRMAN: I wish to have no argument.

TSHEKEDI: Since I am being charged with contravening this law.

CHAIRMAN: You are not being charged with contravening any law. This enquiry is into the facts. The point is that if this man was flogged in the Kgotla, this constitutes an illegal act. This Commission is sitting as a Court of Enquiry. I am not here to answer legal conundrums.

TSHEKEDI: I was referring to the remark of the Magistrate's that my action was in direct conflict with the law of the Territory, and I asked what law was this.

POTTS: The law forbids you to try Europeans in your Kgotla, and that is my answer to your question.

TSHEKEDI: I want my certificate of appointment.

POTTS: I have not got it.

TSHEKEDI: With regard to this law—

CHAIRMAN: You will have to get on with some other questions.

Frustrated in his attempts to get the Magistrate to agree that he was not an appointed Chief and to show that Tswana Chiefs were born, not appointed, as he and his fellow Chief Bathoen had made clear in their protests against the Native Proclamations,[56] Tshekedi was forced to take another tack with Potts. Referring to the circular he had sent out to the white residents, he asked Potts: 'I take it no discontent was made known to you?'

'The European residents of Serowe did not lodge any complaints with me with regard to your action,' Potts replied.

Apparently misunderstanding the direction in which Tshekedi was trying to lead the witness, the Chairman informed him once again that the complaints he had made to the Magistrate would be enquired into by the Resident Commissioner. But just before he could declare the Court closed, Tshekedi intervened: 'I wish to record that I applied to call evidence on the question of the jurisdiction of Chiefs and I was denied.'

Captain Neale then announced the findings of the Commission. In view of the deplorable evidence, which the Commission accepted, McIntosh was to be banished from the Bamangwato Reserve and all other 'native territories'.[57] This decision was received in silence by the Bangwato audience, who were not told what would happen to their Chief. This would be made known by the High Commissioner at the Kgotla in Serowe the following day. As for Phinehas, without the semblance of a trial, without formal charges even being laid against him, he was summarily deprived of his livelihood in consequence of his sentence to banishment, a punishment that had long since ceased to be inflicted in Britain. What is more, his 'crime'—sleeping with black women—was not an indictable offence in the Bechuanaland Protectorate, though it was of course one in the neighbouring Union of South Africa. But not a voice was raised in protest at the way in which this particular British subject was deprived of his basic legal rights.

Immediately after the Commission of Enquiry was concluded, Tshekedi had to go with Buchanan and Kieser to another Enquiry, this time into the 'alleged non-action of the Resident Magistrate, Serowe, with regard to complaints lodged by Chief Tshekedi re P. W. McIntosh, T. McIntosh and H. McNamee.' But before he did so he talked to his people. As one they rose when he approached. He then told them to be seated. As the correspondent of the *Natal Mercury* reported: 'Tshekedi's face betrayed his emotion. On one side of the fence were his followers, ready to do his bidding. Twenty yards away stood a detachment of marines, their bayonets fixed and a Lewis gun at their feet pointing directly towards the assembled natives. It was a dramatic moment but Tshekedi was master of the situation, and before long his tribesmen were winding their way slowly towards their encampment.'[58] Tshekedi then made his way to the second Enquiry, which began just after 3:00 P.M. in the full heat of the afternoon. Under Rey's chairmanship, it was briskly conducted. Tshekedi made it clear at the outset that he was not complaining about the laxity on the part of the Magistrates but their inability to deal with the question of the behaviour of McIntosh and McNamee. Captain Nettelton's own defence was that the Chief was absent from Serowe for much of the time he was relieving Potts. He had been waiting for the Chief to supply the evidence he had requested but this was not forthcoming before he was relieved by

Potts in September. He therefore disclaimed any responsibility for not taking the Chief's complaints further and holding the Enquiry that had been approved by Mafeking.

Tshekedi's response to this was: 'There is no reason why because I dropped my action the Magistrate should have dropped it too. He fully realized the state of affairs existing in the country. The last arrangement was that I should collect evidence. I accept that fact, but, as I said, I was very busy then. I have commenced afresh with the Magistrate Capt. Potts . . . and I definitely insist that firmer action could have been taken. In fact, when the question came up again, it came up from the Magistrate to me—although these lads are European. It was a complaint by Mr. Booker who referred the question to me. But nothing further was done, and I have never raised my complaint about inaction, but what I say is that nothing was done. It is merely a fact. Nobody has any complaint against the Magistrate. All that I asked was that something should be done.'[59]

Potts, who was also present at the Enquiry, then insisted that something had in fact been done in this case. He had reprimanded McIntosh, and the nuisance had ceased. The number of times McIntosh and McNamee had been brought before the Magistrate's Court was rehearsed, and then the Enquiry was brought to a close by Colonel Rey, who was in a hurry to get to the airfield to meet Evans, who was due to arrive at 5:30 P.M. As far as Rey was concerned the accusations about the 'alleged dilatoriness' of Nettelton and Potts 'in dealing with the Chief's complaints against the white villain . . . proved quite unfounded; the real fault lay with Tshekedi himself who had failed to produce the evidence asked for by the R.M.'[60]

Immediately after the Enquiry, Rey had a hasty interview with Serogola Seretse, who was acting as Chief while Tshekedi was confined to the Government Camp, and 'directed him to command the tribe to return to Serowe in accordance with H.C.'s instructions for the meeting to be held on the following day.'[61] According to the Rev. Burns, who overheard this conversation, Serogola replied very firmly: 'I take orders from the Chief only, Sir.'[62] Rey then rushed to the hotel to change into his uniform—he and Ninon had vacated the High Commissioner's coach, since Evans would be sleeping there that night. He then drove up to the airfield and met Evans, who arrived together with Eales and his Flag Lieutenant in a De Havilland Dragon from Johannesburg. So heavily loaded with luggage had the plane been that it had raced along the Baragwanath aerodrome in clouds of dust, not rising until the last minute.[63]

Meanwhile, Tshekedi addressed 'a great gathering of his tribesmen in their encampment. In a notable utterance he exhorted them at all costs to accept the High Commissioner's decision, whatever that might be. A note of pathos crept into his voice as he referred to the events of the day and hinted at the likelihood of

8. Rey meets Vice-Admiral Evans on his arrival by air from Johannesburg (Rey Collection).

having to take farewell of his people forever.'[64] That evening one of Tshekedi's chief advisers told the correspondent of the *Natal Mercury:*'We listened to the inquiry ''as people in the presence of a dying man'', but the Chief's words are wise words. If we had not heeded them we would have been cannon fodder.'[65]

Far away in Balmoral, another monarch was 'horrified over this Bechuanaland affair and feels that these young Scotsmen have brought it on themselves, though of course His Majesty quite realizes that the prestige of the white man must be upheld.'[66]

CHAPTER 4

An African Dreyfus?

After the Enquiry, the Rev. J. H. L. Burns returned once more to Serowe, this time taking Mr Whiteside with him. There he found that many of those who had remained behind in the Bangwato capital had held prayer meetings. One in the church that morning had filled the large building.[1] At the mission itself, Burns met the Rev. Keletlokhile Raditladi, younger brother of Headman Disang Raditladi and the first Mongwato minister ordained by the London Missionary Society. Even though a minister, he was a man of whom Tshekedi was intensely suspicious. For his part, Keletlokhile, as Burns observed, 'never has a good word to say about Tshekedi.'[2] When Burns told him what had happened at Palapye Road, he asked: 'Is that British justice?' Burns later commented sadly: 'I could not answer in the affirmative.'[3]

Back at Palapye Road, Tshekedi was confined to his quarters in the Government Camp, though he was able to continue making plans with Buchanan and Jennings for dealing with the crisis engulfing him. From Serogola Seretse he received assurances that should the Protectorate Administration try to choose a successor to him all approached would refuse to accept the position.[4] In the High Commissioner's coach, meanwhile, Evans and Rey were discussing Tshekedi's fate with their fellow officials. Neale and Liesching had already finished their report on the Commission of Enquiry and presented it to the High Commissioner complete with a verbatim record of the evidence. Summarising their findings, the two Commissioners concluded that 'P. W. McIntosh, who is a European, was tried, convicted and flogged in the Chief's kgotla and that this was done deliberately by the acting Chief Tshekedi, who was fully aware that, as a Native Chief, he had no jurisdiction to deal with a case in which a European is concerned.'[5] On the basis of the report, the five officials 'unanimously agreed that no course was open but to suspend Tshekedi from his duties as Acting Chief during His Majesty's pleasure and that he should be removed to the Tati District.'[6] At least as far as Tshekedi would be concerned, he was only being sent to Francistown, just across the border from the Bamangwato Reserve and on the railway line. That was infinitely preferable to being exiled, as Rey had originally proposed, to Ghanzi in the Kalahari Desert over three hundred miles from Serowe and, as far as communications were concerned, isolated from the rest of the country. In Francistown, he would be in white settler territory and outside the jurisdiction of any of his fellow Tswana chiefs, for the Tati District was owned by the Tati Company, which had been given a concession for it in 1869 by Lobengula of the Ndebele. Within Tati Company territory there was, however, a 'Native Reserve', which Tshekedi was specifically forbidden to enter.

Even the workaholic Rey had not been able to complete the report on the Enquiry he had conducted that afternoon with Liesching into Tshekedi's allegations against the Resident Magistrates. He was only able to give Evans a draft of it without the transcript of the evidence, and so no decision was reached in this matter.[7] It was decided, however, that Henry McNamee should be exiled from the Bamangwato Reserve along with Phinehas McIntosh. After making final arrangements for the *kgotla* at which Evans would announce the decision on Tshekedi's future, Rey was able 'to stagger into bed, dead to the world, with a foul headache and a beastly temperature, cold and cough' at half past midnight.[8]

Rey was up next morning at 7:00 A.M. to watch the Rhodesia Railway lorries 'push off' to Serowe 'laden with sailors and marines and their guns, in the midst of a blinding dust storm, the worst ever—a ghastly morning, hot as hell, and a stifling wind.'[9] Rey had to wait at Palapye Road until 10:45 A.M., when the High Commissioner and he were due to leave for Serowe by road. He was unaware that at least one South African newspaper already carried a hostile editorial about the previous day's Enquiry. Far from giving the Administration the unstinted support he and Evans had anticipated when they launched their expedition into the Kalahari, the *Cape Argus* in its main editorial entitled 'Tshekedi Deposed' wrote: 'Negrophobes and negrophiles alike began to gird up their loins in anticipation of the first shot. Apparently the Bamangwato have not, and never had, any hostile intentions or any weapons with which to conduct the hostilities, and the white man whom the Chief had flogged was probably the least worthy person that the majesty of the British Empire has ever been invoked to aid. . . . In the light merely of the inquiry, the local authority emerge from the situation in rather a poor light. . . . Following the worst military precedents, the presiding officer refused to allow Tshekedi the benefit of legal representation, although such assistance had been authorized by a higher authority, and although it was obviously to the advantage of the court that it should be granted. On the other hand Tshekedi was well able to conduct his own case, and he probably suffered no real prejudice.'

But however sympathetic the *Argus* may have been to Tshekedi, it did agree with the Administration that it was 'most undesirable' that such trials as that of McIntosh by Tshekedi should take place. It also concluded by stating that Tshekedi had been 'deposed'[10] rather than 'suspended', a confusion of terms that was soon to cause alarm in London. The Johannesburg afternoon paper of that same day, the *Star,* in its editorial entitled 'Somebody's Blunder' was equally critical, even though it was no more renowned for its liberal views than the *Argus,* which was published by the same company. It, too, criticized the Commission of Enquiry for denying Tshekedi legal representation. It also considered that Tshekedi's allegations against the Magistrates were so relevant to the whole Enquiry 'and to whatever findings may have been reached by the High Commissioner that the facts should be disclosed at once.' Far from expressing any opinion as to whether or not Tshekedi was right in flogging McIntosh, it contented itself with approving the Commission's decision to exile the young white man: 'As it may be assumed that neither the Union nor Rhodesia will be prepared to receive him, and if it is correct that the man was born in the Protectorate, enforcement of the Court's recommendation may prove something of a problem. Mackintosh [sic] is the type of European who disgraces and degrades the name of white man, and his own evidence yesterday amply proves that he has no legal or moral claim to the privileges or status of a European, and apparently makes no such claim. Whether it was worth while bringing up a naval detachment from the coast, with alarms and excursions of various kinds, creating a feeling of bewilderment and unrest among Europeans and natives alike—and incidently a very bad advertisement for South Africa—on account of such a man as Mackintosh, is a question which we do not at the moment intend to discuss. But a good many people throughout the country will be asking it.'[11]

Although the *kgotla* at Serowe had been set for noon, it had to be delayed for more than an hour because of the difficulties the military convoy had in traversing the thirty-five miles from Palapye Road to the Bangwato capital. Eleven lorries carrying the troops and stores and three six-wheelers towing the howitzers churned the dirt road into almost continuous sand. The drivers had 'persistent difficulties in negotiating the corners and awkward sand drifts with their heavily laden lorries.'[12] The lead lorry got stuck and had to be abandoned, and the marines it was carrying transferred to a lorry carrying stores, which were left by the side of the road to be brought on later. At one time the six-wheelers lost touch with the main column, in which, sandwiched between two lorryloads of marines, Tshekedi was travelling in a car marked 'Number 13 Ex-Chief and Police Guard'. 'His Unlucky Thirteen'

9. Marines arriving at Serowe and unloading their guns (Rey Collection).

was a paragraph headline the London *Evening News* could not resist.[13] At times the convoy was reduced to speeds of five to ten miles an hour while the troops 'sang to beguile the tedium of the journey, and "songs of the sea" had a strange ring in the desert surroundings.'[14] 'Great clouds of white dust from the sandy wastes of the parched Kalahari shrouded the moving lorries and the bluejackets in a moving canopy all the way.'[15] Some of the big six-wheelers got stuck in the sand and only extricated themselves after 'a prolonged roaring and tyre-bursting'.[16] The third gun had to be assisted by its gun crew fixing on their hauling gear and so man-handling the gun along.[17] As Buchanan wrote much later: 'If Tshekedi had not had the Tribe well in hand this procedure would have been an invitation for trouble, as leaving guns aside, three small bands of natives armed with kerries alone could easily have disposed of these widely separated parties without the knowledge of either of the others.'[18] The party of journalists accompanying the convoy managed to reach Serowe ahead of it by making a series of deviations from the road through the bush.[19] They arrived there to find it a 'city of the dead', according to the *Natal Mercury*.[20] The first lorry in the convoy did not arrive at the Serowe showground until 11:45 A.M., a quarter of an hour before the *kgotla* had been scheduled.

The Acting High Commissioner's party finally left Palapye Road just after 11:00 A.M. in a fleet of five cars. Evans and Rey travelled in the first car, while

Ninon and the Flag Lieutenant rode with the Director of Operations in the second. Their procession passed several of the lorries carrying the sailors stuck in the sand, and as a result it had to wait outside Serowe for them to catch up. Shortly before 1:45 P.M. the last gun reached the showground, where in happier days, the Rev. Burns reminded his daughter, the Boys' Brigade used to play cricket.[21]

Rey then went ahead, dressed in the khaki uniform of a Lieutenant Colonel of the Bechuanaland Police, to check that all was well. For him, the scene of the forthcoming ritual was 'a most impressive sight'. A canvas canopy shielded the platform from the sun. In front of it a huge Union Jack fluttered from its tall flagpole. Another Jack covered the table from behind which the High Commissioner would address the Bangwato. These were already assembled behind the whitewash line, 'squatting five or six deep'[22] and numbering 'approximately 3,000' in Rey's estimation.[23] Newspaper reporters were to be more conservative in their estimates. The London *Daily Herald*,[24] which was highly critical of the Administration, put it as low as five hundred, while the *Daily Telegraph*,[25] which tended to support Evans and Rey, gave the highest estimate at two thousand. In fact, the number seems to have been lower than that, judging by the photographs[26] taken of the ceremony, where the lines seem to be at most three deep. The

10. Tshekedi, wearing a dark overcoat, standing with his advisers, waiting to hear Admiral Evans's judgement, with Bangwato men gathered behind a line of whitewash (Associated Press).

correspondent of the *Natal Mercury,* whose reports were the most graphic and detailed of any journalist covering the crisis, assessed the number of Bangwato present at six hundred, 'which was far smaller than is usual for these functions.'[27] Tshekedi had certainly not given any encouragement to his men to attend the *kgotla* for the High Commissioner, and since most of them had gone to Palapye Road and had spent the night there, few would have got back in time for it.

To the left of the platform, and facing the Bangwato, were a platoon of marines, with fixed bayonets and helmets. To the right of the platform sat the white community, many of whom had been there since noon, the women in their best dresses. Rey's guard of twenty Protectorate Police all 'as smart as paint and motionless as statues'[28] represented the authority of the Mafeking Administration.

11. Admiral Evans takes the salute, with Colonel Rey standing behind him. To the right of the dais are members of the European community. Buchanan, Tshekedi's lawyer, stands in the second row (Rey Collection).

The naval detachment and the three howitzers with their crew were positioned to the far right of the platform, ready to give Evans his salute.

Once Rey had checked that everything was in order Evans, in the dark-blue uniform of a Vice Admiral, followed by his officers and officials, among whom Liesching looked particularly resplendent in the plumed hat and gold braid of his diplomatic uniform, advanced towards the platform. As he approached he was received by Rey and Potts, in his capacity as Resident Magistrate of Serowe. As His Majesty's representative in the Bechuanaland Protectorate, Evans was given the Royal Salute by the guard, which he then inspected. When he and Rey, followed by officials and ADCs, mounted the platform, Tshekedi took up position directly in front of them, dressed in a thick overcoat despite the searing heat. He was flanked by four advisers, two on each side. Nearby was Chief Bathoen of the Bangwaketse, who told Buchanan that he had joined his friend because 'I would sooner be in trouble with Tshekedi than out of trouble but in with the Administration.'[29] A bulging briefcase stood at the feet of the man on Tshekedi's immediate left, while behind him in puttees and solar topees and Sam Brownes stood two NCOs of the Bechuanaland Protectorate Police. In happier times Tshekedi would have been dressed in his own uniform modelled on that of an officer in the Life Guards, while his supporters would have been in their own regimental uniforms freely adapted from those of their British counterparts. But the uniform of this day was the drab jacket and trousers of the British working man.

Once Evans and his party had mounted the platform, the howitzers 'crashed out the salute of nineteen guns', to which Evans as Acting High Commissioner was entitled, their 'roar echoing in the hills magnificently.' According to Rey, the 'tribesmen jumped up, prepared to bolt, but we had foreseen the possibility of this and had men posted to reassure them.'[30] Buchanan's perspective on this demonstration was more cynical: 'The throngs of natives were surprised to see that these big guns only made noise and had no effect whatever on their houses and huts.'[31]

The High Commissioner had been received in complete silence, in contrast to the warm welcome and ululations of the women—today nowhere to be seen—that usually greeted a representative of the King's Government. The silence continued almost unpunctuated throughout his speech, which lasted for a full twenty minutes as it was interpreted sentence by sentence into Setswana.

Before he read out his judgement, Evans, who was an accomplished public speaker and popular on the lecture circuit, flung his gloves[32] dramatically on the table in front of him. In measured tones he addressed the errant Chief:[33] 'Tshekedi Khama, As His Majesty's High Commissioner I have come here to address you before your people.

'You have been Acting Chief during the minority of Seretse who is the hereditary heir to a great tribe, mainly kept great by your father and Seretse's grandfather, Khama.

12. Tshekedi and his advisers awaiting Evans's judgement (Rey Collection).

'Although,' he continued, raising his voice as if to emphasize Tshekedi's good points which he went on to list,[34] 'you are known to be a decent, clean-living man, clever, a man of education and great intelligence, you have frequently flouted the Administration whilst professing loyalty and allegiance to the King, in whose name I appear here today.

'You admit flogging a European after judging him in your Kgotla, knowing full well that you had no legal right to do this, and no jurisdiction over him.

'Your duty as Acting Chief was to set a good example.

'You have not set a good example.

'You have', he continued as his voice grew cold,[35] 'set a very bad example to your tribe and other chiefs.

'I have already had to reprove you in the short time I have held the office of High Commissioner although you made a full and proper apology.[36]

'A very great deal of trouble has been taken in your case in order that you should have full justice and that any extenuating circumstances regarding your action in flogging this European should be taken into consideration.

'Very thorough enquiries have been made as to your character, and also as to the way in which you yourself have studied the interests of your people.

'From these enquiries, it appears that you are an extremely capable acting chief, quite able to deal with your people and to lead them, but it appears that your overmastering passion is your selfishness and your study of your own personal rights and privileges.'

At this point there was, according to the Rev. Burns, who was present, 'a murmur of disapproval from the Europeans sitting beside the dais.'[37]

'You have not always acted in the interests of your people, nor have you worked in harmony with the Administration, and without harmony and co-operation the administration to which you profess allegiance cannot hope to function.

'I may tell you that your action in flogging a European has aroused general indignation notwithstanding the character of the European you flogged.

'I am satisfied that the man is not a fit person to live in a Native Reserve, and I have this day given orders for this man and one other to be ordered out of the Native Reserve. If they reappear in this reserve they will be punished according to law.

'In addition to other punishment, normally you would have been fined 300 head of cattle. I shall not inflict this fine, but for the deliberate and flagrant violation of the Protectorate law, well known to you, I shall suspend you from the exercise of your functions of Acting Chief at His Majesty's pleasure, and you will not be allowed to reside in the Bamangwato Reserve.'

At this juncture, although the Bangwato maintained their stony silence and Tshekedi stared fixedly ahead, according to the *Daily Herald,* 'white women, many of them in tears, interrupted with cries of "Stop this!"'[38]

'Tshekedi Khama,' Evans continued, 'I direct that you shall reside at His Majesty's pleasure in the Tati District, excluding the Native Reserve.

'Your tribe must now return peaceably to their homes, and in due course elect an Acting Chief in your place, and a council to work with him.'

It was only then, according to the *Daily Telegraph,* that 'the chief, who, at the beginning had been staring in characteristic native fashion at the Admiral, averted his eyes. He acknowledged defeat.'[39]

'The name of the acting Chief', Evans ordered, 'is to be submitted to the High Commissioner for approval, and the names of the Council to the Resident Commissioner for his approval.

'Finally, to you men of the Bamangwato tribe, I call upon you in the name of His Majesty to conduct yourselves well and in accordance with the customs and best traditions of the great tribe to which you belong.

'In conclusion, I wish to impress upon you the necessity to work loyally with the administration and to follow the advice and guidance of the Resident Commissioner and his officers.'

The speech lasted for twenty minutes, including the time taken by the interpreter, Mahloane, to translate it into Setswana. When he had finished, the Acting High Commissioner picked up his gloves, drew one of them on[40] and then as the guard

saluted he left with the official party and drove off 'in an impressive silence' to the
Residency. There Mrs Potts had prepared a light lunch which, as Rey wrote in his
diary, 'we all needed very much—it was past two o'clock and we were all
famished.'[41] Admiral Evans then flew off to Palapye Road to take the train to
Pretoria. As far as Rey was concerned, the whole ceremony had been a great
success.

Buchanan, who had taken the precaution of eating before the ceremony, was
able to witness what Rey had not: the white community's support for the disgraced
Tshekedi. 'What followed', he wrote, 'was probably unparalleled in African
history. The whole white population, including the parents of the boy, the cause of
all the trouble, went forward in a body and each in turn men, women and children,
filed past Tshekedi and shook his hand and told him how sorry they were for what
had happened and hoped he would soon return as Chief.'[42] Though Buchanan
wrote this nearly twenty years after the event, his memory served him well. In the
account that the Rev. J. H. L. Burns wrote a few days after the suspension he
records the same scene,[43] as did the *Daily Herald*.[44] The graphic description of the
scene by Frew, acting for Reuter and SAPA, the South African Press Association,
was carried in a number of papers both in Britain and South Africa: 'The sympathy
with the Chief felt by many European residents at Serowe and Palapye Road, and
in other parts of the Protectorate, was demonstrated yesterday afternoon after the

13. Evans leaves Serowe (Rey Collection).

High Commissioner had read the proclamation of Tshekedi's banishment. After the High Commissioner had stepped off the platform, many Europeans hurried towards Tshekedi, shook him by the hand, and expressed their regret. This is explained partly by the fact that Tshekedi had been exceptionally kind to European residents in the territory. When wild rumours were flying round the Protectorate on the arrival of the detachment of marines and bluejackets Tshekedi sent a message to European residents, particularly to women whom he knew to be alone, telling them that he had made himself responsible for their security.'[45] But further, according to D. G. McLaggan of Mahalapye, all whites in Gamangwato agreed that the Enquiry was 'a farce' and that Tshekedi 'was tried, sentenced, hanged and quartered, before the Inquiry started.'[46] The Bangwato themselves were resentful that their Chief had been subjected to such 'irreparable' insults in being 'escorted like a notorious criminal, bare headed, standing under the burning tropical sun' to hear 'his meaningless and faulty sentence.'[47]

Tshekedi, after having been humbled before his people, as the *News Chronicle*

14. Liesching, Evans and Rey in a relaxed mood after the suspension of Tshekedi (Rey Collection).

put it,[48] was led off to his car by Lieutenant Lawrenson of the BPP. He was then driven to Palapye Road, where he was to spend the night before catching the train to Francistown the next day. After lunch the Admiral himself drove to the airfield and flew off to Johannesburg in time to catch the train to Cape Town. Rey interviewed representatives of the white community and arranged that a party of marines remain encamped near the Serowe hospital overnight in case of trouble. Then he and Ninon returned by car to the hotel at Palapye Road and on arrival 'were utterly tired out and simply flung ourselves into bed.'[49]

CHAPTER 5

'The Road to Rhodesia'

Tshekedi set off that Thursday afternoon on 'the road to Rhodesia', as the Bangwato euphemistically called exile.[1] It was a road he had made others travel often before. According to Rey's information, Tshekedi seemed quite resigned to exile. On the way to Palapye Road he had told his police escorts that he had been expecting something of the kind to happen for some time. He was not sorry that it had now happened and he proposed to buy or lease a farm in the Tati District. He was merely anxious to know whether the Administration would allow him to do so.[2]

Rey was not surprised at Tshekedi's conversation with the policemen, for it fitted in 'with previous remarks of a similar nature that he is reported to have made, notably in connexion with the removal of Sebele, after which he observed he supposed he would be the next to go.'[3] In Rey's mind there was little doubt that Tshekedi had 'for a long time been determined to force the issue and that he thought the present incident would be a good opportunity.'[4]

Rey undoubtedly hoped that Tshekedi would be out of his way for some time to come and that he could now introduce his administrative reforms unhindered. Indeed, his last order to the Bangwato before he left Serowe that afternoon was that they should immediately get on with the business of electing a new Acting Chief as instructed by the High Commissioner. Furthermore, they should choose a Council to support him.[5] The establishment of Councils to advise and restrain the eight Chiefs of the Protectorate was a central feature of Rey's reforms, which were in large part designed to curb what he considered their autocratic powers. Conversely, Tshekedi and his fellow Chiefs had bitterly opposed these Councils because

96

they had no basis in tradition and because they usurped the functions of the *kgotla*. Tshekedi's own brief experience of a Council when he became Regent had made him intensely suspicious of this new institution. He had also seen how the British Administration had used Councils to restrict the powers of his neighbour, Sebele II of the Bakwena, and how members of those Councils had abused their office. He was thus determined to resist any attempts by the British to foist a Council on him. But with Tshekedi gone, Rey now believed he could impose a Council on the Bangwato even before his reforms were passed into law in the Protectorate as a whole. Once a Council had been established for the Bangwato, by far the largest of the Tswana *merafe,* there would be little difficulty in introducing them elsewhere. But Rey had underestimated not only the resilience of Tshekedi but also the loyalty of the Bangwato to their Chief in his time of adversity. He had in fact had some intimation of the extraordinary power Tshekedi wielded in his community, among both black and white, when before leaving Serowe for Palapye Road the European Chamber of Commerce and 'several Europeans of standing' went separately to see him and stated how serious they thought the position was 'on account of what', as Buchanan put it, 'all considered a gross miscarriage of justice. They all supported Tshekedi in whatever he had done and urged his immediate reinstatement.'[6]

Immediately after Tshekedi was driven off to Palapye Road, Buchanan went to see the Chief's mother, Queen Semane, as she was respectfully known. He found her in tears about what had happened to her son. She had nevertheless been busy in his defence and had drafted a petition to King George V. It was translated into English and forwarded to the Resident Magistrate, who acknowledged its receipt on the 16th and confirmed that he had sent it on to the Resident Commissioner.[7] Buchanan recorded later that he then made sure that a copy was given to the young journalist Frew to send off to the press.[8] The petition read:

To the Government.
I, the widow of Kgama, am sending an appeal to you, my King, as you are my only refuge shown to me by my master, Kgama, who left me in your power—I am relying on you for my living in spite of my grief, and the punishment inflicted upon me. I have no other place of refuge but to you. Do have mercy for my life and the life of your Tribe—"Let the great lion eat the flesh but spare the bones". This is the petition of your servant Khama. In our law, my King, if the ruling Chiefs propose to punish anyone for breaking the law, and that person took refuge with me he is absolved from further punishment as that reminds them of the name of Kgama, their father.

The law is your law, and as I cry and run to you—Do please liberate my son— the Tribe and I are stranded.

This is my petition to you my master—May it be heard.

I am the widow of Khama, Semane.

Addressed to
  The Resident Magistrate,
    Serowe[9]

While Buchanan was with Queen Semane, he talked with Peter Sebina, Tshekedi's secretary, who informed him that he was planning to go into exile with his Chief. When Semane heard of this she told Peter: 'You will do no such thing. You will remain here and help carry on the administration and work of the Tribe just as if the Chief had gone on leave to Cape Town to interview Mr. Buchanan.'[10] In fact Tshekedi insisted that Peter Sebina accompany him to Francistown, but he dissuaded several other headmen, who were reported to have vowed to go to Francistown with him, from doing so.[11]

Later that evening, just as Buchanan and Jennings were about to take leave of Burns at the Mission House and return to Palapye Road to see Tshekedi, Major Webber of the marines arrived. He asked Burns whether he thought it was necessary to retain his troops in the town. Both Burns and Jennings thought that it was not. 'At the same time,' Burns recorded later, 'I expressed the fear that it might not be safe for Phin McIntosh to remain in town.'[12] As yet no arrangements had been made for the young man's exile. But the options open to the British were limited. He and McNamee would have to be found a home in the Protectorate for, as the *Daily Herald* pointed out with regard to McIntosh, 'it is doubtful whether either South Africa or Rhodesia will receive him, since he has committed the sin, unforgivable in their eyes, of having lived with a native woman.'[13] The Administration had been preoccupied by the larger problem of removing Tshekedi from the Bamangwato Reserve.

Once back in Palapye Road, Buchanan and Jennings had further discussions with Tshekedi about future strategies. One plan was that permission should be sought from the Administration for Tshekedi to stay in Cape Town, where he would be near to Buchanan. Another was that Jennings and Buchanan should travel to London to plead his cause.

'Trouble started early'[14] that Friday morning for Rey when it was reported to him that Tshekedi was ill. Obviously fearing that this was a ruse on the part of Tshekedi—with whose prevarications and obstructions Rey was all too familiar—to circumvent the Administration's plans to send him out of the Reserve, he phoned Dr Morgan in Serowe and told him to come up urgently.[15] When Morgan arrived he found that although Tshekedi was suffering from slight nervous exhaustion he was in a fit state to travel.[16] Rey then proceeded with his arrangements to put Tshekedi on the train to Francistown that night. At 11:00 A.M. Captain Nettelton went to see Tshekedi in his quarters in the Court House and served on him the High Commissioner's order confining him to the Tati District—specifically excluding the Native Reserve—since 'it has been shown to my satisfaction that there are reasonable grounds for believing that TSHEKEDI KHAMA, for the time living in the Bamangwato Reserve of the Bechuanaland Protectorate, is dangerous to the peace of the said Protectorate.'[17]

Meanwhile, at Serowe Phinehas McIntosh and Henry McNamee were called to the Magistrate's Office and served with the orders 'issued in terms of Section 3 of Proclamation No. 15 of 1907' exiling them from the Bamangwato Reserve and any other Native Reserve in the Bechuanaland Protectorate.[18] They were told to be ready to travel at noon the next day by the post lorry to Palapye Road, where they would board the evening train to the white settler town of Lobatsi in the south of the Protectorate. Instructions were sent to Sergeant Dixon of the Bechuanaland Protectorate Police at Palapye Road personally to ensure that both men boarded the train.[19]

Buchanan and Jennings returned once more to Serowe. There they learnt that in accordance with Rey's instructions a *kgotla* had been held that morning to elect a successor to Tshekedi. But the people had been unable to come up with a name. The day before, the two had been consulted by some of the headmen as to what they should do but had refused to intervene in the matter, as 'we both felt it would serve no good purpose as far as either Tshekedi or the Tribe were concerned.'[20]

It was not long before Potts learnt of the impasse that had been reached by the Tribe over the choice of a successor to Tshekedi. He telephoned the bad news to Rey, who thereupon decided to come down to Serowe that afternoon to sort matters out. In the meantime Potts called in a delegation of headmen, led by the one-eyed Gorewan, next in line of succession to Tshekedi. After Gorewan had told him that he had informed the Tribe that it was necessary to elect an Acting Chief as well as Councillors, Oitsile stepped forward as spokesman:[21] 'The Bamangwato have heard. They found themselves in difficulties which I will explain,' he told Potts. 'They are black people. They do not elect a Chief unless the Chief has died. They are conversant with their birth rights. Their Chief is still alive and the Chief for whom he is acting is still away. Therefore they do not know what they can say yet. The position of the Chief is a difficult one. The duties he had to perform could not be managed by anyone else they could think of.'

Oitsile then went on to enumerate all the things Tshekedi had done for his people and how burdensome his tasks were. 'The Tribe say', he continued, 'that they fear that as the message from the Government and the deposition took place only yesterday it would be precipitate to elect an Acting Chief now. They say that this is undue haste. They want to consider what has happened because the deposition of Tshekedi has taken place without any trial.'

After Oitsile had finished speaking, Lekhutile explained to the Magistrate the order of succession to the Chieftaincy. First was Gorewan, followed by Serogola Seretse, Edirilwe and Manyaphiri.[22] 'All these men from Gorewan downwards stated that they found themselves unable to assume Tshekedi's duties which were more onerous even than Khama's. They said that they said this because Tshekedi was not only watching the Native side of the work in regard to cases, but had also other administrative duties which bore on the European side. They said that if one of them were elected they could not accept the position because they find the burden too heavy. It was a burden which could only be carried by Tshekedi himself as he had been doing.

'They also said that as Tshekedi was still alive wherever they met him they might find they have not carried out their duties in a correct manner.

'I cannot repeat the statements made by many people but all I can say is that the Bamangwato say they are unable. They make a Chief at the death of one Chief. They do not know how to make one Chief while another is still alive. They say that Tshekedi should be tried as they do not know what has led to his deposition.'

Potts was extremely irritated by the statements of Oitsile and Lekhutile and told the delegation that the Resident Commissioner would be arriving at 3:00 P.M. to hear the tribe's message. He could not accept the great burdens attached to the position of a Chief as a reason for not appointing an Acting Chief. 'Oitsile stated himself that a Chief is not appointed but born. What would be the result if a born Chief was found to be totally incapable of performing his duties?'

Without hesitation, Oitsile replied: 'Councillors from his kgotla would be called to assist him.'

On a more placatory note, Potts said that it was not his intention to rush them into a decision. 'I told Gorewan that this meeting today was to be a preliminary one to name someone immediately to take charge of the Tribe and also to give me an idea as to when the Tribe would be ready to submit the name of an Acting Chief,' he told Rey. But he did warn them that the Resident Commissioner would require them that afternoon to name someone responsible to take charge temporarily and fix a time by which the Tribe could finally be expected to name a successor as Acting Chief.

At Palapye Road Tshekedi, now recovered from his exhaustion, began to make arrangements for his exile. He telephoned Mr Fodisch in Serowe and asked him to send a lorry to his house and collect his belongings for delivery in Francistown. He discussed the situation with regard to his cattle at Nata in view of the information he had just received that the foot-and-mouth cordon was being moved. He requested Fodisch to look after his horse and wagon. Sergeant Dixon, who was present while Tshekedi was making his call, reported that 'he did not want to say or hear anything about the Kgotla meeting this morning but would go into the matter in Francistown.'[23] He also asked Fodisch to get Buchanan to phone him.

When Buchanan did eventually get through to Palapye Road Police Station, Tshekedi asked him to contact Headman Disang Raditladi and get him to tell him about his interview with Potts the previous Sunday, with particular reference to their discussion about the possibility of Tshekedi's being deposed. Tshekedi did not, it appeared, wish to go into any more detail in Sergeant Dixon's presence.[24] He then asked Buchanan to come up that evening and discuss the matter with him.

Tshekedi spent some time making notes of the expenditures he had incurred as a result of the enquiry. He listed a total debt of £19.4.2*d*. to Mr Shaw for three oxen (£11.10. 0*d*.) and two bags of mealie meal (£1.16.0*d*.) to feed his followers, the balance being for other expenses, including petrol. To Mr Buchanan he owed £52.10.0*d*. 'for 'Legal Consultation by Chief Tshekedi on behalf of the Tribe' plus the cost of his fare from Cape Town. There was a series of other expenses listed, including telegrams to the cost of £17.3.8*d*. and cablegrams, £7.3.8*d*.[25]

Evans had landed in Johannesburg early on Thursday evening and almost immediately caught the train to the Cape. Thus he would not have seen either the Johannesburg or Cape papers when he woke up next morning on the long haul through the Karoo to Cape Town. Most of them were very critical of his action. The *Rand Daily Mail* in its lead editorial entitled 'Was it all necessary?'[26] opined that 'anyone who appreciates the delicacy of the art of native administration must have been disquieted by the apparent heavy handedness of the steps taken at the beginning of the incident, and the impression of clumsiness then given became steadily stronger as the affair moved towards its conclusion.' It criticized the despatch of the two-hundred-strong force to Serowe as 'a mere melodramatic gesture' and was convinced that there was no danger that Tshekedi would have opposed the decision of the courts by violent methods. It was very critical of the High Commissioner for his indictment of Tshekedi for 'selfishness' and failure to act always in the interests of his people; neither of these charges had been the subject of the Enquiry, though it had to be assumed that they affected the sentence. The editorial concluded: 'While we fully realise the necessity of upholding European prestige in Southern Africa, we greatly regret that it should have been necessary to take such drastic action on account of a person of Mcintosh's type.'

The *Star* that afternoon was hardly less sympathetic: 'Admiral Evans is a quick worker. Within less than a week he has suspended, tried—if the word can be applied to so farcical an inquiry—deposed and deported the principal chief in the Bechuanaland Protectorate. Aeroplanes, motor lorries, bayonets, howitzers, heavy guns, and doubtless cine-Kodaks, figured in this remarkable affair. . . . The Acting High Commissioner has certainly shown slower-moving folk how to hustle, but whether his conduct of this affair will enhance the prestige of the Imperial authority is another story. Prestige depends upon something more than high-handed, arbitrary action.' As for Evans, he 'knows nothing of natives or native affairs. We can scarcely believe that any man in such a position—any man at least with balance and a sense of responsibility as King's representative—could have acted as Admiral Evans did, without the fullest consultation with the chief local officials, and presumably with their approval. This, however, is only assumption. We sincerely hope that before the Secretary of State confirms the sentence on Tshekedi, he will insist on a full report on all that has happened. . . .'[27]

The Cape Times, though it generally believed that Tshekedi was wrong to have ordered the flogging of McIntosh, was concerned that the Chief had been deprived of counsel. It then drew attention to the central ambiguity of the whole Serowe affair: because Tshekedi's counsel had had no opportunity of stating his case, 'it is by no means clear whether McIntosh was actually flogged in satisfaction of the sentence or whether he was chastised in a rough-and-tumble.'[28]

Even the main Afrikaans newspaper, Die Burger, which, as the London Times noted, 'is very far from being negrophile',[29] gave the Administration little cause for comfort. Although it did not disagree with the findings of the Bechuanaland authorities, it did conclude that the Union Administration knew how to handle 'their own natives' better than the British in their Protectorate did theirs. 'In our eyes it was a mistake, a grave mistake, on the part of the Administration', not to have removed McIntosh, especially as Tshekedi's request for his removal was a perfectly fair one. It was certainly not a mistake that would have been made by 'the people responsible for Native Government in the Union.' They also considered that with regard to the Enquiry 'justice should have been seen to be done. . . . The good name of the Administration would not have been damaged if the Chief had been allowed the services of a lawyer. The refusal to allow this leaves an unpleasant taste in the mouths of the whole Union.'[30] Thus the very white South Africans, whose supposed anger at a black Chief flogging a white man the expedition launched by Evans and Rey was intended to assuage, were in fact more concerned with the denial of legal facilities to Tshekedi and doubted the need to send in a miliary force to defend a white man of McIntosh's standing. Indeed, some papers carried a Reuter report sent in by Frew that even in his hour of trouble, 'while wild and persistent rumours were flying around the Protectorate on the arrival of the detachment of Marines and Bluejackets' and 'when the air was electric about Serowe, Tshekedi sent a message to the European residents, particularly to the women whom he knew to be alone, telling them to have no fear—he had made himself responsible for their security.'[31] Furthermore, the press had raised serious doubts about the quality of the British Administration in the Bechuanaland Protectorate, which Tshekedi had himself long been questioning.

Unaware of these developments, Rey accompanied by Ninon arrived back in Serowe at 3:00 P.M. He interviewed the same delegation which had informed Potts that morning that they had failed to elect an Acting Chief and told 'them that they had jolly well got to do so at once.'[32] He did, however, make it plain that he realized they would need time to make their choice: 'We do not wish to hurry you. *But* it is absolutely necessary that there should be someone *at once* to direct tribal affairs and to deal with the Magistrate, until the Tribe have designated the new Acting Chief. This is essential and I must insist on this.' He suggested that Serogola would be the ideal choice as temporary chief and directed that a full-time Acting Chief be appointed at a Tribal Meeting to be held before 11 October. The name should be submitted to the Magistrate by 14 October. He also wanted the names of members of the Council by that date and suggested that the Councillors should be representative of the different tribes and districts that comprised Gamangwato. He informed them that he would expect their decision as to who would run tribal affairs in the interim by 10:30 the next morning.[33]

Rey then went to see Major Webber and discussed with him the situation in Serowe. They agreed that if all remained quiet and the tribe accepted Rey's proposals, then his troops could be withdrawn on Sunday.[34] After that Rey and Ninon motored back to Palapye Road in time to ensure that Tshekedi got on the train to Francistown which was due to leave at 9:20 P.M.

Tshekedi spent the afternoon at Palapye at the Court House, sitting in a basket chair in the sun and cleaning his gun as he spoke with a group of followers, some of whom had slept the night with him in blankets on the ground. He had been asked by the authorities whether he wanted them to make any arrangements for moving his personal effects to Francistown, to which he replied courteously that he had made the necessary arrangements for their transportation himself.[35] Back in Serowe they were being packed into Mr Fodisch's lorry. The correspondent of the *Natal Mercury* had speculated the day before as to what would happen to Tshekedi's library, 'a handsome collection of books which includes some of the best known works on Africa as well as a number of novels' and which would 'require several packing cases to hold it. His furniture is no less impressive and fits tastefully into the atmosphere of a spacious modern villa.'[36] The only items the Administration did insist on transporting for him to Francistown were his firearms, three in all.[37] According to Buchanan, Tshekedi was able to ensure that confidential files in the Bamangwato Tribal Office were removed to a safe place.[38] One correspondent noted that since Tshekedi was still a bachelor the problem of relocating himself in Francistown would not be too great.[39]

At Tshekedi's expressed request few of his followers turned up to bid him farewell, though there was a large crowd of whites at the station as well as some sailors anxious to catch a glimpse of the Chief they had helped remove. His car did not draw up into the station until four minutes after the arrival of the train. He was accompanied by two police sergeants and Lieutenant Lawrenson, who was in charge of his escort to Francistown. He was smiling as he stepped out of the car and walked with composure towards his railway compartment, greeting those he knew as he passed by. Waiting for him on the train were three advisers who were to travel north with him. Among them was the faithful Peter Sebina. When Tshekedi was asked about his health he replied that he was merely a little run down. 'I am taking this action philosophically,' he told the *Cape Times* correspondent. As he boarded the train, he called out 'Salang sentle Bamangwato': 'Stay well, my Bamangwato people.'[40]

Lawrenson then took Tshekedi to his compartment and closed the door to avoid any demonstration by the crowd collected on the platform. After the train had pulled out of the station, Tshekedi asked whether he could move into the next compartment so that he could be with his followers, but Lawrenson was not prepared to agree to this. He did, however, tell him that one of this followers could join him in the compartment with Lawrenson and the two sergeants. When at last they crossed the Shashi bridge spanning the Shashi River, which marked the boundary between the Bamangwato Reserve and the Tati District, Tshekedi stood up and declared that he was now a free man and could go to his followers. Lawrenson allowed him to do so.

At 1:20 A.M. on Saturday the train arrived in Francistown, where Tshekedi was met by the Resident Magistrate and the Medical Officer. Tshekedi declined their offer of the meal that had been specially prepared for him in the local hotel.[41] Lawrenson then handed him Rey's order confining him to the Tati District and forbidding him specifically to enter the Bamangwato Reserve. The penalty for contravening the order would be imprisonment with or without hard labour for a period of not less than one month and not exceeding six months and with or without a fine not exceeding £100 and a further term of imprisonment in default.[42]

The Resident Magistrate at Francistown had gone to considerable trouble to prepare quarters for Tshekedi. Two sergeants' houses had been vacated for him and furniture and equipment brought up from Mafeking,[43] He spent only the night of his arrival there, sleeping on the ground outside by a fire with his followers rather than using the beds brought up from Mafeking. The next morning he went to stay with a local white trader, Mr Grenfell, having declined all the Administration's offers of food and refreshment for himself and his followers.[44]

For Rey Saturday was a busy day telephoning, telegraphing and writing despatches. One of this telegrams was sent to Francistown to seek urgent confirmation that Tshekedi had in fact arrived there. Confirmation was sent by return telegram along with the information, as Rey sourly noted in his diary, that Tshekedi had 'refused to occupy the Government quarters provided, or to eat any of the food we had got in, and went off to a private farm in the neighborhood.'[45] But otherwise Rey was quite pleased with the turn of events that morning. Taking his instructions of the previous afternoon seriously, the Tribe had met in *kgotla* that morning under the presidency of Gorewan. Accompanied by Oitsile and Baise, Gorewan went to see Potts straight afterwards and informed him that the instructions given by the Resident Commissioner had been read to the Tribe. Potts immediately sent a telephone message to Rey giving him the gist of what Gorewan had told him: 'The Tribe had heard the message. They pointed to Serogola and said that he would be temporarily in Kgotla to attend to Government communications and will continue in the office to which the Tribe has entrusted him. Further the main Tribal meeting will be called.'[46]

Rey was overjoyed by the news and at once telegraphed Evans: 'This morning's Kgotla unanimously accepted my proposals. They have nominated Serogola Acting Chief until the decision of full Tribal meeting which they have agreed to call for 11th October.'[47] The decision even to name Serogola as a go-between was made reluctantly. In the Basimane Ward, for instance, a group of headmen met to discuss the question of the selection of a new Chief in accordance with the instructions of the Administration and 'decided that they did not want any other Chief but Tshekedi, and would emphasize this at the tribal meeting that was to be held.'[48] Indeed, according to Jennings it was only after he had pressed on Tshekedi for the fourth time the need to put forward Serogola's name that he had agreed. Jennings apparently convinced Tshekedi that his chances of being reinstated would be dimmed if he failed to comply with the Administration's wishes.[49]

But Rey was deceiving himself. The Tribe had not appointed an Acting Chief to replace Tshekedi even on a temporary basis. Only Tshekedi himself could do that. Often before, when he was away from Gamangwato, Tshekedi had appointed Serogola, who was of his age, to act for him. On other occasions he had appointed his cousin Edirilwe. But in this instance the Tribe was not prepared to usurp Tshekedi's prerogatives and had merely 'pointed out' Serogola to be 'temporarily in Kgotla to deal with Government communications.' The words were carefully chosen, and Serogola was well aware of the nature of his appointment by the Tribe. At best it was that of a go-between with the Administration. He was especially careful not to use the title Acting Chief in his correspondence with the Administration, although they addressed him as such and although on the occasions when Tshekedi had appointed him to this position he had so styled himself. Furthermore, according to Burns, he had only agreed to act as Chief 'on condition that there should be no council.'[50]

Rey was optimistic that he could manipulate what has been called the iron law of succession by primogeniture observed by the Bangwato.[51] As far as the Bangwato were concerned, while Seretse was still a minor, Tshekedi, as the next adult male in line of succession, was Regent by genealogical right. He was not acting in any capacity, even if the British insisted on describing him as Acting Chief. As

Regent he had all the powers of a Tswana *kgosi,* with the one exception that he was exercising them on behalf of Seretse and would cease to enjoy these the moment the Tribe decided that Seretse was ready to take over the chieftaincy, which would be at any time after he had reached the age of eighteen. As Regent he was also entited to all the courtesies due to a Chief.

Rey had not learnt his lesson from his experience in the Kweneng, where even the local administrators accepted that the man he had chosen to replace Sebele II, though a royal and third in line of succession, was not accepted by the people as anything but a placeman of the Administration.[52] But as far as Rey was concerned, if he was to replace Tshekedi on a long-term basis, which clearly he hoped he would be able to do, he could not operate within the normal rules of succession.[53] As he wrote in an appendix to the Report he drafted on the events surrounding the suspension of Tshekedi, the 'nearest person in direct succession was one Gorewan. This man was an unsatisfactory character, dishonest, and not trusted by the tribe who feared the bad results if he were elected.'[54] Elsewhere Gorewan was written off as a 'senile scoundrel', and his son, Rasebolai, was 'put out as long as his father lives',[55] since there was no way a son could succeeded while his father was alive. Rey believed that Serogola came next to Rasebolai in order of succession, but there were in fact a number of other males who were genealogically closer to the succession than he was, being like Gorewan descendants of Kgamane, Khama's eldest brother. Serogola was only the grandson of Seretse, Khama's second brother. There was no doubt that Serogola was popular in the *morafe,* though as far as they were concerned he was genealogically distant from the succession. But then the problem did not really pose itself to either the Bangwato as a whole or to Serogola himself. Tshekedi was still their Chief, and as Burns wrote to Jennings: 'Tshogan Sebina reports RC told Serogola to act as Regent but Serogola replied that he took his orders only from the chief.'[56]

At the time Rey had been waiting for news from the Bangwato about who would manage their affairs, he received a telegram from Evans asking him for the report on his enquiry into Tshekedi's allegations against Nettelton and Potts. Rey replied that it had been impossible to complete it in the time available because of his involvement in the appointment of an Acting Chief.[57] Now that that was resolved, he set about completing the report, copies of which he informed Evans would be sent by train to Cape Town the next day, with a copy to be dropped off at Pretoria for Liesching.[58] He then prepared a detailed summary of his findings, which he sent by telegram to Evans.[59] In it he exonerated both Nettelton and Potts from any blame. Nettelton had taken all reasonable steps to deal with the troubles caused by McIntosh and McNamee between 1930 and 1932, while 'the non-holding of an Enquiry in 1932 was due to the absorption of the Acting Chief in other matters and his prolonged absence, at the end of which there was a change of

Magistrates'. As for Captain Potts, he had taken all reasonable steps to deal with the problem. 'It is unfortunate,' Rey concluded, 'that the situation, created by the disorderly element among the European population at Serowe, should not have been brought before the Resident Commissioner personally either through ordinary official channels or by the Acting Chief on the occasion of the Resident Commissioner's visits to Serowe; as the Resident Commissioner, by virtue of his authority and position, would have been able to deal with the matter in a more summary manner than those occupying a subordinate position.' Rey ended by regretting that no powers had existed before the promulgation of the Immigration Proclamation of 1932 to regulate the entry of the undesirable European and 'semi-European' into the Territory or where necessary their subsequent expulsion. In sum, as far as Rey was concerned, no blame in the matter attached to his Administration or its officers.

This was certainly not the view of the South African press, as we have seen. Nor was it that of the British press. The whole affair had received tremendous publicity in Britain, rating front-page headlines and lead editorials in many newspapers. Some of the reporting was purely sensational. The *Daily Express,* for example, in a story about the Basarwa ran the headline: 'Where the rawhide whip rules'.[60] The *Manchester Guardian* was, however, optimistic that the Evans expedition had underlined the need for definite allocation of duties and responsibilities as between the Chiefs and the Administration, and 'it will have done no harm if it leads the Dominions Office to realize that the South African protectorates can be made, if the will is there, an example of the enlightened handling of native races by a civilized power.'[61] The *Daily Herald,* in a more apocalyptic vein, headlined its story of 16 September 'Appeal barred for suspended chief. May become Gandhi of S. African negroes.' South African newspapers were generally critical of Evans's action and alluded to reports in circulation that the South African Minister of Finance and General Smuts had been having discussions with J. H. Thomas about taking over the Protectorates.[62] The day before it had opined that 'no doubt the fact that "Evans of the Broke" has "taught the Nigger a lesson" will gratify the Nazi-minded in this country. But it will be long before yesterday is forgotten by the people of Bechuanaland, who once had a childlike faith in British justice.'[63]

The Admiral came in for some further snide jibes by those who had read his schoolboy's adventure book *The Ghostly Galleon,* just published by the Bodley Head. The *Daily Express* informed its readers that it had been written in two days by a man who 'has a temper like a rocket [which] comes to earth as quickly.'[64] Several newspapers in Britain and South Africa quoted what one called 'a typical passage' from 'a swashbuckling story for a young gentlemen with adventurous minds'.[65] As the hero from this sixteenth-century sea yarn confronts Master

Christopher Jolly, the pirate captain, who 'whipped his men to their stations as one whips dogs to their duties', he observes: 'Standing near to him was a big mulatto with a bared scimitar in his two hands, and, as Jolly turned, as the words died on his coarse lips, he struck out at this man, insensate rage revealed upon his features. "Say something, do something, you scum!" he shouted, "and you others get out of my sight or by the pit I'll slice the lot of you." ' Later Evans's hero engages the unfortunate mulatto 'whom I had seen punished by Jolly's whip. He was hurling his double-edged scimitar about his head. I waited coolly for him, dodged a mighty swipe, and gave him the point just through the heart.'[66] Unfortunately for Evans, Tshekedi was not to be so easily despatched.

The *Morning Post* was one of the few papers that supported Evans, stating that 'the issue is simply whether a Bechuana chief has jurisdiction over a European. It would be surprising if British power, which insists on capitulations in Egypt and China, should have waived them in the case of a feeble African tribe.'[67] The *Daily Worker,* true to its ideological colours and alluding to Tshekedi's earlier struggle against the introduction of mining into his territory, wrote in its editorial 'Britain's Iron Heel' that the action had been taken 'because this African Chief refused to fit himself in with the schemes and desires of the British capitalists.' Tshekedi's 'deposition' was a 'glaring instance of the true character of the British capitalist robber colonial regime which exercises its iron grip over the colonial peoples, oppressing them brutally and enabling the firmer fastening of the capitalist shackles which bind the limbs of the working-class in Britain itself.' Its special correspondent noted perceptively in an accompanying news story that the sentence on McIntosh 'is never actually carried out, but the white man is struck in a struggle by Negroes, who apparently had grounds for believing that he was about to assault their chief. In this struggle the tribal authorities come to the aid of the white man.'[68]

For officials in the Dominions Office it was of course the weekend, and news of Thursday's events had as yet come in only through the press. J. H. Thomas had been gravely disturbed by earlier reports in the press based on what he described as a 'very specific message from Reuters' that Tshekedi had been deposed. He had met Tshekedi on his earlier tour of the Bechuanaland Protectorate and considered him 'one of the ablest, best educated and highest moral characters to be found in Africa. . . .'[69] He was thus relieved to learn from Evans almost immediately after their appearance that all he had done was suspend him from office. He made sure that Friday morning's press got the story correct. But he also understood that the South African press was under the impression that Tshekedi had been deposed. 'I regard it as of the greatest importance', he cabled Evans, 'that it should be clearly understood in South Africa both by natives and Europeans that your order does not involve deposition but temporary suspension until such time as whole case can be

considered here. It would also be desirable without of course in any way prejudic-
ing my final decision to suggest that duration of suspension may well turn to some
considerable degree on maintenance or abandonment by Tshekedi of his claim that
provisions prohibiting native Court from dealing with Europeans do not apply to
Bamangwato.'[70] For public consumption officials at the Dominions Office contented themselves with a bland statement of support for Evans's action.[71]

Sir Harry Batterbee, however, did write to the King's Private Secretary, Sir
Clive Wigram, to give him a revealing up-date of events from the Dominions
Office point of view: 'It appeared pretty certain from the first that the European
concerned would turn out to be a quite worthless person.' So it was difficult to
justify severe action against Tshekedi. The Secretary of State had therefore deliberately refrained from specific instructions to the Admiral so as not to hamper him
in an emergency, but 'although it does not seem that any such emergency arose,
the Admiral announced his decision without prior consultation with the Secretary
of State. In this Mr. Thomas cannot but think he was mistaken. As to the merits of
the decision, Mr. Thomas believes it is justified and right.' But he had been
alarmed by press reports of Tshekedi's deposition and 'felt, without any hesitation, that he could not justify such a decision.' Fortunately these reports had
proved to be wrong. 'It is clear that this decision is, in effect, a remission of the
case for final adjudication on this side.' Sir Harry then went on to explain that it
seemed that Tshekedi was not just claiming that he had the right to try McIntosh
because he had in effect gone native, but to try 'and, if he so pleased, to flog *any*
European.' Until he withdraws from this claim 'it is impossible that he should be
allowed to act as Chief.'[72]

In a letter to the Prime Minister that same day Thomas made the same points as
Sir Harry had to the King. As far as any parliamentary questions that might be
asked were concerned, the fact that Tshekedi was claiming the right to flog any
European gives us 'an impregnable defence; in fact, the Chief by making this
claim has played right into our hands.'[73] In writing this letter, Thomas was
fortified by a minute of the previous day from Whiskard, who, in the absence of Sir
Edward Harding on holiday, was the senior official in the Dominions Office.
Whiskard suggested that even though Admiral Evans had announced his decision
without prior consultation, he was acting in a temporary capacity. 'If the real High
Commissioner had so far disregarded your obvious wishes, the matter might have
been a serious one.'[74] Nevertheless, as far as Thomas was concerned 'the case
gave me great anxiety, although it would have been indiscreet of me to betray my
feelings.'[75] Indeed, the whole affair had come at a most awkward juncture. The
day the news of Evans's action in Serowe reached London, the Prime Minister was
on holiday at Lossiemouth; Thomas was still recovering in Hove from the effects
of a narrow escape from drowning while sailing in a storm at sea and was keeping

in touch with his office by telephone; Sir Edward Harding, the Permanent Under-Secretary, was on the Continent; the substantive High Commissioner, Sir Herbert Stanley, was on leave in Britain. As the *News Chronicle* remarked, 'Nothing has done so much as this African question to disturb Mr. Thomas' holiday. A table in his seaside villa is littered with papers and he is now finding very little time for the ordinary recreations of a Cabinet Minister when the House is not sitting.'[76]

A minor consolation for the local Administration was that some elements of the South African press were beginning to have second thoughts about the critical attack that had been launched on Evans's expedition. The *Diamond Fields Advertiser* in its editorial on Saturday morning considered that Tshekedi 'was totally unjustified in taking the law into his own hands' and that it was difficult to see how 'Admiral Evans and his co-commissioners could have acted otherwise in the interests of the maintenance of British prestige and the fullest protection of native rights and privileges.'[77] Even the *Natal Mercury,* whose correspondent had been so sympathetic to Tshekedi in his despatches, suggested that Tshekedi 'stood for an old order of things, and obviously has refused to be guided by the advice of the Resident Commissioner. Under the circumstances his removal became imperative.' It even supported the use of force employed by Evans and Rey, but was disquieted by the fact that the Administration appeared unwilling to face an open enquiry into the most serious of Tshekedi's accusations, that the Resident Magistrates had failed to do anything about his complaints.[78]

On Saturday the naval detachment left Serowe, and a semblance of calm now pervaded Gamangwato. Rey seemed sufficiently confident about the whole situation that when he received a letter from Buchanan asking whether it would be permissible for Tshekedi to travel to England and present his case to the Secretary of State in person, he replied that as far as he was concerned he had no objection. Rey then prepared to return by train to Mafeking. As far as he was concerned everything connected with the suspension of Tshekedi had gone better than he could have hoped. As he noted in his diary after seeing Admiral Evans off at the Serowe airfield, 'Altogether a sound piece of organization.'[79]

There were, however, some who were aware of his real motives for securing the suspension of Tshekedi. As an LMS missionary called Snelling wrote to Chirgwin at LMS headquarters, '*I am fairly convinced* that Tshekedi is being punished for his attitude to the draft Proclamations dealing with the powers of native chiefs. This business of the white man being flogged is the very opportunity that has been awaited by the ''Administrator''—you know who he is—to get at Tshekedi, and indirectly, Jennings and the L.M.S.'[80]

CHAPTER 6

'Flattened Out for All Time'?

The weekend following Tshekedi's suspension by Admiral Evans, the South African Railways were busy relocating the main actors in the Serowe drama. Tshekedi was the first to arrive at his destination. Admiral Evans reached Cape Town on Saturday afternoon. McIntosh and McNamee were put on the platform at Lobatse at noon on Sunday to try to make a new life among a white community that wanted nothing to do with them. Rey reached Mafeking a few hours later. Buchanan and Jennings continued on their way to the Cape.

Meanwhile, a special train had been sent north to collect the marines and bluejackets to return them to their ship at Simonstown. The Johannesburg *Sunday Times* suggested in its gossip column, ' "People Say": That the only people to develop anything like enthusiasm about the Bechuanaland expedition were the men from the Navy. That they appear to have had a very nice inland holiday at the British taxpayer's expense. That "sailors don't care" is proved by their consummation of 1,200 pints of beer in four hours—with 1,500 pounds of ice to make the beverage cool and drinkable. That Admiral Evans' marines might have been more profitably employed in Swaziland in scotching the Wildebeeste menace.'[1] In fact, apart from their consumption of beer, the marines and bluejackets had added to the problems of drought-stricken Gamangwato. Stocks of water had sunk so low at Palapye Road that only passenger trains could be catered for, and, reported the Johannesburg *Star*, 'not even passenger trains can obtain all the water they want.' For the marines and bluejackets water had to be brought specially up the line. Further, 'the picture of the drought is brought home forcibly by the long queues of natives that constantly line up at the wells a few miles outside Serowe.'[2]

The marines and bluejackets did not reach Cape Town until midday on Wednesday, 20 September. On the way back they spent a day at Kimberley, where they marched from the station to the City Hall, headed by the band of the Kimberley Regiment. There a large gathering of the townspeople had assembled to hear their Mayor, Mr T. Looney, extend the naval contingent 'a hearty welcome'.[3] For most of the men, the *Cape Argus* reported, 'the expedition will be a memory of dust, bully beef, dust, and more dust. Those who attended the Inquiry were surprised to find that Tshekedi was a cultured young native and declare that the Europeans of Serowe seemed to have the greatest respect for him.'[4] From Cape Town the train took the men on the short journey to Simonstown, where they took themselves and their guns to the more familiar world of their ships. Already the press were speculating on the cost of sending these sailors on their expedition to the Kalahari. The *Cape Argus* suggested that it had cost as much as £8,000,[5] a very large sum for the time.

On his first two days in Francistown, Tshekedi seems to have been curiously subdued. Usually he was at his most pugnacious and hyperactive in times of adversity; but although he had taken his typist with him to Francistown, his output of letters and telegrams was unusually low. Of course he had just been diagnosed by Dr Morgan as suffering from nervous exhaustion. Though Morgan had pronounced him fit enough to travel, he must have been sufficiently worried about him to arrange for the doctor at Francistown to meet his train. Worse still must have been the psychological effects of the public degradation to which the young Chief had been subjected by Admiral Evans. Even for a man with Tshekedi's resilience the effect of Evans's denunciation of him before his people and under the guns of the marines could have been little less than traumatic. And now here he was isolated in Francistown, unable to travel outside the Tati District without permission from the High Commissioner. But his isolation was only relative. Francistown was the most important commercial centre in the Protectorate. News travelled fast up and down the railway line, and the northern Bangwato territory was just across the river. There was the post office with the telephone as well as the telegraph, a form of communication to which Tshekedi was almost as addicted as Rey. All the same, sitting in Francistown that weekend, the options open to him must have seemed bleak, and it is little wonder that he had already begun to look around for a house and land in the Tati District.[6]

Even so calculating a politician as Tshekedi can hardly have anticipated the ferocity with which Evans and Rey had responded to his trial of Phinehas McIntosh. It had surprised the Dominions Office itself. And now it was clear that while Tshekedi was politically emasculated—albeit temporarily—Rey was going to do his best to try to force his hated Proclamations on the Bangwato. Whatever else Tshekedi had learnt from his encounter with Evans and Rey during the past week, he must have realised that even with all his political skills there was one point on which he could not move the British, and that was over his claim to have the right as Chief of the Bangwato to judge cases in which whites were involved. In no other African colony or Protectorate under British administration were whites subject to the courts of black traditional authorities. Indeed, it was a cardinal tenet of colonial rule that members of the ruling race, of whatever national provenance and of whatever lowly status, were exempt from the jurisdiction of African rulers, however exalted. If Tshekedi did not acknowledge this, there was little hope that he would ever regain his chieftaincy, and without it he would be in a weak position to prevent the imposition of Rey's Proclamations on his people. Even if he went to London, as Buchanan and Jennings had proposed, he could expect little support if he continued to claim the right to try whites and if he pleaded his case as a private citizen rather than as ruler of the Bangwato.

It was to this problem that Buchanan and Jennings tried to find a solution. Travelling together on the southbound train, Jennings and Buchanan spent a busy sabbath plotting strategies for Tshekedi's war with the Administration. In a joint letter about his proposed visit to England they assured him that the 'London newspapers and our friends are apparently getting busy—cheerful are the uses of adversity—you are more popular throughout the whole world than you could ever have been under any other circumstances.' The burden of their counsel to Tshekedi was that they should argue that after he had sentenced McIntosh to lashes 'no punishment was actually administered in respect of the matter under consideration.' Rather, what had happened was that McIntosh's dash towards the Chief 'appears to us to amount to a contempt of Court and it was this contempt that was the main cause of his beating by those present.'[7] Again the ambivalence as to whether McIntosh had ever really been flogged at Tshekedi's instigation was brought to the fore, and yet the flogging was the occasion of his suspension.

Mammon, too, was not absent from Buchanan's fertile legal mind, as he ended his joint letter with Jennings by enclosing his memorandum of fees for legal advice and assistance.[8] But Buchanan gave good value for his money. In a letter to Tshekedi written on the 19th after his return to Cape Town he informed him that he had had lunch with the former Chief Justice, Sir James Rose-Innes, and had cabled Earl Buxton, the former Governor-General of South Africa (and thus High Commissioner): 'It is desirable in every interest that permission should be given Chief Tshekedi to proceed to England to lay his case before Secretary of State.' He had had interviews with the editors of the *Cape Times* and *Die Burger* and would be seeing, among others, H. A. Moffat, a doctor from the famous missionary family who once treated Tshekedi, Rheinallt Jones, the Director of the South African Institute of Race Relations, and four judges. He was not at liberty to mention the names of some of the other important people he had seen.[9] For his part, Jennings made arrangements for his coming journey to Britain and held a meeting on 20 September at Vryburg to explain 'the case of Chief Tshekedi'.[10]

If, as Buchanan and Jennings indicated in their first letter to Tshekedi, the enthusiasm for his cause was building up in England, much more surprising was the tide of support for him that was rising in the ordinarily faction-ridden Ngwato state. Even his most bitter enemy and would-be assassin, Simon Ratshosa, now his fellow exile in Francistown, came to his aid. In a brief letter to Margaret Hodgson, the University of Witwatersrand lecturer and publicist on southern African affairs, Simon wrote that when Tshekedi arrived in Francistown to begin his exile he was 'looking well and undisturbed'. With his letter, Simon enclosed an article entitled 'A Native view on Bamangwato affairs', marked clearly *'Not for publication'*. He also suggested to her that Dr Karney, the Bishop of Johannesburg, might like a copy before he went on leave to England.[11] Simon had used his journalistic talents several times before to attack Tshekedi, and he had fed Margaret Hodgson and her friend and future husband, William Ballinger, with much of the information they had used to criticize the operation of indirect rule in the Bechuanaland Protectorate and in particular the autocratic powers of the Chiefs. But he now came to the defence of his young uncle. Old grudges were put aside as he insisted that 'had the Authorities reprimanded the Chief privately and upheld his decision the persistent immorality between black and white would certainly be brought to an end.

'I would strongly recommend', he wrote in terms redolent of the most extreme statements of Afrikaner segregationists, 'that such a class of men disgraceful before their own race be severely punished—thus to bring to an end the long existing cohabitation between white and black. A mixture of European and native blood breaks family tie, thousands of native women have already abandoned their villages to live in towns to cohabit with certain shameless white men, that they should give birth to bastard children who are better treated by the Government. I can only but to suggest that *sterilization* is the best instrument through which both races may be helped. . . .' Such a measure would help 'to stay the drift of our native girls into town where they so quickly get demoralized in search of a Bastard race preferable to their own.' Then, exhibiting deep resentment of what he saw as the privileged position of Coloureds in Southern Africa, he quoted with approval the late Professor Fremantle of Cape Town University, who had written in the *Manchester Guardian* two years before: 'Nor is the Government clear on its differentiation in favour of the coloured people. Nor is such a differentiation defensible or tolerable. It means that the illegitimate son of a degenerate Bantu woman and a drunken sailor is lord over the proud and pure-bred highly educated patriotic child of a manly race—a horrible thing.'[12]

Simon continued with an attack on the British Administration: 'No one of unprejudiced mind can contend that the High Commissioner to suspend a Chief without giving him a fair trial is the right procedure. It is true that in the past if trouble arose with a Chief he was summoned to head-quarters or before the High Commissioner to explain and if possible justify his action, or to receive censure or punishment if found at fault. . . .' He then went on to criticize the quality of the officials serving in the Administration. 'Since the retirement of Sir James McGregor C. M. G. [1923] the High Commissioner has never been fortunate to nominate men of imagination and ability to understand native mind. I admit that the present Resident Commissioner is an idealist and well cultured man but he has behind him "Sechuana expert officials to oil-influence [sic]", recruited from police not upon efficiency.

'To me the position of the Resident Magistrate in Bechuanaland Protectorate is still one of the unsolved mysteries of the Protectorate Administration what he does he does it with a sway that is peculiar to himself. . . .

'It is known all over South Africa that the natives' respect for the white man speaking the vernacular is less than it is for the man who could [not] speak it.

'The speaking to a native in his language leads to unnecessary familiarity, and from then on respect begins to fail and authority is undermined.'

Simon concluded somewhat surprisingly by singing the, albeit qualified, praise of the man he had once tried to assassinate: 'Tshekedi is a young Christian Chief, well dignified, with determination and bull-dog pertinacity, impatient of opposition not always willing to listen to or to take any advice that did not agree with his own way of thinking. Like his father [he] is very generous to rich and poor people, good-natured but with strong will that bore down everything he thinks unsuitable —witty, wise, tactful and deeply reserved in all his domestic and public life. Continue all these qualities and impulses in one individual and you have exact Khama's son—the most acute and enlightened politician of our modern Chiefs. In diplomacy he is undoubtedly a magnificent example of Khama's blood that I could hardly think for any better Chief of Today replaced for him.

'If this son of Khama could only modify and gave study to his ebullition he would certainly be an immortal Khama.'

Simon ended finally with a strong assertion of the loyalty of the Bangwato 'when their young Chief Tshekedi was being subjected to such irreparable insults when he was escorted like a notorious criminal, bare-headed, standing under the burning tropical sun despite the fact of his recent operation. Behind him stood police men with fixed daggers three big guns pointed to him as if he had committed a serious treason against the King. . . .

'No Chief the past and present has been indignified before his subjects the meaning of this was simply to provoke the Bamangwato that they should be drawn into rebellion against the King's authority: and this undoubtedly proves the weakness and irritating manners of the Administration. . . .'[13]

In a separate letter to Tshekedi, Simon Ratshosa castigated whites for the way they had suspended him. Tshekedi, in a rather icy reply sent two months later, addressed to his 'Dear Nephew' and signed 'Your Uncle', wrote: 'I cannot agree that the European mind will always remain a closed book to the Native, and consequently I am not able to say that no white man will ever understand the Native mind. Of course your statement was made having in mind the type of white men one often meets in the Protectorate, particularly in the Government service. It would be doing serious injustice to the British people if you were to take as an instance of their character in dealing with Natives our local officials. One has to sympathize with the latter, because they have not always been trained for the position which they have filled.'[14]

Tshekedi was able to begin the campaign for his restoration in the knowledge that not only his enemies like Simon supported him but also the vast majority of the Bangwato. From Serogola he received reports of what was taking place in Serowe. Serogola, Rey's supposed Acting Chief, was careful to give Tshekedi all the honours due to one who in his eyes was still his *kgosi*. He concluded his letter: 'I end here, Great Lion, I am Your Subject'.[15] In Serowe, too, Burns was trying to rally white support for him. On the instructions of Jennings he tried to get some white women resident in Serowe to sign a petition, and when Jennings wrote to prod him about it, it was to insist that 'anybody's name is as good as another in a petition—the names of the mighty are not necessary.' Jennings also told Burns that he did not anticipate Tshekedi would have any difficulty in obtaining permission to go to London, and that as soon as he received a telegram with the instruction ' "to give my message to Serogola" ' it will mean asking Serogola to write a letter to the RC for submission to the HC to allow Tshekedi on behalf of the acting chief and the tribe . . . to take up the case in regard to the draft proclamations with the Secretary of State while he is there overseas'. Burns was also to reassure Semane that things are 'looking very bright and the sun may soon shine again'. In a conspiratorial postscript he asked Burns to inform Serogola about the contents of his letter 'for his *discreet* use.'[16]

Rey arrived in Mafeking on Sunday afternoon more than satisfied with the way things had gone over the past week in Serowe. His long-drawn-out campaign against Tshekedi seemed to be leading towards yet another of the 'triumphs' he recorded with such undiluted self-satisfaction in his diary. For Rey, one of the achievements he hoped to be remembered for as Resident Commissioner was the reform of native administration and justice in the Protectorate. The main obstacle to the passage of the Proclamations that would implement this reform—Tshekedi Khama—had been temporarily stripped of power, and if he were to persist in his claim to have the right to try whites he might remain in exile permanently, like Sebele II. Whatever happened, the temporary removal of Tshekedi had provided

Rey with a magnificent opportunity of introducing his reforms into the largest of the Native Reserves even before they were promulgated in the rest of the Protectorate. Rey had high hopes that the *kgotla* he had ordered to be held in Serowe on 11 October would elect Serogola as Acting Chief and nominate a Council to advise him.

On his way to Mafeking by train, or shortly after his arrival there, Rey drafted a report justifying every move he and Evans had made over the past week in connexion with the flogging of Phinehas McIntosh and the suspension of Tshekedi. Entitled 'Report of Events in connection with Tshekedi Affair from Tuesday, the 12th September, to Sunday, the 17th September,'[17] it was first typed and then corrected extensively by Rey's own pen. But it seems never to have been re-typed or distributed in any form. It lies in a file in the Botswana National Archives with a cover note marked 'papers thrown out by HH' (that is, His Honour, the Resident Commissioner). This document, prepared in the immediate aftermath of the deposition, reveals more clearly than anything else written by Rey, including his remarkably frank diary, his real feelings about the 'flogging' and its consequences.

'A great deal of hysterical nonsense', he wrote in a note attached to the main report, 'has been written concerning Mackintosh's [sic] depravity—as if it were a unique and dreadful example in S. Africa. It would be well to consider dispassionately the case of this unpleasant specimen of the white race in Africa before assuming that.

'He cohabited promiscuously with native women, he drank and committed various other minor offences—I use minor in the legal sense.

'But fortunately he is by no means a unique or even a rare specimen in the B.P. His counterpart may be found in several other districts; there is hardly an old settler who has not lived with native women at one time or another; it was by no means uncommon for members of the administration to do so; and I have for nearly 12 months been trying vainly to be allowed to dismiss a member of the staff who not only cohabited promiscuously with native women, but photographed them in the nude. He is in my opinion a far more guilty type than Mackintosh.'[18]

Now, in the wake of the McIntosh affair, Rey, with a view to preventing a recurrence of recent events, was planning to resubmit for immediate re-enactment the Draft Proclamation forbidding sexual relations between the races which he had prepared in October 1932. He also intended to issue instructions to all Magistrates that 'any case of actual or potential difficulty with Europeans in Native Reserves was to be reported immediately by the Chief to Magistrate and then by the Magistrate to the Resident Commissioner personally.'[19] Once more the onus was going to be put on the Chiefs to monitor the doings of their white residents, over whom they were not permitted to exercise legal restraint.

If Rey considered that McIntosh's life style was nothing out of the ordinary, he certainly considered that Tshekedi's methods of trying to curb it were. There was little doubt in his mind that Tshekedi had only used the McIntosh affair as an occasion to force a showdown with the Administration. The main blame for this lay at the feet of the missionaries. 'He has been consistently ill-advised by Mr. Jennings of the LMS, who has for many years taken up an attitude of opposition' to the Administration. Even Buchanan had advised Tshekedi badly. 'I do not believe that the request to proceed to London emanates from Tshekedi himself or that he is really very anxious to do so. I am convinced that it was inspired and is being urged by Messrs. Buchanan and Jennings; and the campaign of misleading press propaganda which has been launched is (as admitted to me by Mr. Buchanan himself) entirely their own effort regarded by them in their own words as "their only weapon".'[20]

As regards the use of force he and Evans had employed, this was, Rey insisted, quite justified in terms of their recent experience with Gobuamang at Moshupa. 'If a display of force was considered necessary in regard to a tribe of 1,000 men, how much more necessary was it in regard to the Bamangwato who have mustered 10,000 in the Kgotla and who were in an admittedly highly excited state.

'It wd. have been out of the question to have attempted any action at all without an escort sufficient to ensure the maintenance of order; and the prevention of the possibility of any recurrence of the Moshupa fiasco, the effect of wh[ich] broadcasted throughout the Terr[itory] has undoubtedly induced the natives to think that the Admn. is powerless if they choose to resist.'[21]

Rey was never one to see fault in himself, even when he was recording events in his own personal diary. The one thing that seemed calculated to give him pause to reflect on the wisdom of his actions over the past week was the overt support given to Tshekedi by the white community of Serowe. But he had an answer for that too. 'The attitude of the Europeans at Serowe is easily understood. They are traders and are dependent for their existence on Tshekedi. He has only to pass the word round the tribe that a particular trader is not favourably regarded, and that trader's business would come to an end—as was in fact done in one well known case by Khama.[22]

'But in addition to this Tshekedi owes large sums of money to many of the traders and the non-payment of these sums would undoubtedly embarrass some of them seriously.

'I was personally approached by some of them a little while ago on this matter. They did not dare to take active steps in the matter publicly so that their names should not become known, but wished to know if the Government would help.'

Rey had told them that if the Serowe Chamber of Commerce approached him as a body he would speak to Tshekedi about the matter and try to induce him to settle.

But they had let the matter drop. The general tenor of Rey's report was that he had been right in everything he had done during the crisis over the 'flogging' of Phinehas McIntosh.

Evans, too, returned to Cape Town fully satisfied with his work in Serowe. There had of course been criticisms of the marines in the Press. But more surprising in terms of the original objectives of sending the naval expedition into the Kalahari was the fact that one of the main sources of support for Tshekedi was still the South African press. Evans himself still seemed oblivious to the extent of the criticisms of his expedition to the Kalahari and his 'trial' and suspension of Tshekedi that had already appeared in the papers. On arrival in Cape Town he told journalists that there had been no criticism of his action except in one London paper and that 'it was easy enough to criticize the handling of a ship if you were only standing on the pier.'[23]

What was even more serious for Evans was that the *Sunday Times* had raised the spiked question of the incorporation of the Bechuanaland Protectorate into the Union. One of the main objectives of the display of force had been to demonstrate Britain's capacity to rule the Protectorates. It now seemed that it had achieved the very opposite effect, for many other newspapers in South Africa were to suggest over the next few days that the time had come to pursue incorporation in earnest. The *Sunday Times* reported that 'it is expected that one of the results of the trouble will be to persuade the European residents in the Protectorate, as well as a large number of the natives, that their future will be as secure with the Union as with the Imperial Government.'[24] This was certainly an issue the Dominions Office in London did not want raised at this juncture.

It was only on Monday morning, 18 September that the Dominions Office in London was able to consider the full implications of what Evans had done in Serowe. Four telegrams from him had arrived on Sunday evening. The first gave the text of his speech suspending Tshekedi at Serowe. The second confirmed that he had never used the word 'deposed' in suspending Tshekedi from office and informed Thomas that Serogola had been appointed Acting Chief temporarily, that Rey's report on the Enquiry he and Liesching had conducted into Tshekedi's allegations against the Magistrates together with the transcript of evidence would be telegraphed the next day, and finally that the naval detachment was returning to Simonstown on the morrow. The third telegram transmitted Buchanan's request that Tshekedi be granted permission to come to England to interview the Secretary of State. The last telegram explained that the occasion for his earlier reproof of Tshekedi had been the latter's action in writing direct to Stanley without passing through the proper channels.[25]

In the Dominions Office there was relief that 'Admiral Evans' army goes home today.' Officials were, however, disconcerted by Evans's 'somewhat long and confused account' of his reproof of Tshekedi for 'a rather trifling incident which appears to have been given a great deal more importance than it really merited.'[26] The only telegram sent to Evans that day by the Dominions Office was a request that he seek the opinion of his legal advisers on Tshekedi's claim that the Proclamations limiting jurisdiction of native courts did not apply to the Bangwato.[27] From the Dominions Office point of view, Tshekedi's reported claim was the principal obstacle to a quick solution of a situation that seemed to be rapidly getting out of hand. Indeed, the Anti-Slavery Society was equally anxious that Tshekedi drop this claim, if in fact he were making it. Buxton advised Jennings that if Tshekedi were to come to the United Kingdom, he must 'first make clear to authorities he has no wish to force constitutional issue but only personally explain his position and that he makes no claim to try Europeans.'[28]

On the second day of his confinement in Francistown, Tshekedi seems to have adopted a rather petulant attitude towards the local representatives of the Administration. He took the Acting Resident Magistrate to task on the grounds that Lieutenant Lawrenson, who had tracked him down to Mr Grenfell's house, was spying on him. He was politely but firmly assured that Lawrenson had only been trying to say goodbye to him, and when he did not find him in the Government Camp had sought him out at Mr Grenfell's house to do so. Despite the fact that only three years before when Sebele II had been sent into exile he had been tailed by the Special Branch for twenty-four hours a day, Tshekedi was assured: 'You are quite free to do as you like in Francistown and none of the officials is spying on you or interfering with your liberty in any way.'[29]

The same day Tshekedi learnt that the Resident Commissioner had forwarded his request to travel to England to the High Commissioner, who in turn had forwarded it to the Secretary of State.[30] What he did not know was that Rey had advised that no decision should be made by the Secretary of State on the request until all documents in connexion with the case had been received and considered by the Dominions Office. As Evans could not get these ready in time for the airmail due to leave the next day, they would have to sent by seamail, which would mean they would not arrive in London till 7 or 9 October.[31] Tshekedi also wrote to his lawyer in Mafeking suggesting that he send a copy of the letter he gave to Mr Germond on the day of the flogging to the newspapers, since this would explain why he had been forced to take action.[32]

By the Monday, Tshekedi's correspondence began to resume its former pace. He had taken with him a supply of his official Tribal Authority note paper which he used with the 'Kgotla ea Kgosi Gamanwato' and his Serowe address ostentatiously crossed out. Sensitive to the accusation that he had only tried McIntosh in his *kgotla* with the aim of provoking a constitutional crisis and worried that the newspapers in Britain were interpreting his action in this light, he cabled Charles

Roden Buxton of the Anti-Slavery Society: 'Disquieting as recent developments have been nothing more disturbing to me to observe that my action is interpreted deliberately as determined effort to force constitutional issue between natives and crown courts. God knows such attitude never entered my mind. Greetings.'[33] No doubt, if Rey had seen this telegram he would have commented sourly, 'He doth protest too much, methinks'. In a letter written to Buchanan the same day, Tshekedi informed him that even if he were given permission to go to England it would be impossible for him to get to Cape Town in time to catch Friday's steamer. He also expressed concern that his action was being interpreted in government circles 'as an action of challenge to the Administration powers', and that the Anti-Slavery Society appeared to be influenced by these comments and for that reason were undecided about helping him: for 'without their co-operation there is difficult chance of success.'[34] Guarding against the eventuality that he would not be given permission to go to London, he instructed his Mafeking attorney, J. B. Kieser, that whenever Serogola asked him to, he should make out forms empowering Buchanan and Jennings to speak 'on behalf of the Tribe'. Both Buchanan and Jennings had promised Tshekedi before he was sent to exile that they would travel to London on his behalf if he were prevented from going himself. At a more personal level, hc made arrangements with Mr Blackbeard, the Serowe trader, now presumably in better financial shape, for a loan of £1,000 and received a telegram from Chief Bathoen asking whether there was any truth in the rumour that he was sailing to England the next Friday.[35]

In South Africa Tshekedi's support was meanwhile growing, although the influential mining magnate, Sir Abe Bailey, was widely reported in the South African and British press when he expressed the hope that Thomas would not receive Tshekedi in London. 'Admiral Evans,' he declared, 'acted wisely in having to support him a force sufficiently strong to impress the natives. In dealing with natives white races must face a danger at once if they do not wish to live in fear.'[36] The no less influential Rheinallt Jones wrote to Lord Sanderson, the former Principal of Ruskin College, Oxford, and a representative of the Peers on the Labour Party Parliamentary Executive Committee, to fill him in about the Tshekedi affair and to ask him to ensure that Tshekedi obtained a full and fair hearing in London. 'In view of my knowledge of the situation I was not too much surprised to hear of the explosion between Colonel Rey and Tshekedi and my own feeling, on hearing the news, was that Colonel Rey had chosen a favourable opportunity of bringing Tshekedi to heel. . . . The general view seems to be that Colonel Rey hastily jumped upon a small incident in order to bring the Chief to heel and that even he now realizes that he has released forces which have gone beyond his control.'[37]

Black nationalist opinion also came out strongly in Tshekedi's favour. The

Johannesburg branch of the African National Congress at its meeting in the Inch-cape Hall was reported as resolving unanimously that 'This mass meeting of Africans held under the auspices of the Transvaal African Congress (Johannesburg branch) strongly protests against the high-handed manner in which the Acting Paramount Chief Tshekedi, of the Bamangwato tribe, was dealt with by the Commission appointed to inquire into the flogging of a European named P. W. Macintosh. The Commission's refusal to allow Mr. Douglas Buchanan, K. C., Chief Tshekedi's legal adviser, to represent him at the inquiry is a flagrant vio-lation of the principles of British justice and liberty of the subject, and in the opinion of this meeting a deliberate attempt to defeat the ends of justice. . . . In the opinion of this meeting it is not the flogging of Macintosh which has en-dangered white prestige, and the defence of moral degeneracy with a force of 200 naval men, armed with machine guns, has not in any way enhanced this prestige. On the contrary, it has proved to us that what the white man cannot maintain by his moral strength he wishes to enforce by means of arms.'[38]

One item of news that was widely reported that day in both the South African and British press which redounded further to Tshekedi's advantage was the one the Administration had earlier tried to suppress: that Tshekedi had sent a circular letter to all the whites in Serowe the very day McIntosh had been sentenced in his *kgotla* explaining why he had ordered him to be flogged. Many papers quoted extensively from this circular, which gave their reading public a picture of a caring and deliberative Chief. More worrying for Evans and Rey, perhaps, was the fact that the Afrikaner heartland, represented in *Die Burger,* still had not come out fully in their support. Indeed, the Monday editorial of that paper entitled 'The Error of Palapye' was even more critical than its editorial of the 15th. Its main concern was that the end result of the whole affair would be increasing interference by 'over-seas and local negrophiles' in native affairs. Two days later, however, *Die Vaderland* came out fully in support of Evans. The fact that Tshekedi was denied legal representation was irrelevant. The cardinal issue was that the 'Kgotla does not have jurisdiction over a white man. Tsjekedi [sic] flagrantly overstepped the bounds of his power, and his punishment is entirely deserved.

'There is no white man worth the name in the Union, who would for one moment consider giving a native Kgotla jurisdiction over a white, however low the latter may have sunk. Such a think is unthinkable, not for the sake of the debased individual in this case, but with regard to the prestige of the white man in South Africa.'[39]

Back in Serowe itself the situation after the departure of the marines remained calm. The Reverend Burns had tried to follow up Jennings's suggestion for a petition from the white women of the town and had even secured Mrs Blackbeard's promise of co-operation. But in the end his efforts were of no avail. Sadly he wrote to Jennings: 'I much regret that the proposed ladies' petition is as dead as chilled mutton. Both Johnson and Fodisch urged this morning that this should be dropped because the Government has promised to introduce legislation to deal with the question of white immorality. Mrs. Blackbeard is clearly not the person to carry through a petition of the kind. The Government people having heard all about it began to work against it. The result is that nobody but Evelyn Haile signed it. I am very sorry, but the attitude of the press in the matter, especially in reporting the expression of sympathy offered to Tshekedi after the H.C.'s proclamation of Tshekedi's banishment, may be taken as a true representation of the feelings of the European women.'[40]

There seems to have been little formal correspondence between the Resident Magistrate and 'Acting Chief' Serogola, who scrupulously avoided use of the title accorded him by the Administration. Serogola did, however, write to the Resident Magistrate on Tuesday the 19th asking for the return of the eleven rifles and six shotguns which Tshekedi had taken from his followers on the eve of the Enquiry at Palapye Road and left with Sergeant Dixon at the police station. These were sent back less two that Sergeant Dixon had given to Peter Sebina on the evening Tshekedi left for Francistown.[41] Serogola then wrote to Tshekedi to let him know that they had been received.[42] That same day Serogola wrote to the Magistrate on behalf of Queen Semane that 'she wants to make it clear that her petition should be sent over seas to the Secretary of States [sic]'.[43] Potts replied by return that her petition had reached the hands of the Resident Commissioner on the 16th and that he would forward her request to the Dominions Secretary.[44]

Tshekedi's allies in London had not rested in their efforts to secure publicity for him in the press and to put pressure on the Dominions Office. The Reverend A. M. Chirgwin, Foreign Secretary of the London Missionary Society, wrote to Jennings that he had spent most of his time during the last week 'supplying the Press of London and the Provinces with information about Bechuanaland, Serowe and in particular about Tshekedi and his immediate relatives. We have got articles, interviews, pictures in all kinds of papers and I believe we have secured a very good Press. Over and above that the B.B.C. gave me ten minutes after the second General News on Thursday, 14th, to speak about Tshekedi himself. The line throughout that we have taken is not to pronounce any opinion whatsoever upon the issue under consideration, but to give information to the British public about Tshekedi and his people giving particular care to represent that Tshekedi is an educated, courteous, cautious Christian man. If the Chief decides to come to this country I think he will find that the way has been prepared for him and that he has widespread sympathy.'[45] Sir John Harris, Secretary of the Anti-Slavery Society, had been equally busy with the press. As he wrote to Tshekedi, enclosing a batch of press cuttings: 'You will have observed from the Press of this country that I have been exceedingly busy in keeping them going, and I trust not without effect.'[46]

The efforts of Chirgwin and Harris clearly paid off. The press was carrying an immense amount of editorial as well as news material about Tshekedi and the Serowe affair. Articles on Tshekedi written by Chirgwin himself appeared in a number of papers.[47] The general tenor of both editorial comment and news reports was sympathetic to Tshekedi. The *Daily Herald* almost went overboard in its support, thus justifying the earlier despatch in the *Cape Times* from its London correspondent who informed his readers in South Africa that 'the Liberal and Labour Press is always inclined to take the side of the black man against the white.'[48] In the *Herald* of the 19th W. N. Ewer, in a major article entitled 'Tshekedi—Victim of British Rule', wrote:

'How Hitler must have chuckled as he read the reports of the case. For this is pure Nazi doctrine. Racial superiority, proved by brute force.

' "Einstein is a genius. Damn him: he is a Jew."

' "Tshekedi is an able chieftain. Damn him: he is a nigger."

'If in Nazi Germany a Jew will cringe and grovel, he may escape whipping.

'If in the British Empire a nigger will cringe and grovel, he may also avoid trouble.

'But once a black man sets himself to the job (which is supposedly the white man's purpose) of lifting his people, of helping them, of building up their self-respect, of standing up for their rights against ill-treatment by the worst kind of whites, then the whole force of white civilization—cocked hats and howitzers and all—must be invoked to break him.'[49]

Some elements of the British press did give their support to Evans. The *Evening Standard* in an editorial of 21 September insisted that 'Tshekedi must not be reinstated.' He had broken the law and insisted he had been justified in doing so. 'It now appears to be suggested that he may recede from the position he took up and recover his chieftaincy at the price of an apology. This would, in our opinion, be far from satisfactory.'[50] The *Daily Mail* considered that Tshekedi's conduct was not permissible and that his sentence had been very lenient.[51] The *Manchester Guardian* tried to take a broader view, opining that the McIntosh case 'raised issues by the side of which the flogging was a trivial affair'. It examined the parlous financial situation in the Bechuanaland Protectorate, the problems of the powers of Chiefs and the question of Basarwa 'slavery'.[52] Some newspapers saw the absurd in the whole escapade. The *New Britain* felt that the 'only place where the British Empire can afford an adventure of the Evans type is in Gilbert and Sullivan opera; but even Gilbert and Sullivan would have made a joke out of the proceedings. Unfortunately the British government cannot do so here. There must be some travesty of justice when even the South African Press cries out in dismay against it.' But the editorialist turned from the absurd to the serious aspects of a situation where 'the British tax-payer had to find the money for 200 marines and for the nineteen guns, and presumably for the incidentals to a trial which should never have taken place. The only possible conclusion must be the dismissal of "Evans of the Broke" and the High Commissioner with him, the reinstatement of the Chief, and an apology on the part of the British Government for a shocking piece of maladministration.'[53]

The Press was not the only form of pressure brought to bear on the British government. Sir John Harris of the Anti-Slavery Society asked Thomas to receive a deputation from a non-party, inter-denominational group that wanted to submit to him certain facts concerning Tshekedi 'which they felt sure you would wish to take into consideration in coming to a decision on recent events.'[54] Indeed, Harris was determined to 'keep stirring people up' until Thomas came to a decision.[55] Harold Moody, President of the League of Coloured Peoples, had already written to Thomas asking for 'a full and just examination of the whole case.'[56] Pressure for an independent enquiry into the whole affair was building up in both Britain and South Africa, where the press was taking a surprisingly 'impartial' line in its editorials. The Johannesburg *Star* considered that the 'Imperial Government should send an independent commissioner to investigate affairs in Bechuanaland or, alternatively, request the Union Government to appoint a judicial commissioner to inquire into and report upon the events of last week and the correctness or otherwise of the statements made by Tshekedi.'[57]

In the Dominions Office, Thomas and his advisers wanted to bring the whole affair to a speedy conclusion and would have liked to see Tshekedi reinstated within as short a time as possible, since 'so long as he is deprived of office he is likely to be the centre of agitation not only within the tribe but in South Africa and in this country.' The nub of the problem for Thomas was the fact that Tshekedi seemed still to be claiming that provisions prohibiting native courts from dealing with whites did not apply to him or the Bangwato. 'It is clear', he cabled Evans, 'that so long as this claim is maintained, it will not be possible to restore him to Chieftainship.' As far as Tshekedi's proposed journey to London was concerned, the only possible point of this would be an appeal by him to be restored to the chieftainship at an early date. But this would be almost automatic once he renounced any claim to deal with whites in his court. So there was little purpose in his coming. Thomas concluded that, since it would only keep alive press and public interest in the case which 'might otherwise well lie down', he would 'prefer that visit should not take place. I am not, however, prepared to prohibit visit; and if Chief persists in his desire, I am doubtful whether it would be wise even to postpone it. I appreciate the force of the considerations in favour of postponement mentioned in your telegram; but Tshekedi and his advisers might well take occasion to represent that he had been prevented from obtaining access to me until my mind had been made up on an *ex parte* presentation of the case.' Evans should, however, make it clear to Tshekedi that if he did come to England there would be no material alterations to the draft of the new Proclamations.[58] Stanley had been consulted about the burden of Thomas's telegram and agreed with his approach.[59]

The next morning—Tuesday, 20 September—a telegram from Eales arrived at the Dominions Office addressed personally to Whiskard. It contained news which suggested that there might soon be a way out of the maze into which Evans had led them. Eales reported that late the previous afternoon, with the Acting High Commissioner's knowledge, he had had a purely private conversation with Buchanan. The latter had told him that he was advising Tshekedi by telegraph to send Evans a message to the effect that 'he recognizes that he should not have dealt with a case in which a European was concerned and undertaking not to deal in future with any European case; that in order to remove any misapprehension that may exist he does not and will not claim immunity from the law of the Protectorate as now in force or as may be in force hereafter; that no one could regret what has occurred more than he does and that he desires to assure the High Commissioner that he would work with the Resident Commissioner and his officers at all times in harmony and loyal co-operation.'[60]

Armed with this knowledge, Thomas attended Cabinet that morning, where Item 1 on the agenda was 'Trials of White Men by Native Chiefs'. Ramsay MacDonald was in the chair as Thomas drew the attention of his colleagues to the public interest aroused by the flogging of Phinehas McIntosh. He informed them that he had received 'great numbers of letters on this episode which had become a matter of political importance. The point of principle involved was that the Chief had claimed the right to try a European and this was a point on which no concession could be made.' Ignorant of how long it took to travel from Francistown to the Cape by train, Thomas told his colleagues that the Chief was sailing for London on Friday the 22nd, but that he was not without hope that Tshekedi would accept the advice of his Counsel and express his regret to Admiral Evans. Were he to do this, Thomas proposed, 'if the Cabinet agreed, to sanction his reinstatement.' Thomas further told his colleagues that he intended to examine the action of the Magistrate concerned though what this involved was not, at least as far as the Minutes relate it, explained to his fellow ministers.[61] Cabinet then concurred in Thomas's proposed action and agreed to sanction Tshekedi's reinstatement if he expressed his regrets to Admiral Evans.[62]

On return from Cabinet, Thomas arranged that Whiskard send a message to Eales indicating that if Tshekedi were to send in a letter along the lines suggested by Buchanan, it should be possible for the Secretary of State 'to advise His Majesty to terminate the suspension forthwith and to make an early announcement to this effect.' Thomas further let it be known that he would be 'glad to be in a position to answer the numerous questions he is receiving in regard to the Magistrate's action. He hopes therefore to receive as soon as possible the summary of the evidence and the report on this question'.[63] That evening a telegram outlining the substance of the report into Tshekedi's allegations against his Magistrates arrived at the Dominions Office. While conveying Rey's conclusions that no blame attached to the Magistrates, and that this was the joint finding of himself and Liesching, the telegram carried a portentous and convoluted rider: 'In associating himself with the Resident Commissioner in this report Mr. Liesching records that while specific complaints of failure to act which had been brought against the magistrates have been disposed of at the inquiry in manner indicated in this report he is of the opinion that there is substance in the complaints lodged by the Acting Chief on the general ground that conditions from which these specific incidents arose were a matter in which responsibility for initiating remedial action rested with the Administration irrespective of particular complaints by the Acting Chief and that it appears that such remedial action of fundamental character was not in fact taken by the Administration.' Evans then informed the Office that a full memorandum setting out the basis of Liesching's opinion would be sent together with Rey's comments on it by the next seamail, along with his overall report on the Serowe affair. The first crack in the edifice of administrative solidarity in South Africa had appeared.[64]

On the morning of Wednesday the 21st Rey received a secret telegram from Evans informing him that Tshekedi might shortly be sending a message abandoning any right to try whites and that if such a message were received he might be able to recommend the Chief's reinstatement at an early date. He informed Rey that Sir Herbert Stanley approved of such a course.[65] Before Rey could reply he received a coded telegram from the Acting Resident Magistrate in Francistown. It contained the text of a letter from Tshekedi. He had followed Buchanan's advice which was sent him in two telegrams on Tuesday afternoon. Buchanan believed that if Tshekedi agreed to do as he suggested 'it will put you in a very strong position in the eyes of the world and may possibly have the effect of putting an end to your suspension even before we sail for England'.[66] Accordingly, Tshekedi— recalling previous reprimands for communicating with the High Commissioner direct—sent his letter of apparent surrender to the Resident Magistrate with the request that it be telegraphed to the High Commissioner 'through the usual channels'.[67]

'As it appears', wrote Tshekedi, 'that there is a feeling that it is my desire to try cases in which Europeans are involved I desire to repeat what Mr. Arnold C. Germond said at the recent enquiry that I said to him on the 6th September 1933 that I wished to stress the fact that I had not taken such a step regarding P. W. McIntosh with the intention of forcing an issue on a point of jurisdiction affecting my Court but I had been compelled in the interests of just Administration and the good of my people to order the punishment of Phineas McIntosh. I hereby abandon any right to deal with a case in which a European is concerned and I undertake not to deal with any European case in future. In order to remove any misapprehension that might exist I did not and will not claim to be immune from the laws of the Protectorates as now in force or as may be hereafter in force. No one could regret more than I do what has occurred and I desire to assure His Excellency the High Commissioner that I would at all times work in harmony and loyal co-operation with the Administration.' Tshekedi may have made it clear that he disclaimed any jurisdiction over whites in the future. But he still maintained that in the circumstances he was right to have dealt with McIntosh as he had.

Rey was overjoyed at the news the telegram contained. As far as he perceived it, 'the net result is that Tshekedi has climbed down. . . . So now we are going to terminate his suspension and reinstate him.

'It has been a huge triumph, and I think our friend has been flattened out for all time, or at all events for a long time to come.'[68]

CHAPTER 7

A Tactical Retreat

Rey's triumphs, recorded with different degrees of hyperbole from a mere 'quiet' to 'my greatest yet', all tended to be temporary in nature. And over the coming days Tshekedi and his allies in South Africa and Britain began to undermine the impregnable heights Rey felt he had occupied just after what he called Tshekedi's 'submission'.[1] His exultation on the day he learnt of it was soon to seem hollow: 'Everyone is simply delighted, except of course the rotten missionary-inspired press, and the missionaries themselves. I have received any amount of congratulations.'[2]

For his part, Tshekedi seems to have found his decision to 'climb down' cathartic, and he once again returned to the struggle with the Resident Commissioner. He called on all the sources of support in Britain and South Africa which he had so skilfully manipulated over the past three years, whether it was in his campaign against mining or incorporation into the Union of South Africa. His first concern was to arrange his visit to London. No doubt he recalled the success that had attended his earlier trip in 1930 when he saw the then Dominions Secretary, Lord Passfield, to protest against mining in his territory. It was then that he had made so many of the friends in missionary, humanitarian and political circles who now came to his assistance. The main objective of his proposed visit was not to discuss the McIntosh case but to secure the appointment of a Royal Commission to look into the administration of the Bechuanaland Protectorate with special reference to Colonel Rey's Proclamations.

In his campaign against the Bechuanaland Protectorate Administration, Tshekedi was in no way challenging British colonial rule as such. Bathoen II, his closest ally among his fellow Chiefs, was to say fifty years later that in their campaign against the Proclamations he and Tshekedi were not embarking on an incipient nationalist campaign. Rather, they were seeking reform of the system of colonial administration as it operated in the Bechuanaland Protectorate because they sincerely believed that it did not conform to British colonial practice as they understood it to obtain elsewhere in Britain's African empire.[3]

Tshekedi's request to go to Britain was not a new one arising from the crisis over the flogging of Phinehas McIntosh. In the telegram he and Bathoen addressed to Sir Herbert Stanley just before the 'flogging', which had caused such umbrage on the part of Rey and Evans, he had requested the appointment of a Royal Commission or failing that permission to travel to Britain and explain to the Secretary of State his objections to the Proclamations. Now, having renewed his request in his unaccustomed circumstances as an ex-Chief, he was careful to keep his options open. He was far from sanguine about the chances of his visit being approved, so he made plans for Buchanan and Jennings to travel on his behalf as the three of them had agreed just before he left for exile. Since he was no longer Chief, he made arrangements for them to be given a mandate by Serogola on behalf of the Tribe. He made similar arrangements for himself, because in the eyes of the British he was now a mere private citizen and no longer had any right to speak on behalf of his people.

Even if Tshekedi's request to travel to Britain were turned down, his presence in Cape Town was required by Buchanan and Jennings before they sailed to England so that they could discuss with him how best they could represent his case against the Proclamations. But he could not travel out of the Tati District without permission from the High Commissioner, especially as the railway line to Cape Town from Francistown passed through the Bamangwato Reserve. So Buchanan sent in a formal application for Tshekedi to travel to Cape Town irrespective of whether he would be granted permission to travel to London. In the same letter Buchanan advised the High Commissioner that he had found 'serious discrepancies' between the official transcript of the proceedings of the Enquiry at Palapye Road and that made by Mr Whiteside of the London Missionary Society.[4]

Buchanan's letter crossed with one Evans had written him that same day enclosing the Secretary of State's reply to his request that Tshekedi be permitted to travel to Britain. The Secretary of State's telegram had in fact been sent before Tshekedi's 'submission', but it was clear from it that Thomas would still be most unwilling to see him. If the real motive of Tshekedi's visit was to discuss the draft Proclamations then 'Tshekedi must understand on this point that there will be no material alterations in the terms of the draft.' Thomas did state, however, that if Tshekedi still desired to come to England he would not be prevented from doing so.[5] The contents of the Secretary of State's telegram were delivered to Tshekedi in Francistown that same day.[6]

The discrepancies to which Buchanan alluded in his letter to Evans were in fact quite minor. The only one of substance was the omission from the official record of the exchange between Buchanan and Captain Neale over his right to represent Tshekedi at the Enquiry. The Administration readily agreed to the inclusion of this exchange in the final version of the official record.[7] Otherwise, on close examination they reveal no matters of substance, and what discrepancies there are were just what one might expect from two different shorthand writers recording long and complicated evidence. Nevertheless Buchanan sent a copy of the discrepancies to Tshekedi, and they served as yet another means of throwing doubt on the already widely discredited Enquiry.[8]

The Dominions Office only learnt that Tshekedi had renounced any claim to try whites early on the afternoon of Friday 22nd. Evans cabled J. H. Thomas, the Dominions Secretary, the full text of Tshekedi's letter together with Colonel Rey's recommendation that Tshekedi's suspension should be terminated. Termination though should be coupled with a severe warning, and Tshekedi's letter of 'submission' should be read out in *kgotla* and be published in the press in both South Africa and England. The two Native Proclamations 'should be enacted at the earliest possible moment. I regard these steps,' Rey had insisted to Evans, 'as essential in the interests of future peace in the Protectorate. Prompt enactment of Proclamations is especially necessary to avoid further argument and possible disagreement between Tshekedi and the Administration.' Evans supported Rey's position and further suggested that he personally go to Serowe to reinstate Tshekedi.[9]

Although Thomas was set against Tshekedi coming to see him in London, he and his officials were not unsympathetic to him. But they did feel that Tshekedi's presence in London would merely exacerbate an already inflamed situation. If by proxy he could put so much pressure on his Office through lobbyists and the press, what would it be like if he were to conduct his operations from a base in London? There was the additional matter that, as yet unknown to Tshekedi, Thomas was anxious to have him back as Chief as soon as possible and for that reason did not want him on the high seas at a time when he would be required in Serowe for his reinstatement. The main bone of contention between the Dominions Office and the Administration in South Africa as distinct from Colonel Rey was not how soon this should be but what form it should take. As Whiskard observed in a pungent minute on Tshekedi's letter of 'submission', while he had to a 'considerable extent accepted the advice given to him by Buchanan', he had repeated his earlier assertion that he had been compelled to act in McIntosh's case, 'owing to the supineness of the administration.'[10] Thus when the Secretary of State announced Tshekedi's reinstatement, he would have to say either that there was no ground for Tshekedi's accusation or that steps were being taken to avoid a recurrence. 'A "severe warning" to Tshekedi would be out of place. The less said the better.'[11]

Whiskard also advised Thomas that under no circumstances should the passage of Rey's Proclamations be linked with the reinstatement of Tshekedi. 'It would be most unwise to let it be supposed that the Proclamations arise out of this case. They have been on the stocks for some considerable time, they are now before the Chiefs for their consideration, and we ought not to put Tshekedi in a position to say that we have used this case to prevent him from criticizing the provisions of the draft Proclamations.' Whiskard then turned to the suggestion made by Evans that he personally reinstate Tshekedi. This was 'probably sound—provided that he does not feel it necessary to be accompanied by 200 sailors and 3 guns; but you will probably agree that it is essential that the terms of the announcement should be concurred in by you beforehand, and that he should confine himself strictly to those terms.'[12] The Dominions Office clearly did vet Evans's statement, because three new files were opened on the subject but unfortunately they were later all 'Destroyed under Statute', so we shall never know what modifications they proposed.[13]

Thomas adopted Whiskard's suggestions almost in their entirety, and thus the irascible Rey lost important ground in his battle with Tshekedi over the Proclamations. Thomas sent off a telegram making further enquiries about the circumstances surrounding Tshekedi's complaints against the Resident Magistrates in view of 'the great attention which this aspect of the case is attracting in Press and other circles here and of the numerous inquiries which are being addressed to me.'[14] Then the following afternoon a long telegram incorporating Whiskard's suggestions was sent to Admiral Evans informing him that Thomas was advising the King to terminate Tshekedi's suspension from the chieftaincy. Thomas agreed that Evans should personally reinstate Tshekedi, but that his statement on the occasion should be agreed with him beforehand. 'As at present advised I am inclined to doubt whether it is either necessary or desirable to couple the reinstatement of Tshekedi with a severe warning, but his message should of course be read out in full.' Then came the bitter pill for Charles Rey: 'I should certainly regard it as undesirable to give any ground for the suggestion that consideration of draft Proclamations has been unduly hurried as a result of this affair, or that Tshekedi has been prevented from making representations on behalf of his tribe which it is the duty of a Chief to make. As soon, therefore, as Tshekedi is reinstated he should be informed that the representations which . . . he has now made through proper channel will be considered as soon as possible, and that a further announcement regarding the proclamations will be made at an early date.'[15] This telegram was sent at 2:50 P.M. on Saturday 23rd, one hour and one minute before a telegram from the High Commissioner arrived informing the Dominions Office that the 'Resident Commissioner Bechuanaland Protectorate has asked with reference to his recommendation that suspension should be terminated forthwith, that special attention should be drawn to provision which relates to enactment of both draft Native Proclamations at earliest possible date.'[16] Rey was too late. It is highly doubtful whether the Dominions Office would at this stage have been influenced by his plea. It was Saturday afternoon, and all but a skeleton staff had gone home for the weekend. In any case, Thomas and his advisers were anxious to resolve the whole problem of Tshekedi as soon as possible. To accede to Rey's request would only delay matters and cause further political problems for Thomas.

Rey had lost important ground in his struggle with Tshekedi. Indeed, he had spent the previous weekend trying to persuade Evans to support the imposition of even fiercer conditions for Tshekedi's reinstatement. He was more and more worried about the prospect of Tshekedi going to London, where he would not only raise objections to the Proclamations but, at the instigation of Buchanan and Jennings, the whole question of the constitutional position of the Chiefs. In a long telegram to Evans on Saturday, he had once more urged that the Proclamations be passed before Tshekedi was reinstated and that a condition of his reinstatement should be that he give a definite undertaking to co-operate loyally with the Administration in working both Proclamations. As for the date for ending the termination of his suspension, he felt that this should be not less than six months hence, which in any case he regarded as too short a time. If he were reinstated earlier 'it would not allow Serogola and Council to function at all. They would merely await Tshekedi's return. Indeed it might prevent election of Council as arranged for 11th October which would be very unfortunate as Council most advisable. I consider 1 year minimum period requisite and in interest of Tribe it should be longer.'[17] Evans, who had already communicated Rey's request to the Dominions Office that the Proclamations be enacted as soon as possible, was furious when he received this telegram. He telephoned Rey on Sunday at 11:30 A.M. and in a long and acrimonious conversation on which Rey made detailed notes, he accused Rey of 'asking me to try and get the Secretary of State to bounce through the Native Proclamations immediately and by so doing score a point at Tshekedi's expense, which strikes me as being unfair and not in accordance with the ordinary, reasonable, what we think, just procedure.'

Rey was not one to be cowed by the Admiral and replied that he stuck to his position as he had put it in the telegram which Evans had already forwarded to the Dominions Office. 'In that telegram I suggested the enactment of these two Native

Proclamations forthwith as a condition of reinstatement. There was no intention whatsoever in my mind of trying to bolt this Proclamation through in order to score over him. That is the last thing I would have thought of.'[18]

The one thing Rey did agree on with Evans was that the High Commissioner should personally reinstate Tshekedi. However, if Evans wanted Rey to undertake this task he was perfectly willing to do so. But he should remember that the Tribe had already been called to assemble in *kgotla* on 11 October. 'You cannot get the Tribe together before then.' Rey then concluded his conversation by expressing the hope that Evans would be sending on his telegrams to London.

It is as well that Evans did not forward Rey's request for a continuation of Tshekedi's suspension for a further six months at the very least, and preferably a year. For it would have been most unwelcome in Whitehall. Evans contented himself with reiterating to Thomas that Rey 'feels very strongly that issue of Native Proclamations should not be unduly delayed. He would have preferred that they should be issued before Tshekedi is reinstated'.[19] Rey followed up his telephone conversation with Evans in a letter typed that same day confirming that he considered it vital to peace and harmony in Gamangwato that the Proclamations be enacted before Tshekedi was reinstated. He went on to say, 'I regard it as deplorable that no warning should be given to the Chief as regards his future behaviour when he is reinstated. As it is he escapes without punishment for an admittedly wrongful act, and this, I fear, will be misinterpreted by him and the other Chiefs in the Territory. It must always be remembered that in dealing with Tshekedi we are dealing with all the Chiefs.'[20]

Lieutenant Colonel Rey, with no direct responsibility to Parliament, could shrug off press and public opinion. But the Dominions Office was being subjected to intense pressure by supporters of Tshekedi in London. The only piece of luck on the Office's side was that Parliament was not at the time in session. This did not mean they were immune to parliamentary pressure. Members of both the Lords and Commons approached Thomas on Tshekedi's behalf. Colonel Wedgwood, Labour member of Parliament for Newcastle under Lyme, wrote to Thomas on the 20th that he was most anxious that 'this bad business in Bechuanaland should not be used by the Union Government to get the Protectorates transferred to them. The worst of Admiral Evans' conduct is that it gives them a lever. Do drop me a line of reassurance on this point.'[21] Two days before, the *Morning Post* had reported that it was 'expected that one of the results of the Tshekedi trouble will be to persuade European and native inhabitants that they would be just as well under the Union.'[22] Godfrey Huggins, the new Premier of Southern Rhodesia, had issued a statement from his office making it clear that if 'as a result of the Tshekedi affair, any question arose as to the future control of the Protectorate, the interests of this Colony would be carefully watched.' If there was to be a scramble for the

Bechuanaland Protectorate, Southern Rhodesia had a long-standing claim to the northern half.[23]

The press, missionary inspired or otherwise, was by and large hostile to Evans and Rey. One exception was the London *Evening Standard,* which went further then Rey would have dared (though no doubt would have liked to) and declared that under no circumstances should Tshekedi be restored. This was a matter of principle. A simple apology would not be enough.[24] Support came also from Colonel Trew, formerly of the South African Police, who wrote to the *Cape Argus* that he felt that 'some of the criticisms of Admiral Evans' action in the Serowe affair are most unjustified.

'I used to know the Bamangwato people fairly well, as for some time I was responsible for the policing of the Transvaal side of the Bechuana border. I have also had more experience than most people in restoring and maintaining order during native disturbances.

'The Bamangwato people are not the angels some writers would lead us to believe. In my day we had continual trouble with them. Armed parties of them used to cross the Limpopo and poach the game on the Transvaal side. When the police attempted to arrest them they had no hesitation in opening fire. On one occasion a native preacher was killed and the police had a horse shot. At that time the Bamangwato could put in the field some 5,000 men armed with firearms. These arms are mostly of the Martini-Henry pattern.

'In my experience of natives it is always essential to make as big a show of force as possible if you intend to carry out any action which may arouse them. This show of force will save bloodshed in the end. . . . It would have been a most damaging thing for the white man if the Admiral had gone up without any force at his back and the Bamangwato had defied him.

'. . . The British Government is to blame for allowing white men to cohabit with native women in their territories, because they will not institute a colour bar in relations between races.

'There is one section of the population of the Union who, I feel sure, will strongly support the action of Admiral Evans, and that is the farmers of the Western Transvaal.'[25]

Another Colonel thought differently. The very day that the Dominions Office was finalising the telegram about the conditions of Tshekedi's reinstatement, the *Manchester Guardian* published a letter from Colonel Wedgwood advocating that Evans should be made to pay the costs of transporting 'all these marines and howitzers to the recesses of Bechuanaland.'[26]

A thoughtful, and characteristically perceptive, essay on 'The Real Moral of the Tshekedi Case' appeared in the *New Statesman and Nation* under the signature of W. M. Macmillan, the brilliant South African historian and journalist. Already acquainted with Tshekedi, he was not over-impressed by him or what he considered the autocratic ways of the Chiefs he had encountered on earlier trips to the Bechuanaland Protectorate. He underscored the real outcome of the suspension of Tshekedi, and that was to 'bring the administration of the Protectorate into the limelight, and it is on that public attention ought to be focussed.' He then proceeded to give his own verdict on the Administration. Its policy had been 'to interfere as little as possible, and to harden the local and domestic powers of the Chief into a virtual autocracy.' Not 'wholly unintelligent' critics of Tshekedi had been summarily banished by the Administration. As far as 'real development is concerned the pace has been slow indeed', though he did give credit to Rey, who had begun 'before the great slump, to take some notice of the real economic potentialities of the country and its people.' He and his colleagues in the other High Commission Territories had alerted the High Commission 'that the powers of the Chiefs it has so long relied on are now an obstacle to development.' To the 'Administration, however, the Chief is little more than a puppet, free to lord it thus as he pleases only so long as in keeping order he does not 'flout the Administration''—in this case by doing work it had itself patently failed to do. In pronouncing judgement, therefore, on Tshekedi, Admiral Evans unwittingly pronounced judgement also on the Administration whose mouthpiece for the moment he was.'[27]

If Tshekedi was seen as an autocrat by Macmillan, in *Umsebenzi: The South African Worker,* organ of the Communist Party of South Africa, he was a hero in the struggle against imperialism. 'Chiefs, like Tshekedi, who are prepared to oppose the imperialists and fight for the independence of Bechuanaland must be supported.' Meanwhile, workers and other 'oppressed people of South Africa must rally in support of the Bechuanas . . . hold meetings of protest throughout the country and send resolutions of protest to the British and Union governments demanding:

"HANDS OFF BECHUANALAND" '[28]

In more sober tones, G. L. Steer in the *Spectator* also put the blame squarely on the Administration, which 'most needs overhaul in the interests of both black and white.' Rather unfairly to Rey, whose Proclamations were given no mention, he complained that the 'chiefs of Bechuanaland have powers which are anomalous in the present profound peace of the Protectorate. It is not their fault that they retain these powers: nor is it reasonable to abolish them and put nothing in their place. Nothing less than a renewal of personnel and a complete change of policy in the Bechuanaland service is required, for the Bechuanaland magistrate receives at best little more than a police training. Chiefs can be deposed, degraded or suspended; but so will their successors be, until the Bechuanaland administration learns that it is better to advise, to maintain constant contact and infinite patience than to punish

15. *Umsebenzi*'s view of the suspension of Tshekedi; Evans is depicted as a pig.

outstanding excesses by a procedure that risks the immediate break-up of tribal life. Black men must not flog white men—or else terrible forces are unloosed. But it is not enough to say that. The situation where Tshekedi flogs a white man, because there is apparently no other authority willing to punish him, must never recur.'[29]

Even if there were some reservations about the powers of the Chiefs, the main thrust of much of the commentary in the press was that the fault lay with the Bechuanaland Administration. Tshekedi was certainly winning the 'press war' with Rey.

If the press did not come out wholly in support of Tshekedi, the churches in South Africa and Britain were almost unanimously behind him. Indeed, they were one of his main sources of support. For them he was the son of that great African Christian, Khama III, and had followed in his father's footsteps. As the Rev.

A. M. Chirgwin put it so picturesquely: 'It may be that there are still chiefs in Africa who wear feathers and skins, who live in the midst of either squalid superstition or barbaric splendour, who are hard-drinking, overbearing, untutored polygamists. If there are such, Tshekedi does not belong to their set. He is an educated, quiet-mannered, competent Christian who neither drinks, smokes nor swears. Though he has reached the age when men of his tribe are usually married, he still remains a bachelor. He is a church member and a regular worshipper at the great church his father built, and he takes a keen interest in the Sunday School, the Boys' Brigade, the Girls' Life Brigade and the Temperance Union. He would certainly be a deacon of the church were it not that both he and the missionaries agree that it is probably not in the best interests of the church or the tribe for a chief to hold office.'[30]

Apart from activists like Chirgwin in the London headquarters of Tshekedi's own church, the LMS, resolutions were sent to Thomas by Church groups in South Africa and Britain. The Anglican synod of the diocese of Johannesburg cabled him to express its regrets that the Chief had been allowed no legal defence and expressed the hope that he would be given an opportunity to state his case before the proper authorities.[31] The Northern Women's District Association of the Congregational Union of South Africa and the General Assembly of the Presbyterian Church of South Africa in session at Port Elizabeth sent similar resolutions to the Dominions Secretary, with the latter emphasizing 'the necessity of any Native Chief in South Africa preserving his people from the disastrous consequences of acts of immorality between Europeans and Natives.'[32] The Women's Christian Temperance Union of the Transvaal 'to which the native women of Bechuanaland are affiliated, assembled in Johannesburg', declared that it 'upholds equal moral standards irrespective of race or sex. We deplore the recent unfortunate happenings at Serowe and are convinced that the acting Chief Tshekedi acted in the interests of morality.'[33]

In Britain numerous churches lobbied the Dominions Secretary, including a meeting of the Society of Friends at Bath which unanimously instructed its Clerk to write to Tshekedi and inform him that 'we rejoice at the stand you have taken for truth and right,—even though this has resulted in persecution and hardship to yourself.' The Clerk, Geraldine Theobalds, also informed Tshekedi that the Friends had written to Thomas 'strongly protesting at the unjust action of our Government.'[34] Charles Roden Buxton, who was now convinced that Tshekedi was not 'trying to force a great constitutional issue', wrote to the Editor of the Quaker periodical, the *Friend,* in praise of the Chief. He 'is beyond all question, not merely an able man, but a singularly thoughtful, high-minded and disinterested man. Whatever he has done, he has done from a sense of duty, and in what he believes to be the true interests of his people.' Buxton then referred to the beginnings of his friendship with Tshekedi three years earlier when the Chief came to London to protest against mining in his territory. 'I do know that he has very strong and conscientious objections to mining development. . . . Judging, as he does, from the experience of other parts of South Africa, he is strongly impressed with the social and political evils which such development brings in its train.'[35]

When the Dominions Office opened its doors on Monday, 25 September, the principal problem outstanding in connection with Tshekedi's return to office was whether his accusations against the Magistrates in Serowe were justified. Whiskard had already minuted on the telegraphic digest of the Report by Rey and Liesching that it was difficult to dissent from Liesching's opinion that it was incumbent on the Administration to have taken action whether or not the chief had complained. In not reporting the matter to the Resident Commissioner, the Resident Magistrate was 'at least guilty of a serious error of judgement.' It was bad enough 'to have Europeans cohabiting with native women outside the reserves, but it is infinitely worse to have them doing so within the reserves, and especially in a place like Serowe where many thousand natives congregate together.' But how was the Magistrate concerned to be disciplined? Sir Herbert Stanley had informed Whiskard that Potts was by far the best of the Magistrates in the Protectorate and that to transfer him from Serowe would not mean a change for the better, while 'a *public* reprimand would impair his usefulness.'[36]

As far as Rey was concerned, no blame could be attached to either the Resident Magistrates or the Administration in Mafeking. He was determined that Tshekedi should not have the satisfaction of seeing his accusations against his Magistrates upheld. But Tshekedi had support for his accusations from an unexpected quarter: Percivale Liesching. Later Tshekedi's Mafeking lawyer, Kieser, would warn him that as a result of his observations of Liesching at the Enquiry at Palapye Road he 'by no means appealed to me as being disposed to you in a friendly way and I opine, no matter what power or authority he can exercise, that you will not receive any favourable support from that quarter. This was my impression of him and I became fortified in the view by the trend of the few questions he put during the enquiry. I trust I am wrong in the conclusion.'[37] He was. For, unknown to Tshekedi, Liesching had explained his reservations about Rey's Report on their Enquiry in an eleven-page document submitted to the High Commissioner on 22 September. He was very critical of the role of the Mafeking Administration in the McIntosh saga as it unfolded between 1930 and 1933, during all of which time Rey had been Resident Commissioner.[38]

Liesching argued that when the whole question of the misbehaviour by McIntosh and McNamee was first raised with Headquarters at Mafeking by Nettelton in December 1930, he had been incorrectly informed that it was impossible to deport the two young men from the Reserve. In fact, the Resident Commissioner and the

High Commissioner did possess the necessary authority under Proclamations No 13 of 1907 and 8 of 1929 to remove them. Indeed, although Liesching restrained himself from making the obvious point, Jennings did not. At a meeting in Vryburg on the 20th he emphasised that immediately after the Enquiry at Palapye Road the Government had used Proclamation 8 of 1929 to deport McIntosh and McNamee to Lobatse so that 'the Administration apparently had the machinery but failed to use it.'[39] For his part, Liesching generally felt that Mafeking had not responded to a serious situation of which, in view of Nettelton's report, it could hardly have been unaware. Furthermore, the matter was not brought to the attention of the High Commissioner, while it 'is not revealed from the documents whether they were brought to the personal notice of the Resident Commissioner.'

With regard to the enquiry which Nettelton was asked to initiate into the alleged misdeeds of McIntosh and McNamee in 1932, when he was relieving Potts as Magistrate at Serowe, Liesching considered that 'responsibility fairly rests with Mafeking; that Captain Nettelton, in view of the attitude of Headquarters both on the strong reports put in on this occasion and on the previous occasion (1930–31), did not pursue the matter further when Tshekedi failed to produce evidence; that these considerations apply equally to Captain Potts when he resumed duty in September 1932; that the correspondence should, in the absence of the Resident Commissioner, have been brought to the notice of the High Commissioner; that if, through an error of judgement, this was not done, the correspondence should undoubtedly have been brought to the notice of Resident Commissioner on his return from leave in October, 1932 for a decision as to whether the Administration should not proceed on its own initiative, notwithstanding the failure of Tshekedi to produce evidence.' Finally, he did not think Captain Potts was wrong not to report to Mafeking the fact that he had severely reprimanded McIntosh in April 1933 since 'the replies received by the Resident Magistrates on the previous occasions had specifically encouraged local action of the kind taken by Captain Potts, and held out no prospect of the more drastic action which both he and Captain Nettelton had strongly recommended.'[40]

Evans clearly felt there was justice in these severe strictures on the Protectorate Administration, but Rey would have none of them. In a second hour-long telephone conversation with Rey on Sunday afternoon, Evans tried to get him to agree to a final version of the Report, in which would appear Liesching's fairly mild rider that remedial action of the fundamental character required had not been carried out by the Administration. 'You could, of course, append a further paragraph', he told Rey, 'but if you do it will spoil the frank sincerity of the whole Report with its fearlessness and frankness as its stands.

'If there has been any Magisterial or Secretarial laxity or failure to take action let there be blame attached. After all, who cares. Do we?' Then, in an attempt to flatter Rey into agreement, he told him: 'Personally I consider the Report as it now stands quite a masterly document and I might add that I should be very proud to present it as it stands—signed by you both.'

But Rey was not to be flattered. He may have agreed with Liesching at the time that appropriate remedial action had not been taken, but subsequently 'I found amongst these papers this action which had been taken by me, viz. the circularizing of Chiefs, Magistrates and everybody and the preparation of a law to deal fundamentally with the root evil of this white and native business, which was scotched by the High Commissioner by the way.'[41] Liesching would not have been very impressed by Rey's power of recall, as the Colonel had attacked Tshekedi quite viciously for his lack of the very same thing during the Enquiry.[42]

Under Rey's barrage of opposition, Evans capitulated and sent off a telegram to the Dominions Office which basically exonerated the Magistrates and the Administration from any blame. But before Rey had finished with Evans on the phone, he told him there were some other points he wished to discuss. He understood Tshekedi was coming down to Cape Town on the train next day. 'The only communication he has had from me is the one saying he could go to England. If he breaks the law he will be arrested by the first Policeman he meets. That is the standing order until I countermand it. He has been advised to remain where he is at the present.'

Rey then took up the question as to who should reinstate Tshekedi, about which he had been reflecting since they discussed it in the morning. 'Well, Sir, as you are the person who moved him out—admittedly on my recommendation—I feel it would be placing you in a false position if you were not the person to move him in.'[43]

Rey may have lost the battle over the immediate enactment of the Proclamations, but he had succeeded in denying Tshekedi victory in the matter of his allegations against the Magistrates. Indeed, when the Dominions Office received Evans's telegram putting forward Rey's interpretation of the follow-up to the complaints against McIntosh and McNamee, Whiskard felt that the Administration on 'the whole seems to have made out a reasonably good case for themselves. Where evidence was available of criminal offences action was taken and the men concerned were punished. Cohabitation with native women, however, as such is not a criminal offence. . . .'[44]

Although Thomas was most reluctant to see Tshekedi, he had made it clear that if he insisted on coming to London 'he would not be debarred from doing so.'[45] The Secretary of State's strong reservations about Tshekedi's proposed visit to London were communicated to him by the Acting Resident Magistrate in Francistown, who invariably addressed him as Chief rather than ex-Chief or plain Tshekedi Khama.[46] But before Tshekedi received this message he had already sought permission from the Magistrate to travel to Mafeking by train in order to hold consultations with his lawyer there and also to see the Chief Veterinary Officer about 'the serious loss of my cattle', which he estimated at some four hundred head. This 'severe loss' has been 'occasioned merely by the cordon restrictions, and yet there were many ways by which this loss could have been prevented.' The Government Veterinary Officer in Francistown had told him that 'it had been suggested that the cordon will be shifted back for five miles, and while appreciating this relief I am compelled to state that the grass along the north bank of the Nata river is of very little use to the cattle, it is grass we call ''Motshikhiri'' and it is grass more useful for thatching our huts than for cattle food, particularly when the cattle are in the condition they are now.'[47] But as soon as Tshekedi learnt that 'if I still desire to go to London to interview the Secretary of State I will not be debarred from doing so', he cancelled his request to spend time in Mafeking and informed the Magistrate that he had booked a passage on the boat sailing to England on 6 October from Cape Town. As he needed to consult with his lawyer in Cape Town before he sailed, he planned to catch the southbound Rhodesia Express the following afternoon. Since he would no longer be visiting Mafeking, he made a special request 'for a reasonable relief to my cattle, there is plenty of room to do this without breaking the cordon.'[48] Tshekedi also applied for passports for himself and Peter Sebina, sending one pound in revenue stamps to cover the cost together with certified photographs which, in the case of Tshekedi, the Magistrate regretted 'are not all they might be, but perhaps they will suffice.'[49]

Not only Thomas was averse to Tshekedi's proposed journey. Rey was also firmly set against it, although it was he who had first encouraged Buchanan to believe that there would be no objection to it. In Cape Town, Shirley Eales from the High Commission did his best to persuade Buchanan that he and Jennings 'would be ill-advised to take Tshekedi to England' and that if he did go it would be 'as a private individual and not as a Chief.' When Buchanan told Eales he thought that this 'would put him in a better position with the public', Eales replied that that was a matter of opinion.[50] Evans himself cabled Thomas on the 26th to inform him of Tshekedi's renewed request to come to Cape Town, and he gave his opinion that in 'view of intended early reinstatement and for other reasons it seems desirable that Tshekedi should not leave Protectorate until your decision has been announced and it would be helpful if I could receive telegram from you which I could communicate to Tshekedi . . . saying that it is your wish that he should remain in the Protectorate for a few days later when he may expect to receive a further communication.'[51]

Thomas, who as one of his officials minuted did 'not want Tshekedi to come to England to discuss constitutional principles',[52] replied that same day with a somewhat equivocal message that if Tshekedi wanted to discuss the Proclamations with him he should be informed that his communications on this subject were receiving 'most careful consideration' and that he did not consider 'any useful purpose would be served by a discussion with me. If there are any points which he considers he has not made sufficiently clear in the representations already put forward by him, he should submit to you through the Resident Commissioner at a very early date an explanatory statement by which he desires to supplement them.

'I appreciate of course that, pending Tshekedi's reinstatement, he is not entitled to submit statements on behalf of the tribe. As, however, I hope that it will be possible to make an announcement of his reinstatement within the next few days, we can, I think, waive this point.' What Thomas did not do was supply Evans with the requested formal statement that he wished Tshekedi to remain in the Protectorate.[53]

In the circumstances Evans felt compelled to give Tshekedi permission to come to Cape Town, while making it clear to him that Thomas did not want to see him in London and that any further representations he might like to make concerning the Proclamations should be made to Rey for onward transmission to the Secretary of State. In a telegram to Rey explaining his decision to allow Tshekedi to come to Cape Town, Evans emphasized that he had 'not of course lost sight of the fact that we should have no control over Tshekedi's movements outside of the Protectorate but I think we must assume he will not disregard Secretary of State's wish that he should not proceed to England.'[54] In a further telegram to Thomas he informed him that in view of the repeated requests by Tshekedi 'to be allowed to consult his legal adviser and as a refusal would have inevitably given rise to the suggestion that he was being prejudiced, I have given him permission to come to Cape Town.'[55]

By the time Evans's telegram reached the Dominions Office, Tshekedi was already on the train to Cape Town. The terms of his exile had effectively been cancelled. He was now permitted to travel outside the Tati District, to pass through his own territory, and to leave the Protectorate and enter the Union of South Africa, where he was no longer subject to the jurisdiction of either the Resident Commissioner or the High Commissioner.

CHAPTER 8

Out of Exile

Tshekedi caught the the southbound Rhodesia Express on the afternoon of Wednesday, 27 September. His exile in Francistown had lasted only eleven days. But he was still suspended from the chieftaincy and although he had been informed that he might soon be reinstated he had no indication as to when that would be. Uppermost in his mind as he made the forty-eight hour long journey to Cape Town, with the train stopping at every little station in the Protectorate, was the question of the Proclamations. He was as determined as ever to prevent their promulgation, and though he had not yet been given formal permission to sail to England, it was with the object of catching the boat leaving on 6 October that he had set off on his thousand-mile journey to the Cape. On an earlier occasion in 1930 the Administration had done all it could to prevent him travelling to London, but he had eventually got there and had had two interviews with the Secretary of State for Dominion Affairs. He was no less determined now.

Soon after leaving Francistown, the train crossed into the Bamangwato Reserve and then continued through it for nearly two hundred miles before it entered the Bakgatla Reserve. Technically Tshekedi was not passing through his own territory, since the land for fifty yards on either side of the track belonged to the Rhodesia Railways and did not come under his jurisdiction as Chief. Tshekedi was not so foolish as to leave the station at any point on his journey south. If he had, he would have risked being accused of entering his own territory, thus contravening the order exiling him to the Tati District. But some of his people as well as the white inhabitants of his Reserve learnt that he was on the train and turned out to greet him. At Mahalapye, according to D. G. McLaggan, the local white trader, he had a 'splendid reception but there was no demonstration whatever, the proceedings were marked you might say with a sincere feeling of respect for the British Empire and also Tshekedi. The natives, there were not many, were not at all demonstrative, but quiet and almost reverend, their demeanour was that of a supplicant pleading for justice, and a contrast to the recent display of force.'[1]

Tshekedi told those he talked to at Mahalapye that he felt his position dreadfully but that he was 'full of courage, knowing that he had the support of all decent thinking people in the country.' From his brief remarks it was clear that he thought that the Government was prepared to reinstate him without delay. He was going to Cape Town to find out what the conditions were. He did not want 'to incur unnecessary expense by going Home, but would if he found the conditions impossible.' With regard to the election of a new Regent which Rey had ordered the Bangwato to carry out on 11 October, Tshekedi told the small crowd that he thought that this would now be postponed.

Before the train left the station one of the white residents of Mahalapye on the platform told Tshekedi about the petition that McLaggan had taken round Gamangwato for signature. Signed by thirty-nine 'European residents in Khama's country' and addressed to J. H. Thomas incorrectly as Secretary of State for the Colonies rather than the Dominions,[2] its contents must have given Tshekedi heart as his train steamed out of Mahalapye station on its way to Mafeking, the Protectorate capital.

'We are not conversant with the differences that existed, and possibly still exist between the Government and Tshekedi,' the petition began, 'but as loyal British subjects, trust we are still privileged to state that in our humble opinion the employment of a naval force to support the demands of the Government was quite unnecessary, and has created a very bad impression throughout South Africa, especially among the natives.

'Most of us have spent many years in Khama's Country, where we have always been treated with the greatest kindness and courtesy by the Chiefs and their followers, whom we have found most loyal, and never once to our knowledge, has the authority of the Government been defied by the natives as a whole.

'We have been, and still are passing through most trying times, which have been considerably aggravated by "Foot and Mouth" disease and drought, and this has added very considerably to the anxieties and difficulties of those placed in authority, Native Chiefs as well.

'Under the circumstances, the thrashing of a degenerate like Mac Intosh [sic] by orders of Tshekedi, although admittedly wrong, we consider should have been treated with more leniency and privacy.

'Many of us have our wives and children in the country, and never once has a European Woman been maltreated or openly insulted in Khama's Country by a native—a record the Chief and his followers can be justly proud of—probably unequalled in other native territories, and we always feel our women folk are safe. Can the same be said of Europeans, who are considered the superior race, in their treatment of natives?

'We are disgusted with, sincerely deplore and condemn the behaviour of a degenerate like Mac Intosh and ask you, Sir, immediately to introduce legislation that will make miscegnation illegal.

'Legislation on these lines was talked of years ago, but for reasons that are perfectly obvious to many of us, was postponed, and had it been introduced, the country would have been saved the recent upheaval and the expense that has been incurred thereby.'

Not all the whites in Khama's Country had been willing to sign the petition. McLaggan, its organiser, was able to persuade all the white residents of Mahalapye to sign it, with the exception of members of the Administration and those employed by the Rhodesia and South African Railways. But he had greater difficulty elsewhere. 'The Serowe people to a man are all pro-Tshekedi,' McLaggan reported to a friend, 'but quite a number, although heartily agreeing with the letter, would not sign it. All manner of excuses were made but few gave the real reason which is very obvious. However I battled on and got a fair number of signatures and then went to Palapye Road. I met with similar opposition and as the leading people would not sign, saw it was hopeless to try and get the smaller fry to.'[3] McLaggan reported that all the whites he approached agreed that the Enquiry was a farce and that the 'behaviour of the Chief was splendid and the sailors I hear were greatly impressed with the Chief. Mr. Blackbeard, the oldest resident in Serowe, I may add he signed, told me that a sailor said to him that the Chief was a man.'

McLaggan had heard that it had been suggested by some people that Tshekedi had 'leanings toward Communism, is this not absurd?' What was clear to McLaggan was the strong support Tshekedi enjoyed among his people. Although the Bangwato had been told to hold a *kgotla* on 11 October and elect a new Regent, 'the natives are leaving Serowe. Now it has always been the custom that before the rains fall for the natives to live in Serowe and only go ploughing when given permission by the Chief. I have known Serowe for 21 years and never to my knowledge has it been so deserted. Serowe people think that there will be few natives in Serowe on 11th Oct. and as the Govt. has suspended the Chief it is up to them to appoint a successor. . . . Of course I do not know what the Govt. intend doing but if Serowe opinion can be relied on it seems evident that the line of passive resistance is to be followed by the natives. What will follow remains to be seen. There will be no trouble, I mean by this bloodshed, and the Government have a stiff hurdle in front of them.'

McLaggan, who described himself in a later letter as having been 'brought up amongst Pukkah Sahibs'[4] in India, was convinced that there would have to be 'a searching inquiry into the way the country has been run, and there will be some very unpleasant truths to face.'[5]

A less enthusiastic note about Tshekedi was struck by Kgaleman Tumedisho Motsete, the most highly educated Mongwato in the Protectorate. Born in Serowe in 1889, he had been educated at Tiger Kloof, where he had passed his Junior Teacher's Certificate in 1918. He then went to London in pursuit of further education, gaining bachelor's degrees in arts, theology and music. On his return to Serowe in 1930 he began by supporting Tshekedi but soon became disillusioned by what he considered his autocratic ways and his refusal to share power with, or at least seek advice from, the small but lively educated élite in the Reserve. Like educated élites elsewhere in British Africa, Motsete and others in Gamangwato (albeit with less education than he) resented the power of traditional rulers and saw themselves, rather than these heirs to the past, as the future leaders of their people. The relationship between the Bangwato educated élite and Tshekedi became the more complex since essentially he was one of them. Although he had not been able to complete his studies at university, he continued to read widely, and was as enthusiastic a moderniser as they were in the fields of development and education, provided that it was he who determined their direction. But while Simon Ratshosa, that older doyen of the educated élite, had now closed ranks with Tshekedi and given him qualified support, Motsete did not and basically felt that the young Chief had received his just deserts.

Though Motsete had not suffered as much at the hands of Tshekedi as had the Ratshosa brothers, he had moved out of Tshekedi's jurisdiction into the Tati Reserve to set up his Tati Training Institute with funding from the Carnegie Corporation and the Phelps Stokes Fund. He was a friend of Colonel Rey, whom he had met in London, and it was he who introduced the Resident Commissioner-designate to the Setswana language prior to his departure for the Protectorate in 1929. In a long letter to Margaret Hodgson, Motsete wrote that, while he was shocked by the suddenness of the drastic step taken against Tshekedi by the Administration, some of those who had 'been watching his relation with the Government expected something to befall him at some more or less distant future.' In a long list of Tshekedi's wrongdoings, such as his banishment of his rivals and oppression of minorities, he concluded that the 'removal of Tshekedi, I believe, from the Bangwato Chieftainship was a foregone conclusion and this affair of the thrashing of the European P. W. MacIntosh [sic] was only a little match that chanced to fall upon the bomb that was there already, but it served as a plausible excuse on the part of the Government of precipitating their drastic step.' His conclusion was: 'A worse ruler, we Bangwatos, have not had in the lifetime of this generation, I mean.'[6]

A letter from Simon Ratshosa to Margaret Hodgson written on 25 September listed many of the same criticisms of Tshekedi's rule that Motsete had mentioned, but it was more charitable to Tshekedi, who 'could have been a better chief had he been well guided in the first day of taking over the chieftainship [by] the Government but instead they left him uncurbed and told him his word is law. . . . We must be fair with Tshekedi and blame the Government.'[7] Simon also enclosed an article marked 'Strictly Confidential' and entitled 'Wait and See'. In it he suggested that a large number of Government officials were sleeping with local women. Miss Hodgson should '*wait and see* the outcome of Tshikidi's [sic] affair: it will have good results on Tshikidi and disgraceful results on the administration.

'They will all have to be dismissed from the service.

'The Bamaywato [sic] cannot understand why the Chief should be made to suffer as the result of protecting the honour and prestige of a European race.

'I make bold to say my views support their actions.

'The Bamaywato have no intention whatever against any private European residents who are at present in full support of their chief's action.'[8]

Simon concluded by expressing the hope that his papers would only be used by Miss Hodgson and Mr Ballinger and that they would not divulge them, for if the Administration got to know about them they 'would exile me for ever or use other means to hurt me.'[9]

Tshekedi arrived in Mafeking on the morning of Thursday, 28 September and had a brief discussion with his lawyer, Kieser, before his train went on to Cape Town. Kieser advised him strongly against attacking the official record of the the Palapye Road Enquiry because of any discrepancies with the unofficial record kept by Whiteside. In a letter confirming their brief conversation on that subject written shortly after Tshekedi departed, Kieser warned him that 'such a course might be fraught with danger to you both in relation to your early re-instatement—a fact which we are hoping may be accomplished before you sail—and to the future administration of tribal affairs in the Protectorate.' Kieser's own opinion was that the official record 'reflected, in substance and in fact, (with one exception)[10] what took place. . . . To attack it or query its correctness, means in effect, that the officials are charged with mala fides or it may be construed by the Administration that the intention is to say that the records have been falsified to suit its own ends. The shorthand notes were taken by the Admiral's own stenographer and whilst he may have, in some instances, summarised what happened instead of giving a verbatum [sic] report I cannot help feeling that it is substantially correct. Our notes are unofficial and when it was transcribed, in several places, Mr Whiteside had not quite gathered what was said and it was left to us to put it in order, so that it will be equally dangerous to advance the contention that ours is a complete and true record of the proceedings.' Kieser concluded his advice by suggesting that to raise the question of the discrepancies might merely have the effect of getting the Acting High Commissioner's back up, 'and we may be met with the retort that if we are not prepared to accept the bona fides of the officials of the enquiry how can the Administration expect you to co-operate with it in terms of your undertaking in your letter of the 21st instant to the Magistrate.'

Kieser also talked to Tshekedi about his forthcoming trip to England. The lawyer felt strongly that it was not vital for Tshekedi to undertake it. 'I still adhere to the view,' he wrote afterwards, 'that to press your viewpoint again in person, *specially at this juncture,* may not have the effect that you will have hoped for. To press for the appointment of a Royal Commission is highly desirable and more to the point but can this only be achieved by your visit to England? To say that you will be heard in person appears to be problematical. Failing this, must you not rely on outside influence and intercession? Do this help and aid demand your personal appearance?'[11]

As far as Tshekedi was concerned he was still determined to go to England. But in case he were not given permission to sail, he confirmed with Kieser that an authority from the *morafe* was being prepared for Buchanan and Jennings to represent them in London.

After Tshekedi left for Cape Town, Kieser sent off a petition to Serogola in connection with the forthcoming *kgotla* to elect an Acting Chief and a Council.[12] This clearly had Tshekedi's hand in it, for it was sent to Serogola at the request of Tshekedi's secretary, Peter Sebina, with Kieser's instructions that 'it will be necessary for you to have this re-typed on the Tribe's ordinary paper, and then for such Petition to be signed by those persons, you may consider entitled to do so. . . . I trust that the contents of the Petition, in light of present circumstances meet with approval. I fear that I had to modify some of the sentiments, as I considered this course advisable at this juncture.'[13] The petition, though never sent since it was overtaken by events, clearly expressed the views of the opponents of Rey's Proclamations. The petitioners asked 'to be permitted to say most respectfully that our Native Laws and Customs will not permit of us to elect an Acting Chief to rule and govern us in a permanent capacity, until such time as the rightful heir to the Throne succeeds, in a position such as has arisen in consequence of Tshekedi's suspension. All we feel we can do is to respectfully suggest that a responsible member of the tribe, who may be styled an Acting Chief, would be appointed temporarily until such time as the question of Tshekedi Khama's suspension has been definitely settled. The temporary appointment, according to our laws and customs, does not carry authority with it to bind the tribe without the approval of the Kgotla but its value lies in such person acting as an intermediary between the Government and the Tribe.'

The putative petitioners went on to say that Serogola had already been appointed to act in this capacity and to request that his appointment 'in a temporary capacity' be extended indefinitely 'or until such time a definite decision has been arrived at by the Secretary of State in regard to Tshekedi Khama's suspension.'

As for the election of a Council, Serogola had acted without a Council to the satisfaction of the Tribe and, they believed, to that of the Administration, and in the past 'we have felt, and we still feel, that there is no need for such a body. May we, therefore, be permitted to suggest the abandonment of this proposal more particularly under the existing circumstances and the further fact that such a procedure, as far as our Tribe is concerned, is without precedent. The proposal is, we respectfully wish to say, an innovation and is contrary to our Laws and Customs.' The petitioners ended by stating that they trusted His Excellency would 'for the present at any rate, defer if not entirely abandon, the election of a Council as contemplated, and permit, in accordance with our wishes, the extended temporary appointment of Serogola.'[14]

A copy of the draft petition was sent by Kieser to Tshekedi in Cape Town.

When Tshekedi reached Vryburg station he received a telephone message from Buchanan that his suspension from the chieftaincy had been terminated.[15] In fact, the morning newspapers in London and South Africa all carried the news that Tshekedi had been 'reinstated', for on the 28th, while Tshekedi was travelling south from Mafeking, the Dominions Office issued a long press notice concerning the termination of his suspension. The first item in the notice consisted of his letter of 'submission' printed in full. Then came a detailed summary of the findings of the Rey-Liesching Enquiry into Tshekedi's allegations against his Magistrates. There was, however, no reference to Liesching's reservations about the Administration's failure to respond adequately to Tshekedi's complaints. The press notice merely informed editors that in view of the facts outlined, the High Commissioner 'is unable to accept the statement made by Tshekedi, as a reason for dealing with this case himself, contrary to the law, instead of referring it to the Resident Magistrate, that he was "compelled in the interests of just administration and the good of his people" to order the punishment of McIntosh.' But, since Tshekedi had abandoned any right to deal with a case involving a white man and did not, and would not in future, claim to be immune from the laws of the Protectorate and had promised to work in harmony and loyal cooperation with the Administration, 'the High Commissioner has recommended to the Secretary of State for Dominion Affairs that His Majesty should be advised to terminate forthwith the period during which Tshekedi is suspended from the exercise of the functions of Acting Chief.'[16]

For Rey the publication of the press notice by the Dominions Office must have constituted a minor victory in his war with Tshekedi. Since the 17th he had been pressing Evans to issue a statement putting forward the Administration's point of view on the Serowe affair. In a coded telegram to Evans he had urged that 'in fairness to the Administration' a full statement should be issued setting out the whole position leading up to the Enquiry and the suspension of Tshekedi. 'At present situation is judged on enquiry only which gives absolutely false impression and Buchanan and Jennings are inflaming Press to utmost possible extent.'[17] But Evans considered it preferable not to issue any official statement for publication and stuck to this position even when Rey urged that it was important to issue a statement before Tshekedi's return. 'The publicity', Rey complained, 'has been so far entirely one-sided and wholly inspired by Jennings and Buchanan as evidenced by their continuous nursing of reports during and after enquiry at Palapye Road . . . position of publicity is grossly unfair to this Administration. . . . If position is not promptly corrected it will leave a permanently unfavourable and undeserved impression regarding this Administration both in this country and at home.'[18] But while Evans sympathised with Rey, he felt that to issue a statement at that stage would merely 'revive newspaper controversy which now appears to be dying away.'[19] In London, officials at the Dominions Office regretted that Rey had not considered 'the effect the incident as a whole would have on public opinion.'[20]

Only when it was decided to reinstate Tshekedi was sanction given to the publication of the Government point of view. Rey was allowed to check the press notice before it was issued and approved of it but for one minor reservation. A copy was sent to all Resident Magistrates, who were thus informed that Tshekedi had climbed down and that no blame attached to either of the Resident Magistrates concerned in the saga. However, the exchange of correspondence between Tshekedi and the Resident Magistrates on which Rey and Liesching had based their report was shortly after released to the press and put the administration in a less favourable light.[21]

On the whole, the commentary in the press was more sympathetic to Rey's position than at any time since the crisis erupted two weeks before. Both the *Times* and the *Manchester Guardian* saw the whole episode as highlighting the need for regulation of the relationship between the Administration and the Chiefs. Indeed, the *Guardian* almost explicitly backed Rey's position over the Proclamations when it emphasised the need for statutory limitation of the powers of Chiefs and the formation of fully representative native councils.[22] The *Times* even went so far as to defend Admiral Evans, who until then had received little support in the press. 'As for Admiral Evans, and his body of marines, the whole paraphernalia may seem a little ridiculous in the light of the complete tranquillity in which the gallant seamen, unexpectedly thrust into an unfamiliar and very difficult position, conducted the proceedings at Palapye-road. But there was always the prospect of a large assemblage of deeply interested tribesmen and the history of South Africa records a good many serious disturbances which might have been averted by similar precautions. There is no reasonable criticism to be made of the admiral's landing party.'[23] This was not the view of Ramsay MacDonald's own political party 'News Letter' which rapped Evans on the knuckles.[24] The opposition Labour party *Daily Herald* was delighted 'to find in the Prime Minister's organ . . . a remark that the "parade of marines and howitzers cannot be excused." '[25] The *Cape Times* in a long editorial hoped that one result of 'the revelations in the case of Macintosh [sic] will be that the law of the Protectorates will be brought into line with the law of the Union which makes it a criminal offence for white men to cohabit with native women. For, as we said at the time, it is highly undesirable that there should be enclaves within the Union which may become Alsatias for white men who act in violation of the accepted code of South African morality. Finally, we think it right to say that Tshekedi, though he erred in a serious degree when he assumed in September a jurisdiction which he must have known he did not possess, has acted since his arraignment with a dignity and loyalty which do him the highest credit, and which have won for him a large measure of sympathy.' The editorialist was less kind to the Administration: 'The world's searchlight has been turned upon it with rather dazzling effect in the past fortnight. If it results in improved efficiency and closer supervision it will be good for the natives and good for the Administration itself.'[26]

The High Commissioner's office in Cape Town was still nervous about handling Tshekedi, even though he had now been reinstated. Fearing a demonstration at the Monument station, where normally he would have terminated his journey, a message was sent to Wolseley station just outside Cape Town to tell the driver of the train not to make an express run to the city as was customary, but to stop at the suburban station of Bellville so that Tshekedi could get off there. A posse of a dozen police was sent to Bellville, twelve miles up the line, as a further precaution, though, as the city-late edition of the *Cape Argus* reported, Tshekedi's arrival was not marked by anything unusual. He was met only by Buchanan and Jennings and taken by car to the former's chambers. Meanwhile, at the Monument station 'a crowd of not more than 20 natives, all fairly well dressed, gathered to greet the Bechuana chief. The train arrived ten minutes early. The group was completely orderly and dispersed without a sound when informed by railway officials that Tshekedi had left the train at Bellville.'[27]

The Administration were also still worried that Tshekedi might try to sail for England on 6 October before Evans could formally reinstate him. The day before Tshekedi's arrival, Shirley Eales had sent for Buchanan to come and have what he hoped would be considered a purely confidential talk to make the whole position 'definite and clear', because he was anxious 'that Tshekedi should make no mistake'. When Buchanan discussed Tshekedi's plans to go to England, Eales showed him the telegram from the Secretary of State that was handed to Tshekedi the day before he left Francistown. Buchanan still insisted that Tshekedi planned to sail on the 6th. Eales then asked Buchanan: 'Don't you understand the Chief has no permission to proceed to England; that the chief is in the habit of not reading his communications carefully and if this communication is carefully read he will see that the Secretary of State says as far as the suspension is concerned that he is to await his further communication and that his leave to proceed to England on that boat is cancelled.'[28] In fact, it was Eales who had not read the Secretary of State's communication carefully. In no place does it say expressly that Tshekedi was forbidden to travel to England. It merely said that the Secretary of State was not prepared to discuss the Proclamations with him.

The next morning, before he went to meet Tshekedi, Buchanan had another interview with Eales, at which they discussed the order Rey gave to the Bamangwato Tribe to elect a Council on the 11th. In the circumstances Eales suggested that it was probably best to cancel the order altogether. They also discussed the Admiral's allegations about Tshekedi's selfishness. Anyone in Serowe, European or native, Buchanan insisted, would say the opposite about the Chief. Tshekedi was there to look after the heir, Seretse, 'and did not want it said when the boy came to the throne that he had given away the boy's rights.'

Before Buchanan left, he was asked by Eales 'to keep the Chief quiet until the Admiral had made his speech at Serowe.'[29] As he was leaving the office, he met the Private Secretary to the High Commissioner, Captain Holbech, who remarked that he and Tshekedi got on very well together. Last time the Chief was in Cape Town he had won a sovereign off him on a race. After further discussion Holbech asked whether there was any little thing the Admiral could do, and Buchanan suggested that it would be a very good thing 'if he looked up the old Queen' in Serowe. Buchanan was then told that this would be arranged.[30]

As it happened, Queen Semane was herself in South Africa. She was on her first visit to Johannesburg to attend the second annual convention of the 'native' branch of the Women's Christian Temperance Union. The Johannesburg *Star,* which accorded her the title of Queen, reported that she had been awarded the Union's banner for recruiting the highest number of adherents to the temperance cause during the year. Her total was ninety-eight, beating 'Mma Shaw', the widely known and loved wife of the trader who had looked after Tshekedi at Palapye Road, by six. No doubt Queen Semane reinforced her son's support among Christians in South Africa with her declaration to the *Star:* 'I am very proud at having won this honour. Temperance is gaining ground among the Bamangwato, not only among the women but also among the men of the tribe. The missionaries are helping us greatly in our fight against liquor, and I only wish we had more missionaries in the Protectorate.'[31]

A crowded programme had been arranged for Queen Semane's visit to South Africa. On the day her son was on the final stage of his journey to Cape Town, she addressed the convention on temperance work in the Bechuanaland Protectorate. And when he arrived in Cape Town she was visiting Pretoria, where she toured the Union Buildings, the impressive government offices standing on a hill overlooking the city and designed by Sir Herbert Baker. While her son would be spending the weekend dealing with the Admiral, Semane was scheduled to go shopping in Johannesburg, to attend church and finish her visit with a morning at the zoo. It was a curious feature of visits arranged for African dignitaries in the 1930s, whether in southern Africa or in London, that their programme frequently included a visit to a zoo, as though they would find it interesting to see in cages many of the animals they had seen or could see in the wild.

Tshekedi spent his first afternoon in Cape Town discussing strategies with Buchanan in his chambers in Wale Street just opposite Parliament. There he received a telegram from the Acting High Commissioner notifying him that his suspension had been terminated. This was followed up by a formal letter which commenced vocatively, 'Tshekedi Khama', without the customary 'Dear' or 'My Friend'. It reiterated much of what was in the press statement and concluded by informing him that Evans would personally reinstate him 'as soon as the necessary arrangements can be made, and you will be informed as soon as possible of the date of your reinstatement.'[32] Tshekedi, no doubt on Buchanan's advice, drafted a reply in which for the first time in two weeks he used as his address 'Kgotla ea Kgosi, Gamanwato'. Acknowledging receipt of the telegram stating that His Majesty had been pleased to end his suspension, Tshekedi asked the High Commissioner to convey the following message to King George V: 'I humbly thank Your Majesty for your gracious message, and would express my unbroken and unswerving loyalty to Your Majesty's throne and Person.'[33] According to the *Cape Argus*, Tshekedi spent the remainder of the afternoon discussing 'the terms of the Proclamations to be read to the Bamangwato when Tshekedi is restored to the regency.'[34] Buchanan, like his friend Jennings, was very suspicious of the motives of the Administration in restoring Tshekedi. The two had cabled the LMS in London that they believed the intention of the reinstatement was to foreclose any enquiry into maladministration and force through the draft Proclamations.[35]

On Saturday morning Tshekedi went to the High Commissioner's Office and asked to see Evans. He was told that the Admiral was busy and could not receive him. Tshekedi said he would wait, but was told several times more that the Admiral would not be able to see him, since his new flagship, *HMS Dorsetshire*, had just arrived and he was busy dealing with officials from one of the other High Commission Territories where some trouble had developed. But Tshekedi's patience paid off, for in the end the Admiral invited him for tea on board his flagship that afternoon.[36]

Buchanan and his wife drove Tshekedi and Peter Sebina to Simonstown. Tshekedi, dressed in an overcoat, went on board the flagship with Peter, and took tea with the Admiral in the Captain's cabin. Detailed notes were made of the interview, at which Tshekedi asked whether he could use his secretary to interpret for him 'as he was not very fluent in his speech.'[37] Thus the Chief who had defended himself so ably in English at the Enquiry used the old ruse of employing an interpreter to give himself more time to compose his replies to the admiral. Tshekedi then began the interview by complaining that he was not at all pleased by some of the newspaper comments which suggested that he had not in fact reported McIntosh to the Magistrate and had given no reasons for his decision to sentence him to a flogging. He had absolute proof that he had done both, and declared that 'his side of the story has not yet been heard'. Evans replied 'in the language that the Chief would better understand—"You do not have to go to a game reserve to hear jackals bark."' He then pointed out that while some newspapers were bitter against the Chief, some were also critical of himself. 'The Chief should take no notice of what is being said in the press.'

Tshekedi also complained that the press had reported that Evans did not believe that in sentencing McIntosh he had done so in the interests of both justice and administration. He was bitter that he should be thought guilty of telling a lie, and if Evans believed this to be the case he should have discussed it with him before. 'Finally the Chief pointed out that he was very loyal to His Majesty's Government, and even during the last few days when he had to undergo all he bore, he remained calm and trusted to the Government, and to which remark the High Commissioner said the Chief had behaved very well indeed.'

After this initial petulance, Tshekedi got down to the essential business of his interview. He told Evans that he was still determined to go to England, even though the Secretary of State had said it would serve no useful purpose. He wanted to go there to get the advice of certain people 'who are the friends of the Native people and who get on very well with the King's Officers in the Dominions Office.' Evans replied that Tshekedi would have to put his request in writing and submit it to the Resident Commissioner, who would send it on to him, and he would in turn submit it to the Secretary of State recommending him 'to grant such leave.' Tshekedi said 'he saw no necessity of going through all that because like every British subject he has his personal liberty, and if he wished to go to England, say on holiday, he would not be debarred from doing so, but in the present case he would not be going to England for a holiday, but for the express purpose of getting his views and those of his people to the Secretary of State, failing which those of his friends who would advise him what to do under the circumstances.'

At this juncture, Shirley Eales intervened by pointing out to the Chief that even if he went on holiday to England he would need to get permission from the Secretary of State. He was 'not like any other private individual who may go to

England without the consent of the Secretary of State, but was like an Officer of the Government.' The High Commissioner reinforced Eales's point, but Tshekedi countered by saying that 'on several occasions he had had occasion to leave his people, sometimes coming to the Cape on tribal matters, and what he did only was to inform the Magistrate of his absence, without ever asking for leave to go or not to go.'

Evans then told Tshekedi that he planned to reinstate him the following Wednesday and promised him that after the ceremony they would hold an interview at the Magistrate's house to discuss the matter of his visit further. Tshekedi reiterated that he was anxious to get to England before Sir Herbert Stanley returned to South Africa, and Evans replied that if he put everything in writing before their Serowe meeting, he would recommend his application to go to London.

Finally, before Tshekedi and Peter Sebina were shown round his flagship, Admiral Evans promised the Chief that after reinstating him in Serowe he would shake him by the hand in the presence of his people and call him his friend and added that it was Colonel Rey himself who had recommended that Tshekedi 'should again be put in his position as Chief as he had promised never to try Europeans in a Native Court.' Evans, attempting to heal the breach between Tshekedi and his Resident Commissioner, made a special point of the fact that it was Rey personally who had recommended his reinstatement,[38] though Tshekedi was not to know, but surely must have suspected something of the kind, that Rey had in fact argued for a delay of at least a year before he be allowed to return to Serowe.

What this account of the interview does not record is that part of the conversation which Tshekedi and Peter recounted to Buchanan and his wife as they drove back to Cape Town. When Evans asked Tshekedi whether he was glad that he personally was going to reinstate him, Tshekedi replied: 'That depends.' 'On what?' asked the Admiral.

'On whether you are going to say the same things about me when you reinstate me as your Excellency did when you took me off the stool.'

To this the Admiral replied, after clearing his throat, that he supposed he would have to say much the same.

'Then,' said Tshekedi, 'I am not at all pleased.'

'Why?' asked the Admiral.

To this Tshekedi answered somewhat as follows: 'Well, Sir, suppose you were the Captain of this big battle-ship and suppose your superior officer had assembled the whole ship's company on the big deck and said to the company: "You see this man. He is not fit to be your Captain, he has set a bad example to you all, he has been disloyal to His Majesty, he has been guilty of misconduct and behaved as no Captain should and I am depriving him of his office as Captain." Well, Sir, if a fortnight later you assembled the same ship's company on the same deck and after repeating all the charges you had previously made you ended by saying: "However I am reinstating this man as your captain and I hope he will behave himself in the future", do you, Sir, think that such a captain would have any control of his ship's company? No, Sir, if you are going to say the same things about me as you said before, then I am not at all pleased at being reinstated in such a manner.'[39]

In Serowe, meanwhile, instructions had been received for the arrangements to be made in connexion with the reinstatement of Tshekedi. Potts was informed that the Acting High Commissioner and the Resident Commissioner would be arriving on the train early on Wednesday morning. They would then drive to Serowe for the ceremony. The Tribe were to be called for a meeting that morning, probably to be held at noon. 'This should be as large as possible,' Rey directed him, and would take place on the showground arranged as before with the same platform and the flagstaff. Though no troops would be coming this time, an escort of Bechuanaland Police would be sent up and Lieutenant Moseley should be brought in to Serowe immediately to take charge of the policemen and 'put them into shape'. Potts was also instructed to arrange for transport for the police—three white NCOs and fifteen Batswana—from Palapye Road to Serowe early on the Monday morning. Six cars were also to be found, and these 'should be good cars as some failed last time.' No mention was made of Tshekedi himself in the telegram, but Potts was told to inform Serogola about the change in the date for the meeting.[40]

Potts arranged with the local white communiiy to provide six cars and one lorry. The post lorry was taken out of service for the day to provide for the transport of the three NCOs. Chairs were borrowed from the church. Mrs Potts offered once again to lay on lunch for the High Commissioner's party after the reinstatement ceremony, and Potts sent a telegram to Rey to this effect, trusting that he would be coming with Mrs Rey. But this time Ninon was not going to accompany her husband as she was unwell. Rey cabled Potts that he was coming by himself and confirmed that the ceremony would start at noon. A notice was sent out to the white residents of Serowe announcing the time of arrival of the High Commissioner at the showground and asking that all 'motorists kindly park their cars well behind the platform'.[41] Serogola, still addressed as Acting Chief, was informed that 'His Honour the Resident Commissioner expects that the meeting will be as large as possible and it should be understood that the meeting fixed for the 4th October will take the place of the meeting announced for the 11th October.'[42]

On Monday morning Evans and Tshekedi both boarded the northbound Rhodesia Express. The High Commissioner's personal coach was attached to the train, and Evans, dressed in a lounge suit and black velour hat, arrived at the station with Shirley Eales, Captain Holbech and his Flag Lieutenant, who were travelling with him. His Norwegian wife, who had not hidden her distaste from her husband about his handling of the Serowe affair,[43] came to see him off. Tshekedi himself did not arrive until ten minutes before the train was due to leave, but the faithful Peter Sebina had already had their nine pieces of luggage stowed away in their compartment in a second-class carriage, the highest class in which a black—even a Chief of Tshekedi's rank and means—could travel. About a dozen blacks had turned up at the station to see him off. According to the *Cape Argus* reporter, Tshekedi seemed very subdued and was reluctant to be photographed, though he did agree to be once he was seated in his compartment. Among the blacks, who raised their hats as the train left the station, was one clergyman. Also waving good-bye was his lawyer and devoted friend, Douglas Buchanan, while his former missionary, Alfred Jennings, was travelling on the same train but getting off at Vryburg. Before departing Jennings told the *Argus* that he hoped to have a reply to Tshekedi's application to go to England by the next Thursday. If permission were granted, the Chief would probably sail on the boat leaving on Friday the 13th, and Jennings himself would be accompanying him.[44]

In Serowe on Wednesday, 4 October, Evans, this time dressed in a white drill uniform rather than navy blue, drove up to a scene strongly reminiscent of that at which he had suspended Tshekedi almost exactly three weeks before. The only major differences were the absence of the marines and their guns, and the much larger crowd of Bangwato who had assembled to witness the Vice Admiral's second dramatic performance.

Once again Tshekedi stood silently before the dais on which Evans and Rey, accompanied by their respective officials, sat behind a table bedecked with the Union Jack. Tshekedi was dressed in a dark suit and accompanied by some of his headmen.[45] Without emotion he heard the High Commissioner read out the text of his letter of submission, which was then translated into Setswana. The final text, vetted by the Dominions Office, had, however, been a matter of some negotiation between Evans and Rey. Rey asked Evans that in his reference to the Resident Commissioner the phrase 'who has always had the welfare of the Tribe at heart' be substituted for Evans's draft version which described Rey as having 'always been your friend.' This Evans accepted. But he was not prepared to add after his statement that it 'can never be for the good of the people that a Chief should break the law' the warning that 'such action cannot be tolerated.' Evans did, though, heed Rey's advice that he make no reference to the question of Tshekedi's supposed selfishness.[46]

Evans read the text approved by Rey and the Dominions Office to Tshekedi and his assembled subjects with his customary sense of the dramatic.

'Bamangwato, on the 14th. September I announced to you in this place that I had made an order suspending Tshekedi Khama, your Acting Chief, from the Chieftainship of the Tribe during the pleasure of His Majesty the King.

'The reasons for which I made that order are known to you. I did not make it because I thought that the man McIntosh did not deserve to be punished. On the contrary I expelled McIntosh and another European from your Reserve. I made it because the Law does not allow Europeans to be tried in Native Courts, and no man can be Chief unless he is ready to obey the Law. I have now received from Tshekedi the following message.'

Evans then read out to the crowd Tshekedi's letter of 'submission', after which he told them that he could not accept the statement in the letter that Tshekedi was compelled to act as he did in the interests of just administration and for the good of the people.

'It can never be for the good of the people that a Chief should break the law.

'Nevertheless, in view of the statement in the message which I have now received from Tshekedi that he regrets what has occurred, that he will not deal with any European case in future, that he does not claim to be immune from the laws of the Protectorate and that he will at all times work in harmony and loyal co-operation with the Administration, I have felt able with the advice of the Resident Commissioner to recommend to the Secretary of State that he should advise His Majesty the King to terminate the period of Tshekedi's suspension and thereby to reinstate him as Acting Chief of the Bamangwato.

'Tshekedi Khama, the message which you have sent to me has been read to the people of your Tribe, and they have heard the promises you have made as to your future conduct. I believe that you earnestly intend to keep those promises. Because I believe this, I have felt able, at the request of the Resident Commissioner, who has the welfare of the Tribe at heart, to recommend to the Secretary of State that the period of your suspension should be terminated and with it the Order directing you to reside in the Tati District, and the Secretary of State has accepted that recommendation and has advised His Majesty the King accordingly.

'Bamangwato, I now announce to you that His Majesty the King has been graciously pleased to direct that Tshekedi Khama shall be reinstated as Acting Chief of the Bamangwato Tribe and that the Order requiring him to reside in the Tati District shall cease to operate.

'The direction which I gave on the 14th. September for the election of an Acting Chief and Council is no longer operative.

'Acting Chief Tshekedi Khama, you are now restored to your position as Acting Chief of the Bamangwato. In that capacity you are in the position of a Trustee for the young Chief Seretse, with all the responsibilities and duties which trusteeship entails.

'You have promised that you will at all times work in harmony and loyal co-operation with the Administration. I charge you not to forget that promise.'[47]

Evans then beckoned Tshekedi to join him on the dais and shook him warmly by the hand. According to the *Rand Daily Mail,* a friendly smile broke out on the restored Chief's face.[48] Rey then stepped forward to shake Tshekedi's hand but Tshekedi 'coolly and studiedly ignored it in the presence of all', according to one eyewitness.[49] It is not clear from other reports that such a breach of manners, untypical of Tshekedi, took place in full view of both the white and Bangwato communities. But it would certainly have expressed Tshekedi's deepest thoughts, for he was well aware who his real enemy was. The Rev. Burns, when asked about Tshekedi's action by Mary Benson many years later, reported that it 'rings a bell in my memory but I am sorry I cannot trace any record of the incident in my papers.'[50]

Tshekedi then joined Evans at the Resident Magistrate's house, where he was given the promised interview about his request to go to England should it not be agreed to appoint a Royal Commission to enquire into the proposed Native Procla-mations. Tshekedi also reiterated to Evans that even if the Secretary of State did not want to see him about the Proclamations, he still desired to go to London to seek the advice of certain friends there. The High Commissioner promised to transmit his request to the Secretary of State. Afterwards the Reuter correspondent felt confident enough to report that it is 'considered unlikely that permission will be refused.'[51]

After lunch with Potts, Admiral Evans motored back to Palapye Road, where his coach was hitched to the southward-bound Rhodesia Railways Express due to arrive in Cape Town on Friday. Rey travelled with him as far as Mafeking. Before they left, a telegram was sent to Rey that must have warned him that reinstatement in no way meant an end to their troubles with Tshekedi. In the afternoon, shortly after Evans and Rey had left, a deputation of headmen had been to see Potts. Led by Serogola, they requested that the 'Chief be given permission to go overseas.' The reason Serogola gave for this request was that 'during the course of this affair a statement has been made that we profess loyalty to the Government whilst we act disloyal. This statement injured our feelings because even if a fault has been discovered in the Chief we have never been told of it.

'Seeing that the Chief is our leader we feel that the statement made about him refers to us.

'We regret very much that when a fault is found in us we are not told about it.

'We have not come to make a case but ever since this case commenced we have not had an opportunity to discuss it.

'We have not come to argue but to ask permission for the Chief to go overseas to deal with the matter of the Proclamations on the powers of Chiefs'.

Supporting Serogola were fifteen of the most important royal and commoner headmen, including Gorewan, Phethu and Oteng Mphoeng, Disang Raditladi, Radiphofu, Rasebolai and Oitsile. The last named noted pointedly that Potts had taken down their names and affirmed that they endorsed what Serogola had said.[52] Potts, in communicating the gist of his exchange with Serogola to Rey, informed him that he had told the erstwhile 'Acting Chief' that he was questioning His Excellency's actions. 'I informed delegation that Chief's visit to England was a matter for negotiation. To my mind the deputation represents an overt act of loyalty to the Chief or it constitutes the habitual attitude of these people to the Government.'[53]

CHAPTER 9

Tshekedi's Victory?

Rey was determined to put as brave a face as possible on Tshekedi's return to power. Copies of the speech made by Admiral Evans at Serowe on 4 October were sent to all Resident Magistrates with the instruction that it should be as widely circulated as possible 'to the natives of your respective Districts, explaining and stressing the fact that it was only on the grounds of Tshekedi's complete submission that his suspension was terminated.'[1]

After his reinstatement Tshekedi gave no indication that he had in any way submitted to the Administration or that he felt at all chastened by his experiences over the past two weeks. Indeed, he seems to have become more aggressively self-confident than ever. Fifteen years later, headmen opposed to him in the crisis over his nephew Seretse's marriage to an Englishwoman reported to the District Commissioner of Serowe that Tshekedi came back from exile in 1933 'to inform heads of villages that he was not happy about the fact that the Government states that he is merely Regent to the Bamangwato. He said that Seretse is his child, it was not for the Government to tell him that and that he wants to be addressed as "Paramount Chief" and not "Acting Chief" '.[2] Apocryphal or not, this accusation symbolises the renewed strength Tshekedi felt in his position after what he clearly considered was a battle in which he had gained the laurels. On not a few occasions thereafter Tshekedi was to refer to himself as Paramount Chief.

Tshekedi lost little time in renewing his campaign against Colonel Rey and his Proclamations. Barely had he shaken hands with Evans after being reinstated than he was off to his office to arrange for a letter to be sent to his friend Chief Bathoen. After describing the ceremony he told him that at 2:00 P.M. he would be seeing

Evans at the Magistrate's residence to resubmit his application to go to Britain, 'or else I will have to request a Royal Commission to come here so that we can inform it of our feelings. . . .' He went on to urge Bathoen to seek permission to accompany him to Britain. He should be prepared to sail on the ship leaving Cape Town on 13 October.[3]

For some Bangwato, Tshekedi's return from exile within so short a space of time was little short of miraculous. Moanaphuti Segolodi, whom Tshekedi had sent into exile two years before, believed that he was re-instated 'because his mother prayed for him to His Majesty the King.'[4] In fact Semane's petition, though widely published in the press, was not even forwarded to the Secretary of State until early October and she was not informed that it had been laid before the King until late the following month,[5] by which time of course it was irrelevant. But, as some elements of the press pointed out, the effect of Tshekedi's speedy restoration was bound to add to his prestige among his own people. The *Natal Mercury* saw what it called 'the precipitous reversal of the judgment pronounced only a fortnight ago' as 'a sharp rebuff' for both Admiral Evans and the Administration of the Protectorate. It considered that, even though Tshekedi had tendered his apologies, 'no harm would have been done if his period of suspension had been prolonged for a few months. As the matter now stands, however, the Crown's decision can be represented to Native opinion as a virtual justification of the criticism directed against the High Commissioner's picturesque intervention with a display of armed force.'[6]

Not a few newspapers saw Tshekedi's reinstatement as victory for him and defeat for Admiral Evans and Colonel Rey. But Tshekedi was too shrewd a tactician to consider that he had won anything but a battle in a long-drawn-out war. Almost immediately he set about collecting as much evidence as possible both about white residents of Gamangwato who had accepted his jurisdiction before the McIntosh affair and about the events leading up to the 'flogging' of McIntosh himself. Thus on 7 October he sent a letter by bearer to R. P. Garrett, a Justice of the Peace living at Palapye Road, who was an old established trader and former partner in Khama's trading company. With the bearer Tshekedi sent a number of Bangwato 'whose statements I have taken down, and I should very much like these people to swear to these statements before you in your capacity as a Justice of the Peace.

'As a friend of my late father, and also a personal friend of myself, I might just as well tell you that the matter in connection with the recent developments is not over yet, and I am getting these evidences not for offensive but defensive purposes, as they may at some future time be required, and I wish to be prepared for any emergency. There is still a bitter feeling on the part of my superiors to ruin me.'[7] This was not some ploy dreamt up after his reinstatement. Tshekedi had clearly had it in mind whilst in exile, for the Resident Magistrate at Francistown had reported with some mystification Tshekedi's request for a list of all Justices of the Peace in the Protectorate.[8] Indeed, even while he was in in exile in Francistown he had made use of Garrett to take a statement from McIntosh's mistress.[9]

Tshekedi had two immediate objectives in view with this exercise. He wanted to have as much evidence at his disposal about the activities of Phinehas McIntosh to be sure that at any future enquiry he could prove that the young man's activities had become so outrageous that he really was 'forced to to to give a check of some kind to this sort of thing',[10] as he had told Germond on the 6th. His second aim was to find as many attested statements as possible from whites that they had in fact accepted his justice before he sentenced Phinehas to a flogging.

Tshekedi, now back in office, had no difficulty in obtaining sworn statements about the activities of Phinehas and other white men who had been having sexual relations with Bangwato girls. Even Baikgantshi Dikgobo gave evidence about Phinehas beating her, 'but I did not complain of his beating me because he was my husband.'[11] How reliable the evidence he collected was, is difficult to determine. Clearly, it was not hard for him as chief to obtain evidence favourable to his position. More important in the context of the 'constitutional' issue concerning his jurisdiction over whites, Tshekedi obtained sworn statements from two whites who had appeared in his *kgotla* and accepted his justice. E. P. Cavanagh testified before Garrett that his wife had gone to Chief Tshekedi and complained about him. The Chief called him to his *kgotla* and in his judgement 'said that I should give my wife eight head of cattle', which he did. Tshekedi noted in his own hand on this testimony: 'N.B. a white man.'[12] Similarly, he noted that Frederik Johannes Mollentze, residing at Palapye Road, was a white man whose late wife, also white, had gone 'to Chief Tshekedi and complained that I did not support her and also that I was living with a native woman, Mmadinalo, as husband and wife.' Mollentze duly appeared before Tshekedi in his *kgotla* and was told 'to support my wife and that I should live with her and also that the native woman I was living with should be sent back to her people and that I should give my wife some Cattle to live by.' This he had done, giving her thirteen head.[13] But Tshekedi's overall aim in collecting this evidence was for a petition he was preparing to send to the King should he not be allowed to sail to England, which both Rey and the Dominions Office were determined he should not do.

Rey had many other matters besides Tshekedi on his mind at the beginning of October. For him it was the start of an 'awful month owing to Ninon's illness which started on the 1st and lasted well into November—the worst time I've ever had since her great illness in England.'[14] Ninon had regularly taken to her bed ever since the death from dysentery of her two sons in rapid succession in Ethiopia.[15] Over and above the problem of his wife's poor health Rey had still to worry about the foot-and-mouth cordons, the restrictions of the importation of cattle into the Union, the continuing Depression and the affairs of the other seven Reserves as well as the white blocks of the Protectorate. In London Tshekedi would raise many more problems than he could in southern Africa. So it was with great relief that Rey learnt that the Secretary of State had turned down Tshekedi's request for a Royal Commission to advise on the Draft Proclamations and by implication his visit to London, which he believed would delay 'progress of various measures for re-establishment of native industries in and exports from territory as nothing would be done by acting Chief in Tshekedi's absence.' It would 'cause unrest among other chiefs' and the 'cost of journey would be considerable.' Evans concurred with this view and believed that Tshekedi was being egged on by Jennings.[16]

Tshekedi was told on 9 October to submit any comments he wished to make on the Proclamations to Sir Herbert Stanley, the substantive High Commissioner, when he returned from leave. And he was specifically instructed that he should submit them through the Resident Commissioner. 'In these circumstances,' J. H. Thomas concluded with a by now well-worn phrase, 'no useful purpose would in my opinion be served by Tshekedi proceeding to England to discuss the matter with me and I consider that his proper course is to remain in South Africa.'[17] As far as the Dominions Office were concerned, Whiskard had put the official point of view pungently in a minute to Thomas: 'There is clearly no ground for the appointment of a Royal Commission. Apart from any other consideration such a Commission could hardly avoid going into a number of questions as to native policy in South Africa generally, which might prove very embarassing vis-à-vis the Union Government . . . you will also, I am sure, agree that it would be very undesirable for Tshekedi to come to England at the present time. He would certainly be lionized by the Press, which would be exceedingly bad for him; and apart from that, as you are aware, the King has expressed a strong view on the subject.'[18] The problem was how best to put him off. The solution was to tell him that the Proclamations would not be promulgated until he had had a chance to discuss them further with the substantive High Commissioner rather than Thomas himself. A similar message to that given to Tshekedi was sent to Bathoen in answer to his own request to see the Secretary of State.[19]

Tshekedi was in no way surprised by the decision to deny him permission to travel to England. If he could not go, Buchanan and Jennings would go on his behalf. They might not be lionized by the Press as he would be, but with all their missionary and humanitarian support in London they would serve his cause well. Thomas had already had an intimation of the continuing pressure Tshekedi could put on him from distant Serowe. On 6 October the Anti-Slavery and Aborigines Protection Society had informed him through their Secretary, Travers Buxton, that they wished to send a deputation to see him to make representations regarding the rights and powers of Tribal Chiefs.

Tshekedi left Serowe for Cape Town to see Buchanan and Jennings on 10 October, but not before he had signed a letter to the Secretary of the Chamber of Commerce at Serowe asking him to send the following circular letter 'to the European Residents in the Bamangwato Country':

'In a recent meeting of the Kgotla I was asked by the members of my Tribe to thank all European residents in the Bamangwato country for their sympathy and support which they have shown both to myself and to the Bamangwato Tribe during our most troubled time.

'The support and sympathy shown in this case are very great items of mutual understanding, and co-operation which existed between the white people and the natives of this country, and which we, the inhabitants of this country, have of course always known. May this understanding and co-operation so continue.

'Please accept my thanks and those of my Tribe.'[20]

Buchanan and Jennings were sailing on the *Balmoral Castle,* due to leave on Friday, 13 October. As his train did not arrive until Thursday, Tshekedi had little time to discuss the approach they should take to Rey's Proclamations. He also wanted them to go over the petition he had drawn up for presentation to the King. As a result the three of them could have had little sleep that night, for the petition which Tshekedi had drafted in Serowe was finalised, retyped together with annexures running to a total of sixty-four pages, and signed in front of a Notary Public[21] before Buchanan and Jennings boarded their ship.

The burden of Tshekedi's petition was that he had been unfairly 'tried' and 'convicted' at the Enquiry at Palapye Road. In the first place, he had not been granted the fourteen days he had requested to prepare his defence and consult his advisers.[22] In consequence, his counsel, residing as he did 1,165 miles from Serowe, had only been able to reach him a few hours before the Enquiry.[23] In the second place, notwithstanding 'the High Commissioner's recommendation, your Petitioner was denied the privilege of appearance by Counsel at the said Enquiry.'[24] The nub of the petition showed that Tshekedi had not really put his heart into his letter of 'submission', and that in writing it he was merely making a tactical withdrawal: 'The Commission of Enquiry found your Petitioner guilty of "a deliberate and flagrant violation of the Protectorate Law" . . . and, although your Petitioner has since been re-instated in his office as Acting Chief of the Tribe, this conviction stands on record against him.

'Your Petitioner was barred from raising at the Enquiry the legal issue as to whether or not he had contravened the law of the Protectorate, and, whilst he agrees that in future no European should be tried in a Native Court, he says that in trying *PHINEAS WILLIAM MCINTOSH* on September 6th. 1933, he neither intended to, nor did he in fact, contravene the Law of the Protectorate. . .'.[25]

In seeking to justify his trial of McIntosh in his *kgotla,* Tshekedi recapitulated at great—almost tiresomely excessive—length the legal arguments he had tried to raise at the Enquiry. Central to his argument was that the law as it stood at the time of the trial of McIntosh and as amended in 1922 referred only to 'appointed Chiefs' in the Protectorate and was promulgated during the chieftainship of his father, Khama III. But since neither Khama nor his son, Sekgoma II, was an appointed chief but both were born to the office, the law 'did not have the effect, in fact, of precluding *KHAMA,* or *SEKGOMA* as his successor, from exercising jurisdiction, with knowledge of the Administration in matters Civil and Criminal in which Europeans were concerned. Both Chiefs continued after 1922 to try cases in which Europeans were concerned.'[26]

Tshekedi then went on to insist that as Chief of the Bangwato he, too, had 'tried cases in which Europeans were concerned as parties, but only with the consent of parties, and where Europeans themselves have brought their cases to be dealt with by the Kgotla in preference to the Magistrate's Court. In so doing your Petitioner did no more than his father *KHAMA* and his brother *SEKGOMA* did during their respective chieftainships.

'European witnesses were in attendance at the said Enquiry on September 13th. 1933 to give evidence in this regard, but your Petitioner was barred from leading such evidence.'[27]

Tshekedi, still smarting from Evans's public denunciation of him in front of his people, asserted that although he had only been charged with contravening the Proclamation concerning the trial of whites by tribal courts, he had been found guilty of frequently flaunting the Administration and 'that your Petitioner's over-mastering passion was selfishness, and a study of his own personal rights and privileges. No evidence was led at the Enquiry as to these findings, and your Petitioner, as a son of *KHAMA,* and whose interests are solely for his Tribe, under the Protection of the Crown, prays that an opportunity be given him to meet these grave findings, which reflect upon his personal character, and incidentally upon the tribe.'[28]

Like a terrier with a rag doll, Tshekedi continued to worry at Evans's accusations. Thus he prayed that he would be given an opportunity of showing that he did indeed order the punishment of McIntosh 'in the interests of just administration and the good of my people', even though Evans had publicly rejected this assertion when he reinstated him on 4 October.[29]

In conclusion, Tshekedi prayed that 'Your Majesty may revoke, annul and declare void, the *findings* of the Enquiry held at *PALAPYE ROAD* on September

13th. 1933, published by Your Majesty's High Commissioner for Bechuanaland at a formal Tribal Assembly summoned by the Chief at the order of the Resident Commissioner at Serowe on September 14th. 1933, and confirmed subsequently by Your Majesty's High Commissioner at a duly constituted Kgotla of the said Tribe at Serowe on October 4th. 1933.'[30] Armed with this Petition, Jennings and Buchanan set sail in the *Balmoral Castle* on the two-week journey to England.

Tshekedi was not the only one to prepare his defences. Rey and his Administration were not yet out of the woods with regard to Tshekedi's accusation about the failure of his Magistrates to do anything concerning his complaints against McIntosh and McNamee. Investigations in the office of the Resident Magistrate at Serowe led to a certain amount of acrimony between Nettelton and Potts. On 2 October Alfred Mahloane, the Senior Native Clerk and Interpreter to the Magistrate, swore before Germond, in his capacity as a Justice of the Peace, that about a week before the return of Captain Potts from leave, 'Captain Nettelton cleared his baskets of considerable outstanding correspondence. Included in the "File" basket was the correspondence . . . dealing with a proposed enquiry into the conduct of Phineas McIntosh and Henry McIntosh [sic].

'On going through the Files for filing I was struck by the absence of any action taken in connection with this matter and I took the correspondence to Captain Nettelton in order to ascertain whether the instructions to file were not a mistake. To the best of my recollection Captain Nettelton stated: "I have been waiting and waiting for the evidence which the Chief promised he would furnish, but he has done nothing." I accordingly filed the papers away as "General Correspondence" and produced them to Captain Potts recently when the McIntosh affair arose.'[31] Potts used this statement by Mahloane to defend his own inaction in the matter, sending a confidential handwritten note to Rey in which he said 'it is a great pity that this correspondence and an explanation of the action taken was not placed before me by Capt. Nettelton when I assumed duty. . . I venture to say that I have not consciously either shirked a duty or evaded forcing an issue when necessary.'[32]

Despite public repudiation of Tshekedi's allegations, privately Evans considered that there had been 'some laxity of the local administration in turning out the offending Europeans from the reserve', and he communicated this opinion to Thomas in a personal letter sent on 25 September even before he publicly reproved Tshekedi for suggesting that this was the case. Later, on 10 October, Evans wrote officially to the Secretary of State commenting on Liesching's criticisms of the Bechuanaland Protectorate Administration. His own view was that if the complaints made to Captain Nettelton had been brought before Sir Herbert Stanley, he would have had the two young men removed from the Reserve under the powers vested in him by Proclamation No 15 of 1907, which in fact was the Proclamation that Evans as Acting High Commissioner used to banish them from the Bamangwato Reserve. 'In the circumstances I feel compelled to record the opinion that the omission of the Authorities at Mafeking to bring to the notice of the High Commissioner Captain Nettelton's Minute of the 28th April 1932 was an error of judgment. As you are aware Colonel Rey was absent on leave in England at the time, and Captain Reilly who was acting as Resident Commissioner in his absence is at present on leave in England.'[33]

Though Rey was effectively exonerated from blame by Evans, he received a copy of this letter with fury. His reply to Evans of 19 October barely observed the customary restraint of letters addressed to the representative of the Crown: 'I appreciate', wrote Rey, 'the fact that it is stated . . . that ''Colonel Rey was absent on leave in England at the time'', and although I am not therefore personally concerned, nevertheless I regret that I am unable to associate myself with the view expressed by Your Excellency.' Once again Rey laid the blame on Tshekedi for not providing Nettelton with the evidence he had requested.[34] Under no circumstances was he prepared to accept that Tshekedi's allegations were in any way justified, despite the evidence of Senior Clerk Mahloane and the censure of Potts.

Two days before he had sent his angry reaction to Evans's letter, Rey had decided to anticipate the arrival of Buchanan and Jennings in Britain with a propaganda campaign of his own. He addressed a letter enclosing a document entitled 'A note on the Serowe incident' to a series of notables connected with colonial affairs. To Lord Lugard, Sir Alan Pim, Lord Wolmer, Lord Buxton and Mr Pybus[35] he wrote that in view of 'the grossly misleading statements (mainly inspired by the London Missionary Society) which have appeared in the South African Press, and the public's ignorance of the position out here, I enclose some notes which may be of use to you in case of need, regarding the Serowe incident.

'The Secretary of State has very wisely declined to receive Tshekedi, but Buchanan . . . and . . . Jennings have sailed for England and will doubtless let loose a certain amount of poison gas.

'The attacks on Admiral Evans have been grossly unfair; he behaved magnificently, and I have no hesitation in saying that his prompt action averted what might have been a serious situation.

'He commands the complete and unswerving support of every member of the Administration.

'Of course, owing to my official position, I cannot ''take the field'' or be quoted publicly; I don't care a row of pins for the attacks on myself, but I do resent the misleading and distorted attacks which have been made on Admiral Evans, for whom, as my Chief, and as a man, I have the most unbounded respect, who supported me unhesitatingly, and indeed, acted on my advice while accepting full responsibility.'[36]

Rey's 'Notes' made no points that he had not already made, except to damn Tshekedi even further and to recognise that the real issue was not McIntosh but his own Proclamations. 'So far from the incident standing alone, or even of it being the real cause of the trouble, it was the culminating point of 8 years' trouble with a swollen-headed youth whose openly expressed desire and ambition has been to be the ruler of an independent sovereign nation.

'Trouble with this youth Tshekedi had started long before I became Resident Commissioner and had been allowed to grow unchecked.'

Rey then proceeded to outline the aims of his Native Proclamations, which 'are designed for the benefit of the 200,000 people of the Territory, and as such were naturally bitterly resisted by Tshekedi who was out for one thing—and one thing only—to maintain his present rights and privileges.

'As I always have been, and still am, of the opinion that our duty is to safeguard the interests of the 200,000 natives rather than to preserve the personal privileges of half a dozen autocratic, half-educated, and to some extent, thoroughly rotten young Chiefs, I have pressed these proposals continuously and steadily and they are now within an ace of becoming law.

'Realising this, Tshekedi determined to try at the eleventh hour to sidetrack the enactment of the new laws by raising a constitutional issue. He did this by the flogging of McIntosh.

'It was a deliberate challenge to the Administration. He knew perfectly well that even under the existing law no white man, with or without his consent, could be judged, on any excuse whatsoever, in any Native Court. Nevertheless, Tshekedi dragged McIntosh before the Native Court, not—be it observed—on any immorality charge, but on a charge of common assault, namely striking a native. Tshekedi was not carried away by passion, nor did he do anything in the heat of the moment. He waited a whole month after the case had been before the Native Court, and then in cold blood, at the end of the month, without reporting the matter to, or notifying in any way, any officer of the Administration, he ordered the man to be flogged.'

Apart from his diatribe against Tshekedi, Rey attacked his long-standing enemies, the London Missionary Society. 'I am prepared to believe that this Society has done good work elsewhere, but so far as this Territory is concerned they have done nothing but harm. . . . They have endeavoured to establish a religious monopoly here . . . and so far as the Bamangwato country . . . is concerned, they have succeeded. But having kept out all other Missions from there, they have achieved nothing else. They have not a single Medical Mission or Medical Officer in the whole Territory. . . . They are represented in the Protectorate by a poor type of individual . . . ' and the 'man Jennings, who is now going to England to try and raise trouble, is the most troublesome specimen of them all. The Advocate, Buchanan, whose name has appeared in connection with this matter, is an amiable negrophilist who is doubtless merely doing the job he is paid for.

'He and Jennings have, however, consistently fed the Press here with a series of misleading and even lying statements representing the facts in a totally untrue light; and of course owing to my position, I have been unable to answer them.'[37]

Rey's attempts to put over his own case were to be of little avail, for Tshekedi was not only better placed to arrange publicity for his position but had become a consummate manipulator of the press, Parliament, public opinion and pressure groups. Not for nothing was his personal library full of books on the British constitution, imperial history and methods of colonial administration. Tshekedi appreciated more keenly than any other chief in Britain's African empire of the day did that real power lay not with the local administration but in the distant metropolis. Even if he could not go there personally to mobilise these four pillars of politics in the imperial capital, he had the necessary agents to do so on his behalf.

Tshekedi was of course working within a well-established tradition in southern Africa when he appealed to London. His own father, along with his fellow rulers of the Bakwena and the Bangwaketse, had done so on their visit to the imperial capital in 1895 to protest successfully against the possibility of the transfer of their territories to Cecil Rhodes's British South Africa Company. In 1909 the Basotho had sent a delegation to London to lobby against any possibility of incorporation of their territory into the planned Union of South Africa. In that same year a Coloured and Native Delegation left the Cape for London to try to have the racist provisions of the act establishing the Union modified. More recently, Sobhuza II of Swaziland led a delegation to England in 1925 to try—unsuccessfully—to regain some of his lands that had been alienated to white farmers.[38]

The media had been largely with Tshekedi during the period of his reinstatement. He personally monitored the press closely and arranged with a son of a pillar of the London Missionary Society, Oliver Whiting, manufacturer of fancy leather goods and 'Leatho' products of Regent Street, to procure press cuttings for him from the Woolgar and Roberts press-cutting agency in London. These Whiting (with whose father, J. E. Whiting of Farnham, Tshekedi had stayed in 1930), sent off in regular parcels. On 22 September, for instance, he sent a packet containing 'about 300 cuttings' from a press which he reported was 'favourable'.[39]

While the press in Britain, and indeed South Africa, continued on the whole to be sympathetic towards Tshekedi, in the absence of continuing high drama such articles as they did carry on the Protectorate tended to be more reflective and more searching. Though the majority were still critical of the Administration, some of the criticism was directed specifically at the British system of indirect rule as it operated in the Bechuanaland Protectorate whereby, they suggested, too much power was left in the hands of the chiefs. Thus the *Manchester Guardian* gave prominence to the pamphlet opportunely published by Margaret L. Hodgson and W. G. Ballinger on *Britain and South Africa, No. 2: Bechuanaland Protectorate*, reporting that the crux of the authors' attack was that 'the rule of the chiefs is inefficient, wasteful, and tyrannical, and it is the British policy, which—out of a wish to save expense as well as from mere inertia—has left the substantial power of the chiefs virtually untouched that is responsible for the backwardness of the Bechuanaland Protectorate today.'[40] Similarly, Leonard Barnes, friend and erstwhile collaborator of Hodgson and Ballinger, wrote in *Time and Tide* that 'British policy has contrived to fossilize the old organic chieftainship into an irresponsible autocracy, unadapted to the changes in tribal society introduced by education and by the industrial revolution in progress all over South Africa.'[41] Barnes's conclusion was that the new laws being drafted to regulate the administrative and judicial powers of the Chiefs were a welcome step in the right direction, provided they did not 'stifle the growth of native institutions beneath the weight of white officialdom.' Perceptively, he saw that 'Tshekedi is a long-headed tactician, and it is safe to assume that he was looking far beyond the McIntoshes of his world. He was not contending for jurisdiction over Europeans; he was contesting the Government's claim to regulate the municipal affairs of his tribe.' In the same issue of that magazine appeared a letter from 'Imperialist', which must have delighted Tshekedi when he read it among the other press cuttings sent by Oliver Whiting. 'The South African Protectorates should be made a political and economic laboratory, capable of instructing the Union Government by example. Hitherto they have been treated more like a waste-paper basket. I hope that the Tshekedi case will provide an opportunity for really vigorous reform here.'[42]

The aim of Tshekedi and his spokesmen, Buchanan and Jennings, was to show that the Proclamations violated native law and custom in a way that would be unacceptable in other British African territories, which were administered by the Colonial Office as distinct from the Dominions Office and practised orthodox indirect rule as developed by Sir Donald Cameron in Tanganyika as a result of his experiences in Nigeria. And thus whenever the press carried suggestions that the Bechuanaland Protectorate be transferred to the Colonial Office or criticized the past performance of the Administration in the Bechuanaland Protectorate, Tshekedi felt his cause was being advanced. He believed that an independent Commission from outside would not only understand his reservations about Rey's Proclamations but also realise that the Chiefs were not the autocrats that Rey tried to suggest they were. So his heart must have been warmed when the conservative *Daily Telegraph*[43] wrote in an editorial on his reinstatement: 'We cannot read the record without feeling a lack of seriousness and energy in the administration. While we insist, as we must, that white men should be exempt from the punishments of tribal courts, it is incumbent on us to insist that British officials should effectively protect the black man from the crimes of the white.' There was widespread unease at the general state of the Protectorate, 'sunk into the slough of bankruptcy, stagnation, and decay, where it seems likely to remain, to the increasing material and moral distress of it inhabitants. These things are not figments of the negrophile imagination; they loom out of the solemn pages of the [Pim] Commission's Report. It is they, and not the McIntoshes and the howitzers, that matter.'[44]

Rey and the Administration may have been impotent in putting over their case in the press, but they did have some support. For instance, J. Wentworth Day in the *Saturday Review* defended Evans and accused the Prime Minister and the Dominions Secretary of heaping insults on him. 'Is it not enough that a Socialist Premier, to whom the very idea of Empire is anathema, a man ridden by the twin devils of political opportunism and mob pressure—working hand in glove with Mr. Thomas, the playboy of public banquets, the aitchless enunciator of after-dinner inanities—should, by virtue of the power residing in their hands, have condemned the wisdom and reversed the judgement of Vice-Admiral Evans?'[45] But even where the Administration had access to the British Parliament through the Dominions Office, Tshekedi and his allies in London had comparatively greater success. Parliament was, perhaps luckily for the Dominions Office, in recess at the time of the Evans expedition to the Kalahari. The new session did not begin until 17 November. Questions about the goings-on in Bechuanaland did not get attention in either House until the following month, by which time Buchanan and Jennings had been able to lobby both MPs and Peers of all political colours.

Between 12 and 14 December a number of questions were asked in the House of Commons that were either directly inspired by Buchanan and Jennings or were responses to the immense amount of publicity Tshekedi's case had generated in the press. On 12 December, Mr Lunn asked the Secretary of State for Dominion Affairs whether the Chiefs in Bechuanaland had been consulted about the Draft Proclamations. He was assured by Thomas that they had been, 'in great detail', and that 'the drafts had been revised in order to meet, as far as possible, the suggestions which the chiefs have made.'[46] Colonel Wedgwood then asked whether the House would have an opportunity to discuss the draft legislation before it was enacted. Thomas responded rather lamely to this radical suggestion, since colonial legislation of this sort was rarely discussed in the House. 'I do not know, but whatever is the usual practice will be followed in this case.'[47] Mr Lunn then inquired whether before the Draft Proclamations were adopted the Secretary of State would consider setting up an independent Commission of Enquiry 'to deal both with the system of government by the chiefs and the British administration, and their relation to one another.' But Thomas did not consider there was adequate ground for adopting this suggestion.[48] Next Mr Parkinson asked Thomas whether he had received further requests from Tshekedi to come to London in connection with the administration of the Bechuanaland Protectorate and the Draft Proclamations and whether he would consider inviting him for this purpose. To Tshekedi's considerable later anger,[49] Thomas answered that no such request had been made since the beginning of October 'when it was explained to him that I considered that the proper course was to await the return of Sir Herbert Stanley, the High Commissioner'. Then, repeating a familiar phrase he affirmed, 'I do not consider that a visit by the Acting Chief to this country would serve any useful purpose.'[50] But Parkinson was not to be put off and asked: 'If no satisfactory arrangement is arrived at, will the Right. Hon. Gentleman consider allowing the Chief to lay his own case before a Committee of this House?' At this point Thomas said he did not know whether Parkinson was speaking for the Chief but 'I would remind him that it is very dangerous, when a High Commissioner in these territories is conducting a very difficult and delicate task, to allow a suggestion that his discretion in matters of this kind will be overruled, and we shall give no encouragement to it.' At this juncture Parkinson lost his cool and accused Thomas of hurling an insult at him. But then, showing clearly that he was effectively representing the Chief, he asked how many members of the Bechuanaland Protectorate Administration were recruited from the police.[51] One of Tshekedi's constant criticisms of those set in authority above him was that they were not properly trained for the job.

Later that afternoon, Parkinson asked the Prime Minister whether 'in view of the difficulties which have been disclosed by the negotiations with Chief Tshekedi, he has considered the desirability of transferring the South African Protectorates from the Dominions to the Colonial Office?' The Prime Minister replied that he did not feel that recent events afforded sufficient reason for such a transfer.[52] Colonel Wedgwood, who had in many ways made the McIntosh affair his own crusade, then waded in with a question asking whether modifications would be made as soon as possible to 'ensure the same standard of public services in the Dominions as has hitherto existed in the Colonial Office services? I mean with regard to the better selection of the officials?'[53]

Over the course of the next two days questions were asked as though Tshekedi himself were in the House. Had officials with experience of native administration, especially in Tanganyika, been consulted about the drafting of the Bechuanaland Proclamations?[54] Would the Secretary of State consider separating the office of the British High Commissioner to South Africa from that of the High Commissioner for the three South African Protectorates?[55] Would the Secretary of State indicate 'in what respects and on what dates Chief Tshekedi Khama has flouted

His Majesty's administration, as stated by the High Commissioner in announcing his supension?' Did he not think that 'it is grossly unfair to bring forward all these charges without attempting to substantiate them?' Did the reinstatement of Chief Tshekedi involve 'the withdrawal of the serious charges on which his suspension was based; and what steps have been taken to make it clear to the chief's people and to the public what is the present position?'[56] To all these questions the answers were evasive or non-committal. And when Colonel Wedgwood asked, 'Who is to pay the bill for sending these marines up to Bechuanaland?' he was requested to put a question on the Paper.[57]

At the same time an extensive debate in the House of Lords was held on conditions in the South African Protectorates, where once again Tshekedi's cause was championed, this time by Lord Snell, the former Labour MP whose entry in *Who's Who* listed him as a speaker on labour and religious topics. While not assuming that Tshekedi 'is either blameless or that he is an easy person to work with', Lord Snell told Their Lordships that they must understand that Tshekedi 'was not the hereditary paramount Chief, and I know that his desire was and is to hand over unimpaired the full prerogatives which he has in his charge. . . . I am far from satisfied that he was treated with either courtesy or consideration. I fear he was harassed and systematically and scientifically bullied to grant concessions to which he was opposed.' As to the events that led to his suspension, it was 'a great misfortune to Bechuanaland and the British Empire that when this happened the High Commissioner should be away, and that the situation was dealt with by quarter-deck swagger instead of statesmanship, a military parade, and one feels that, if it had been possible, the whole Fleet would have been taken on that occasion. I very much fear that the aim on this occasion was to break the opposition of the Bechuanaland Chief to the draft Proclamation to which he was asked to submit, and to produce a tamed and obedient Chief.'[58] Tshekedi could not have said it better himself. Lord Snell, who had met Tshekedi on his visit to London in 1930, then sang his praises as a 'man of high capacity and character, and he has the almost unique distinction of having won the respect and even the regard of every white man and woman in his territory. I formed the opinion that he was not an unworthy son of his great father, and that perhaps is as good a recommendation as he would wish to have. I believe his sole mistake was in doing for himself what millions of decent Englishmen would willingly have done for him.'[59]

Lord Lugard, former Governor-General of Nigeria, appealed, as a one-time colonial administrator, for a little more sympathy for the man on the spot. 'The recent incident relating to Chief Tshekedi seems to indicate a considerable lack of co-operation between the native rulers and the Administration, and an absence of definition of the real powers and duties of the native Chiefs. But this, as the noble Lord has said, has been a growth of many years, and is not specifically to be attributed to any particular individuals at the present time.'[60] Lugard was followed by Earl Buxton, former Governor-General of and High Commissioner to South Africa, who, with little modesty, told his noble colleagues that if the affair had arisen when he was in office, 'we should have heard nothing about it.' The situation had been handled 'in a somewhat sensational way', but the Secretary of State and Sir Herbert Stanley, who was then in England, were to be congratulated on the way they had managed the matter.[61] Lord Strathcona and Mount Royal, speaking for the Government, deprecated Lord Snell's sarcastic remarks about Evans's expedition and insisted that the Acting High Commissioner 'took only such measures by way of safeguard as the local administration thought advisable, having regard to the very important fact that at the time the bulk of the Protectorate police were away, engaged on a campaign for the prevention of foot-and-mouth disease.'[62] Perhaps the most important statement to be made in Lord Strathcona's very cogent defence of the Protectorate Administration was one dear to Tshekedi's heart. He re-affirmed the pledge he had made the previous July that Parliament would be consulted before any question of the transfer of the Protectorate to the Union of South Africa was considered, and that the Government would not 'make any decision until the native population and the white population have had a full opportunity of expressing their views.' Finally, there would be no support by the Government for transfer 'if it involved any impairment of such safeguards for native rights and interests as the Schedule of the South Africa Act was designed to secure.'[63] All in all, the questions in the House of Commons and the debate in the House of Lords had served Tshekedi's cause well and kept alive issues that the Administration were trying to contain for purposes of discussion within South Africa.

A month before these debates, Tshekedi had written from Serowe to Sir John Harris, the Parliamentary Secretary of the Anti-Slavery Society, to thank him for the press coverage he had secured for his cause and regretting that he had not been able to come to England 'to have personal interviews with you, although Messrs. Buchanan and Jennings will do their very best on my behalf. . . . We fully realise, and in fact I had to express it openly to a big meeting of my Tribe, that my hasty reinstatement has been occasioned by the pressure from the English public.'[64] Indeed, one of the most extraordinary aspects of the whole McIntosh affair is the way it made Tshekedi a hero with the British public and also gained him sympathisers and admirers in South Africa and, indeed, other parts of the world. In a letter to Alfred Jennings written just before he left for London, the Rev. A. M. Chirgwin reported that at the Autumnal Assembly of the Congregational Union held in Nottingham he was able to announce the news of Tshekedi's reinstatement before it was carried on the BBC. 'It was received with torrents of applause and by a great audience standing. The interest in the Tshekedi case has been quite remarkable. I remember nothing quite like it.'[65] The *Northampton Evening Telegraph* reported that the 'congregation rose in their seats, and there were demands for the singing of the Doxology and the National Anthem, but the Chairman (Dr A. G. Sleep) restrained the meeting in order to allow Mr Chirgwin to proceed.' Harold Moody, the Jamaican President of the League of Coloured Peoples, told the Assembly, 'I am delighted with the way you have received this wonderful news. When I think of Admiral Evans, with his guns and aeroplanes, and of Tshekedi, cool, calm and dignified, I ask myself, "Which is the representative of the so-called civilised race? Which is the Christian?" ' The Chairman then declared the announcement of Tshekedi's reinstatement to be news that would 'make the bells of Heaven ring in their hearts.'[66]

Some indication of the remarkable interest in Tshekedi's case to which Chirgwin referred can been seen in the file of 'Letters of Support' Tshekedi kept in his personal archive.[67] To many of these letters he seems to have sent replies, though only a few have carbon copies. A number of his correspondents were former missionaries who knew either Tshekedi or his father. Others were former Serowe residents. All exude warmth for Tshekedi and his people.

One letter came from as far away as Canada. Mrs Catherine Wright of Renfrew in Ontario, who was as she put it 'one of your race', informed Tshekedi that 'the white man got just what was coming to him, and if more men of the African race were like you, I am sure we would get some where.

'There are too many men like that around, we should have a few of your kind of men over here with some spunk.'[68]

A young Irish nurse wrote to congratulate him on his 'very lovely photo. I have also seen your showing on the pictures, and you are such a charming man, I just love you. I do hope I am not making to [sic] free but I just had to write you.—I want to tell you about myself well I am a young nurse a Typical Irish Beauty. . . .' Enclosed in the letter were three pressed ivy leaves—heart-shaped.[69] Nurse Anne Murphy had no doubt seen the British Movietone News interview with Tshekedi shown as 'Meet Chief Tshekedi in Exclusive Talk. Bechuanaland tribal head deposed for flogging a white man, praised English hospitality in 1930.' In the minute-long interview, filmed on Tshekedi's visit to London in 1930, he comes across as a handsome and very charming young man with a shy but melting smile. 'Your people', he told the interviewer, 'have been rather too kind to me.' From the film it is easy to see how he won Nurse Murphy's heart.

Quite a number of letters came from South Africa. One from J. Bryant Lindley of Claremont in the Cape assured Tshekedi that nineteen out of every twenty people were on his side. 'I love the brown people for they have always been very kind to me.

'There are one or two of your enemies I would like to put a knife into.

'As a whiteman I apologise for the injustice done to you.'[70]

Perhaps the most extraordinary letters in the collection are two from a young Afrikaner surveyor at a gold mine in the Transvaal, who told Tshekedi that 'I have always thought at heart that it was not your fault entirely, and since your letters between you and the Magistrate have been published, it is quite clear how the trouble came about.'[71] But this was not the burden of Mr de Koek's letter. What he wanted to do was set up a friendship with Tshekedi. He asked for his photo, assuring him that it was not through curiosity or inquisitiveness that he had written him. Tshekedi clearly replied to this odd letter, for on 26 January de Koek wrote to thank him for his letter and suggested that the two of them go on a camping tour of the Transvaal 'or some other province. Do you think you could come? I have a little Standard car and we could just go until we feel like stopping, and enjoy ourselves. Don't you think this would be fine? Let me know what you think about it—I would just love it—but of course we must picnic and make food too—by the way, I can't cook tho', can you? We'll be able to roast chops and sausage anyway, eh? . . . Please tell me something of your daily life—remember I want to be a friend of yours, tho' no one else will or need know it, everything is said in confidence unless of course you wish to tell others as there is naturally nothing secret about our friendship. I will be pleased of a photo of you Tshekedi so don't disappoint me.'[72]

The consideration with which Tshekedi replied to what nowadays would be called his fan-mail gives an indication why his white friends remained so loyal and devoted to him. In one of his letters enclosing press cuttings for Tshekedi, Oliver Whiting had offered the services of his sister as guardian for young Chief Seretse if Tshekedi followed through with his idea of sending him to school in Britain. On 4 November Tshekedi acknowledged receipt of the letter as well as the parcels of press cuttings which were waiting for him on his return from a tour outside the capital: 'It is some time since I last corresponded with your family—though oceans divide us and letters not constantly written—it is impossible for me to forget the kindness which your family extended to me in England. . . .

'I deeply appreciate the offer that your sister, Miss Mildred Whiting, would be a mother to my nephew in the event of my sending him to England for education; I have, however, now changed my plans after further consideration, and I have decided that it would be unwise for the boy to be brought up away from his people, and we think it would be better policy to send him to England only to complete his education, when he will be more or less a man. Nevertheless we very much appreciate the spirit of friendship of your family to my family which is continually being made manifest.'[73]

To Mr Edward Little, a friend of Whiting's father, he wrote assuring him that 'we in this Dark Continent are ignorant of what goes on the world, but even the most ignorant Native of this Protectorate, seeing the white man's flying machines and steam engines all around him, cannot help realising that he has not got the ability to fight Great Britain. But our case is different: we have been taught friendship with Great Britain from our babyhood, and we have no inclination to show a display of force to the Officers of the British Government. The present display of force was therefore very bewildering to us, and even today we cannot understand what has happened. However I confidently trust that His Will will in the end be done.'[74] Tshekedi was also careful to thank those who had helped him in his hour of need, as in his very fulsome letter to the Rev. Whiteside acknowledging that his 'short-hand notes have been of the greatest help to me, I fully believe Providence had sent you to come and be of such help to us.'[75]

Tshekedi's letters to his supporters overseas made them feel as though they were somehow personally involved in the affairs of his distant people and that their help was indispensable. Most important of all to his campaign in Britain was the group of lobbyists who intervened on his behalf with officials at the Dominions Office, or explained the 'truth' about the Bechuanaland situation to members of both Houses of Parliament and planted questions for them to ask Government ministers. Most notable among these was Sir John Harris, once for a brief spell himself an MP and now Parliamentary Secretary of the Anti-Slavery Society. When members of his Society had been convinced that Tshekedi was not making claims to be 'above the law', Harris mobilised them into supporting the Chief's cause. As early as 15 September Harris had written to the Dominions Office in response to the many enquiries he had received about the Bechuanaland Protectorate, asking that his Society be allowed 'to see the terms of any official document which debars the Chief of a Native Territory from dealing with a white man who has become a nuisance and a danger to the public.'[76] It was not until 6 October that the Society formally requested the Secretary of State to receive a deputation to discuss the Bechuanaland situation.

Two weeks before that, another influential group of moderate colonial critics—the London Group on African Affairs—had asked Thomas to receive a deputation of three of the members of its executive to discuss the 'recent trouble in Bechuanaland', whose fundamental causes 'were concerned with the Administrative system.' The Administration, they suggested in their memorandum, were isolated, locally recruited, and sub-standard. Tshekedi's action was the 'not unnatural outcome of the autocratic powers allowed him by the Administration'.[77] The deputation from the London Group comprised Lord Sanderson, Professor W. M. Macmillan, Mr Leonard Barnes, Mr Harold Moody and its Secretary, Mr Livie-Noble, who had previously worked in South Africa for the Council of Education. Thomas, received them on 14 November 1933 and began by saying in what was to be a remarkably frank discussion, 'Do not let us waste a moment about the

European. If there was any law to shoot him I would have shot him. I do not hesitate to say that, and I would say it publicly, because he disgraced the white race, he disgraced humanity, and he was not worth two moments of consideration, a man who lived in kraal as he did, and the life he led, that was not involved, and therefore at no moment of this case was I worried about him. I was more worried that I did not have powers to punish him. But I could not allow Tshekedi to establish a claim to try a European'. These high-minded statements ring a little hollow when read by those who recall that two years later Thomas was driven from office in disgrace for carelessness over confidential information relating to the budget.

Few new ideas were put forward at the meeting with Thomas, though Professor Macmillan, from his own experience of 'native administration' in South, East and Central Africa and in the Bechuanaland Protectorate itself, where he had met Tshekedi in 1931, suggested that Cameron, currently Governor of Nigeria, and Sir Philip Mitchell, the Governor of Uganda, be consulted about the position of the Chiefs in the Bechuanaland Protectorate.[78]

The deputation from the London Group on African Affairs to the Dominions Office was in no way a mouthpiece for Tshekedi. That sent by the Anti-Slavery Society in January of 1934 very much was. Indeed, little was said at it by members of the Society itself. Rather, all the talking to Thomas was done by Tshekedi's representatives, Buchanan and Jennings. The two had landed at Southampton on 30 October and had quickly started drumming up support for Tshekedi. Buchanan had a wide range of contacts in the legal profession, in academe and politics. He was a man of considerable charm and irrepressible enthusiasm. Jennings, of course, had the wide Congregationalist network to manipulate in Britain. They contacted Sir Herbert Stanley a few days after their arrival and reported to Tshekedi that their discussion was 'so confidential that we are not at liberty to give you full details by letter. We found him very friendly to us and youself, and we went into the various points you asked us to deal with. On none of these did we find him opposed to our views.'[79] The two went to see the Legal Adviser to the Dominions and Colonial Offices and presented him with an extraordinary document on 1 December. This was a draft of a new 'Treaty' between the British Government and the Chiefs and Tribes of the Bechuanaland Protectorate. Under the 'Treaty' it would be agreed that its object 'is the development of the said Bechuana Tribes into civilised self-governing communities within the Commonwealth of the British Empire.' The draft went on to set out the main points of the 'Treaty':

2. In pursuance of this object the Chiefs and Tribes hereby voluntarily agree to place themselves under the tutelage of His Majesty's Government of Great Britain as hereinafter set forth.

3. His Majesty's Government hereby agrees to undertake such tutelage.
4. His Majesty's Government agrees to administer the territory through the Colonial Office until the aforesaid object is accomplished or until this Treaty be cancelled or amended as hereafter provided.
5. This Treaty may be amended at any time by mutual consent or terminated by His Majesty's Government upon giving suitable notice in writing to the Chiefs and Tribes concerned.
6. On the aforesaid object being accomplished or on receipt of written notice as aforesaid all Sovereign Rights shall fully revest in the said Chiefs and Tribes including full Sovereignty and Dominion in their respective portions of the territory annexed as "Crown Lands" in 1901.
7. At any time after receipt of such written notice as aforesaid the Chiefs and Tribes shall be entitled, should they desire to do so, to negotiate a Treaty with any other Protecting Power on such terms as they may deem fit.
8. No hereditary Chief or Councillor shall be deprived of his hereditary office except in accordance with Native Law and Custom or after due and proper trial before an impartial Judge in accordance with the principles and practice of criminal trials in His Majesty's Courts at Westminster on a specific charge of incompetence, mental or moral disability, or failure to observe the terms of this Treaty.'

The draft then detailed the methods of administration to be employed by the tutelary power and, with McIntosh still well in mind, concluded with a clause that specified that all cases 'connected with miscegenation between Europeans and Natives shall be heard and determined by a special Native Court comprised of a Magistrate or higher Official who shall act as Judge and the paramount Chief and two Councillors who shall sit with such Official and act as Assessors.

'All other cases in which Europeans are concerned shall be heard and determined by a Magistrate or superior judicial Officer save that on prior written request by the European concerned such cases may be heard by a paramount Chief in his Native Court.'[80]

Although, according to Buchanan, the Legal Adviser accepted the 'Draft Treaty' gladly, he did say that it was a matter of politics rather than law and offered to see Sir Edward Harding, the Permanent Under Secretary at the Dominions Office, about it.[81] Sir Edward, not surprisingly, rejected the 'Treaty' out of hand, for it was quite revolutionary in its intent. Effectively it placed the colonial relationship on the basis of a contract between two equal parties, with both having the right to withdraw from it at will. Under its terms the Chiefs and Tribes of the Bechuanaland Protectorate could take independence whenever they wished, or transfer their administration to another Protecting Power. Not even the Class A Mandates of the

League of Nations made such provisions. As Harding put it, 'I am bound to say that we should regard any such document as wholly unsuitable to form the basis of future administration in the Protectorate, and it would not appear, therefore, that any useful purpose would be served by talking over this document with you.'[82] As far as Tshekedi was concerned, he would have to proceed on the basis of the Draft Proclamations and discuss any reservations he might have with Sir Herbert Stanley. Buchanan was so put out by the letter from Harding that he wrote to him from holiday in Kitzbuhel in Switzerland that it 'did not require a lawyer to grasp that the basis of the Draft Proclamation is complete annexation in breach of the Treaty made with Sir Charles Warren in 1885 as explained by the then Secretary of State in 1887 and so understood by Khama and his people and reaffirmed in 1895 in the agreement between Chamberlain and the Chiefs Khama, Sebele, and Bathoeng [sic].' Indeed, it completely changed the relationship between the Protecting Power and the Batswana as accepted by Khama. But increasingly over the next year Tshekedi was to argue that the way to settle the differences that existed between himself, as representing his people if not the other Chiefs, was to draw up a Treaty which would specify quite clearly the obligations of both parties.

Buchanan went further, in what was an intemperate letter for a lawyer to a senior Government official, suggesting that 'Admiral Evans, as Tshekedi and his people thought, on the advice of the Resident Commissioner', had 'attempted to start a rebellion by sending an inadequate armed force into a peaceful and friendly state, by conducting a flagrantly unfair trial, by parading the Chief through his capital in a lorry labelled "Ex-Chief Tshekedi Khama and Police Escort" even before judgment had been announced, etc. etc.—it seems this was all part of Britain's scheme to annexe the Territory.'[83] Harding was, to say the least, annoyed by Buchanan's letter, and wrote back that he had 'read it with considerable surprise.' He made it clear that it was not possible to accept him or Mr Jennings as representatives of Tshekedi and asked him to read once again the last paragraph of his letter, 'since I cannot believe that you really intend to make the very serious allegations which it contains.'[84] Despite this contretemps with its senior civil servant, Buchanan and Jennings were not cut off entirely from access to the Dominions Office. Arrangements were finally made for the Anti-Slavery Deputation to see the Secretary of State on 16 January, and Tshekedi's two 'representatives' were to be part of it.

While preparing the ground for their formal presentation to the Secretary of State, Jennings and Buchanan had received a number of letters from Tshekedi and in turn reported their progress to him. On 30 October Tshekedi sent them further evidence about miscegenation in the Protectorate, which no doubt formed the basis of Buchanan's assertion to Malcolm MacDonald, the Junior Minister at the Dominions Office, that 'the reason why the Administration Authorities did not act more swiftly and effectively regarding Mac Intosh [sic] is that miscegnation is so common. This applies to officers of the Administration as well as to other Europeans, and Mr. Buchanan thought it probably affected 75% of the white population.' According to MacDonald, Buchanan considered this state of affairs to be 'very serious' and that it had 'to be dealt with' or they would be storing up fresh troubles.[85]

Tshekedi also informed his 'representatives' that he and Bathoen had asked for an interview with the High Commissioner about the Draft Proclamations. In that same letter he wrote bitterly about Rey's order that copies of Evans's speech on the occasion of his reinstatement be circulated to the other tribes of the Protectorate. 'The purpose is obvious but this attitude is very damaging not only to my character but to my position because the announcement is given out with the intention that I had been really reinstated because I had apologised, this is of course tantamount, if I had done so, to admitting that I had committed a wrong or breach of the Proclamation which I did not feel I have ever done . . . it was a well intentioned scheme to degrade me before the eyes of my people and it is not uncommon to hear of any incidents which have happened little before or after my deposition that such incidents happened before or after ''The Chief's arrest'' this is very disturbing against anybody's character and I therefore hope that you will see your way to having my petition presented to the King.'[86]

On the eve of the Deputation of the Anti-Slavery Society to the Secretary of State, Tshekedi wrote another pained letter, this time to Jennings alone, saying that he had no faith in the Dominions Office after reading the correspondence between Harding and Buchanan. The Dominions Office was clearly convinced that the Chiefs were autocratic, and it was 'entirely blind to all arguments' and clearly 'determined not to alter the basis of the Draft Laws.' He had still not seen the High Commissioner. 'I am therefore of very strong opinion that my petition to the King should have been presented; it is the only hope I see of obtaining any redress not only in connection with the recent trouble but I feel that its presentation, and with luck attention given to it, would very greatly assist in altering the attitude which the Officials are adopting.'[87]

Unknown to Tshekedi, some officials were in fact nervous about the prospect of his petition being formally presented to the King. In an unsigned brief for Thomas's meeting with the Anti-Slavery Society, it was noted that Tshekedi still maintained that he had not acted contrary to the law and was contemplating a petition to the King. Perhaps recalling Tshekedi's surprise victory at the Judicial Committee of the Privy Council in 1931, the anonymous official drafting the brief wrote that it 'must be admitted that we cannot be certain what view the Courts might take on the legal point if it ever came before them.'[88]

Buchanan and Jennings decided not to proceed with the presentation of the petition, but rather to use the occasion of their membership of the Deputation to the Secretary of State to put the record straight and to bring Tshekedi's reservations about the Draft Proclamations forcefully to his attention. The Deputation was led by Lord Rhayader, who had been a Liberal MP and was well known as a speaker on politics and anti-liquor temperance, and it met with J. H. Thomas early in the morning since there was a meeting of the Cabinet at 11:00 A.M. Present with Thomas were Malcolm MacDonald, Harding, Whiskard and H. N. Tait, a more junior official in the Dominions Office. Thomas began by flattering his potential adversaries by saying how proud he had always been 'that there are people who are purely disinterested, only looking at the human side of life, whether it be for white or black, and who can, without reward or hope of reward, feel that they are rendering service by protecting those who unfortunately cannot protect them- selves, so no apology is ever needed from any of you, either in connection with your work or effort, or your representative position.'

Buchanan was the first to speak and immediately stressed 'the desirability of cancelling the conviction which stands against Tshekedi. In terminating the period of Tshekedi's banishment . . .'

At this point Thomas interrupted Buchanan in mid-sentence and told him that he thought it would be disastrous from everybody's point of view to reopen the matter. 'I do not intend to reopen it at all, and anything that would tend to let it be supposed that I was going to reopen it, even by the cancelling of the conviction would be wrong, because so far as the relationship with Tshekedi is concerned, I have wiped that incident entirely out and all my staff and administration feel the same, and not one of them will harbour any feelings of any sort; on the contrary our instructions are, and my policy is, to forget that incident, and let the administration and work go on as if it had never happened. You may take that from me, and I do not want the matter reopened.'

'I am very grateful to you for those words which you have just spoken,' Buchanan told Thomas, 'and it will be a great joy to repeat them to Tshekedi.'

In the general spirit of bonhomie that now prevailed in his office, Thomas replied: 'You are perfectly at liberty to do that, and if it would help you in that matter I would not hesitate to confirm that in a letter, which would be far more important than the repetition of what was said here.'[89] But dogged lawyer that Buchanan was, after thanking Thomas, he insisted on going over the whole question of Tshekedi's 'conviction' again. He told Thomas that the local Admin- istration had 'caused to be announced in the Kgotlas of the other Bechuanaland tribes such conviction and termination of suspension, thereby causing further pain to Tshekedi Khama, the most loyal and devoted subject of His Majesty the King. Tshekedi was charged with X, convicted of Y, and sentenced for Z, but was not guilty of either X, Y or Z.

'Prior to the trial the name of British justice stood as high in South Africa as anywhere, and had been the refuge of the natives and the admiration of the Colonists. When I returned from the trial and entered the Club a well-known member of the side-bar shouted across the vestibule, "Hallo, Douglas, where is your British justice now?" I answered promptly, "Wait and see", never doubting but that when the facts were known to you, Sir, justice would triumph and British prestige be restored.'

But Thomas remained adamant that he would not reopen the case, and the rest of the interview was concerned with Tshekedi's objections to Rey's Proclamations. Thomas did, though, keep his promise to write a letter for publication confirming what he had said about Tshekedi. It was written for Thomas by none other than Harding, who informed the Anti-Slavery Society, 'Mr Thomas then explained that he regarded the whole incident as finally closed. While, however, he was not prepared to re-open it, it would not be allowed in any way to prejudice the future relations of the Government with the Acting Chief; he regarded the Acting Chief as an upright and straightforward man who was trying to do the best for his people. It was his desire that the local Administration should continue to work in the most friendly and amicable way with the Acting Chief for the purpose of promoting the best interests of the Bamangwato.'[90]

The next morning Jennings and Buchanan wrote enthusiastically to Tshckedi about their interview with Thomas: 'This matter in our view has been very happily settled in this undertaking by the Secretary of State, as it makes it impossible for the matter to ever be mentioned by the officials of the B.P. for all time.'[91]

EPILOGUE

Myths and Ambiguities

The crisis precipitated by the 'flogging' of Phinehas McIntosh continued to have repercussions in southern Africa as well as in the imperial metropolis long after the Dominions Secretary declared the incident finally closed. The participants in the drama that unfolded as a consequence of Tshekedi ordering the flogging of the young wagon builder in his *kgotla* were actors in a play with many themes and many sub-plots. But white or black, peasant or politician, they were all playing on a stage whose sets included Serowe, Mafeking, Cape Town and London. And whatever the part played, whether that of imperial proconsul, missionary lobbyist, Serowe trader, Mongwato headman or Bangwato chorus, their roles in the drama were inextricably intertwined. For they were all elements in a socio-political situation that linked black and white together.

This drama showed nowhere more clearly than in the roles performed by Tshekedi Khama and Phinehas McIntosh that the conventional distinctions between white and black, ruler and ruled, educated and illiterate, senior and junior partner, did not operate consistently in the southern Africa of which Gamangwato formed part. In both cases there was a reversal of the conventional perceptions of the role of black and white. Phinehas McIntosh by his own admission lived as a 'native' in a Bangwato hut, with a Mongwato 'wife', and readily accepted the authority of 'his' African Chief as well as the headmen in whose ward he had his hut. Only his skin—not even his clothes—distinguished him from other Bangwato, posing them with the problem that Headman Peter Sebina had elaborated on before the Enquiry: 'Our difficulty is that he lives like ourselves, but his colour is different to us.'[1]

186

Phinehas did not and could not reverse his role completely. He was protected by the colour of his skin as Tribal Policeman Matome made clear in the evidence he gave when McIntosh was tried in the *kgotla:* 'On several occasions I came into contact with the doings of McIntosh, and had McIntosh been a Native I should have dealt with him long before now, but because we had instructions not to treat white people in the same way as we did the Natives, I did nothing to McIntosh even when he provoked me. I further put a question at the Kgotla as to whether I should let McIntosh go on with his evil actions, without exercising the right I have as a Policeman. I put that question because I have so often seen McIntosh do wrong things, and I did not know what authority I had over such a one.'[2] On the other hand, when confronted with a choice of supporting his Chief or his Magistrate, McIntosh was consistent in his loyalty to Tshekedi. Indeed, he was the only actor whose role in the drama that ensued on his 'flogging' was a completely honourable one. He never sought to suborn the Chief who had ordered his flogging. He made it clear that he was 'quite satisfied with the judgement the Chief passed on him,' as the Rev. J. H. L. Burns wrote to his daughter.[3] He refused to become a pawn of the British Administration. He did not even protest publicly when that Administration sentenced him to exile without even the semblance of a trial, which at least Tshekedi had given him. He did not seek out the press to put his side of the case, so that the only version of his amorous activities presented to the outside world was that purveyed by Tshekedi and the Administration. Though he was sentenced to a flogging for assaulting a Mongwato youth, he was punished as much for his sexual peccadilloes as for his readiness to use his fists, even though sexual intercourse between black and white was not against the law in the Protectorate. Among white residents in Serowe he was not alone in his attentions to Bangwato ladies; nor did the majority of Batswana have as puritan a view of extra-marital sex as did the Administration and Tshekedi. Not long afterwards Tshekedi himself was to find himself in deep trouble with his missionaries when he fathered a child by a woman to whom he was not married. For both Tshekedi and Rey, McIntosh was but the occasion for a struggle over much grander matters. It suited Rey to make a major issue out of what was a minor incident; Tshekedi could have chosen Henry McNamee or one of a number of other young white residents for the 'flogging' he knew would provoke Colonel Rey.

When McIntosh and McNamee went into exile in Lobatsi they were put on a road gang comprised of whites who at first refused to work with them.[4] Indeed, the white residents of Lobatsi got up a petition to the Resident Commissioner in which they asked for the immediate removal of 'the two Europeans banished from the Native Reserves and dumped into this District without any consultation with the Residents nor any regard to their feelings.' The petitioners feared that 'their presence here may exert a bad influence on Natives and Europeans. . . . We understand that they have already attempted to attend a European dance at Hilda-vale and we object most strongly to their attempting to associate with the European girls in the District.'[5] Rey asked the local Resident Magistrate to make enquiries into these complaints. All the Magistrate could report was that the foreman of the road gang was pleased with the work of McIntosh and McNamee and that as far as the dance was concerned they had gone to it with the rest of the road gang but had remained outside and had not taken part in the dancing. They had also attended church but had not attempted to force their company on anyone.[6] In view of this Rey refused to entertain the demands of the petitioners.

So good was the behaviour of the two young men in exile that the Administration felt able to pass their requests to return for short visits to their families in Serowe on to the Chief for approval, which he readily gave. In 1935 Phinehas married a white girl in Lobatsi, and in late 1935 Tshekedi gave him permission to spend a whole month in Serowe, to which he wanted to return on a permanent basis. Permission for him to stay on a month-to-month basis was granted by Tshekedi in 1937 on the recommendation of Captain Nettelton, once more stationed in Serowe as British representative, this time with the new title of District Commissioner. As Nettelton told the Government Secretary, 'My information and observations show that McIntosh's behaviour is very good and he is an industrious young man who might be employed on boring machines, etc., if there is any work available. He is now married and has apparently changed his habits being thus markedly different from McNamee.'[7] A year later the order banishing Phinehas was revoked, and he established his home in Serowe. He spent much of his time away from Serowe working for the Protectorate's geological survey services. He became quite friendly with Tshekedi and would often go out shooting for him, whether to kill lions troubling cattle or to obtain game for the people in times of hunger.[8] He eventually settled in a house next door to Tshekedi's Red House. Clearly neither he nor Tshekedi bore any rancour towards each other over the drama that took place in September 1933. The young tearaway now pursued a 'respectable' life, observing the conventions he had once scorned. After retiring from the Geological Service he went into business on his own account drilling boreholes for the water which has always been in such scarce supply in Gamang-wato.

McIntosh's behaviour, as even Rey admitted, was far from unique. At the very time of his 'flogging' a much more serious case involving an administrative officer, Mr Stanley Langton, Clerk in Kanye, was causing Rey considerable discomfort. He had not only been sleeping with many local black girls but was also alleged to have burnt down the administrative office to cover up irregularities in the accounts. Indeed, Simon Ratshosa went as far as to suggest that the reason the Administration had failed to deal with Tshekedi's complaints against McIntosh and McNamee was because 90 percent of the British officials were living 'side by side with native women.' Thus the Administration 'could not for a moment accuse McIntosh when he was reported to them by Tshekedi because he would certainly expose them.'[9]

What McIntosh unintentionally did was to raise the whole question of sexual relations between white and black in a part of Africa where most whites held strong views on the subject. Across the border in South Africa such relationships were illegal. The reason that the reaction by white South Africans to Tshekedi's 'flogging' of McIntosh was not the one of deep horror Evans and Rey anticipated was that the crime of punishing a white man for sleeping with a black woman was less heinous than the crime being punished. And if the white Administration would not deal with the matter, it was just as well that a black Chief had done so. Of course it was not only whites who disapproved of such relationships: many blacks like Simon Ratshosa and Tshekedi himself did, too. Colonel Rey had hoped that such behaviour would be regulated by a law similar to that in operation in South Africa, as had Tshekedi. But in the event racist legislation of this kind was never introduced into the Protectorate, so that it was possible a decade and a half later for Seretse legally to return to Serowe from England with a young Englishwoman as his wife, even though under pressure from South Africa the British refused to let him assume the chieftaincy and exiled him to Britain. Tshekedi, true to form, bitterly opposed this marriage, both because he had not been consulted and because he still disapproved of such unions.

Although no changes were in fact made to the existing law on sexual relations between blacks and whites, the McIntosh affair did revive a miscegenation 'scare' in the Protectorate. One of its consequences was the attempt in both Kanye, the capital of the Bangwaketse, and Molepolole, the capital of the Bakwena, to introduce residential segregation of black and white. Proposals were put forward to have 'undesirable Europeans' removed from the 'native reserves'. There were renewed efforts to restrict 'immorality' between the different groups in the Protectorate, including Indians and so-called Coloureds. Colonel Rey's proposal to create a special reserve for them beside the Molopo River was, as Jeff Ramsay has put it, 'pure apartheid'.[10] There continued to be many pressures for the introduction of a law on the South African pattern, and these pressures came not only from the British Administration but also from missionaries and members of the Batswana élite they had educated. But they came to nothing.

The sexual adventures of Phinehas McIntosh had only been incidental to the major struggle between Tshekedi and Rey over the introduction by the latter of 'reforms' that would dramatically alter the existing power relationship between black Chief and white Administrator. Potts even went so far as to suggest that Tshekedi was quite cynical in his attitude to McIntosh. In a private note to Captain

Neale he reported that 'Tshekedi has actually living in one of his houses—next to the European School—a European named Plotz who pays poll tax and works as a well-sinker for Tshekedi who is cohabitating with a native woman and has been doing so I understand for the past seven years . . . he is not averse to poor whites having native wives. They are thus brought down to the native level.'[11] In the larger struggle over the Proclamations, Admiral Evans, as temporary High Commissioner, was similarly incidental to the struggle, a bluff sailor whom Rey hoped to use to impose his Proclamations. At first Evans went along with Rey's schemes wholeheartedly. According to Rey, he even anticipated him by calling up the naval force to fly the flag in the Bechuanaland Protectorate. It was only when the Dominions Office showed itself less than enthusiastic about his expedition that Evans placed a restraining hand on Rey.

The swashbuckling expedition which the negrophobe Evans sent to the Kalahari cost his reputation dearly. His heroism in the Antarctic and on HMS *Broke* during the First World War did not protect him against attacks by the press or in Parliament. Indeed, in March 1934 when the Supply Committee of the House of Commons was debating a grant to the Bechuanaland Protectorate of £177,000 for the alleviation of distress, Evans and his expedition were pilloried from both sides of the House. There were strong protests against the fact that £4,000 of this sum was being set aside to cover costs involved in the Evans expedition. Members protested against either the British taxpayer or the 'natives' of the Bechuanaland Protectorate having to bear any part of the expenditure of the expedition. Mr Grenfell (Labour) was concerned that Evans 'had made a demonstration which drew the attention of the whole world, and rather disturbed a good many people in this country because of the display of force—unnecessary force we believe—on that occasion, and now we find that unnecessary display, accompanied by guns, the rattle of drums and the presence of soldiers, is to be at the expense of the Treasury to the extent of not less than £4,000.' Grenfell asked whether Admiral Evans was 'authorised to go under the conditions and with the accompaniment of the force which was displayed on that occasion and whether it was necessary to spend £4,000 of public money of this country in making a demonstration of force against a people unarmed, friendly, and generally content with their relations with us.' Grenfell then suggested that Evans be surcharged with the cost of his 'adventure'.[12] Colonel Wedgwood (Labour) supported Grenfell's demand that Evans be made to pay the costs involved in his 'wild-cat expedition'.[13] Malcolm MacDonald, the Parliamentary Under-Secretary in the Dominions Office, admitted that Evans had undertaken the expedition on his own authority but assured the House that as Acting High Commissioner he had the full discretion to do so.[14] He said that the £4,000, which Captain Crookshank (Conservative) suggested had been smuggled into the House as an item of expenditure,[15] was needed to pay for the cost of the railway transport of the naval party through the Union and in the Protectorate.[16]

Evans seems to have been little scarred by the attacks of politicians and journalists. His career was not held back in any way: he was made a Knight Commander of the Order of the Bath in the New Year's Honours in 1935, promoted to full Admiral and after the Second World War made a Peer by the Labour Government. On the other hand, the Dominions Office, after its experience his brief spell as acting High Commissioner, decided never again to have the Commander-in-Chief of the Africa Station assume duties as High Commissioner. Thereafter the senior civilian official in the High Commission took over whenever the High Commissioner went on leave. As far as Evans himself was concerned, he had no regrets about his actions. In his autobiography, *My Life,* published in 1946, he recorded that both the South African Minister of Defence and another Cabinet Minister had 'sent telegrams of appreciation and pointed out that had not decisive action been taken they could not say what repercussions Tschekedi's [sic] action in beating up a white man would have had amongst the natives, who were getting very much above themselves and threatening trouble on the mines and in other parts of South Africa.'[17]

Evans was also proud that he had established a precedent for taking imperial troops across the Union,[18] but in fact this caused some heart searching in the South African press and within the South African Government itself. The *Natal Mercury*[19] and the Bloemfontein *Friend* both raised the question as to whether Evans's expedition had violated the Union's sovereignty. In the words of the latter, 'As the Protectorate is outside the Union's political borders and the Union Government has no jurisdiction in Bechuanaland, the passage of the contingent through the Union raises the question of this country's neutrality in a concrete form.

'It must be assumed that the Union Government has, in some way or other, sanctioned the facilities for the dispatch of the naval brigade to the Protectorate. If this permission, however, has not been obtained, the omission would be tantamount to a positive breach of the Union's national rights.'[20]

As it was, Oswald Pirow's eagerness to help Evans was questioned by Dr Bodenstein of the South African Prime Minister's Office in interviews with both Eales and Liesching. Apparently Pirow had failed to inform the Prime Minister, General Hertzog, that he had given permission for Evans's Royal Navy detachment to cross Union territory on its way to Serowe. Eales assured Bodenstein that Evans had been fully aware of the constitutional implications of his action, and that was why he had written to Pirow immediately after their interview on 9 September to confirm that 'the Union Government would have no objection to the transporting of a Naval armed escort from Simonstown to Mafeking.' According to Eales, Bodenstein took the view that 'the Minister of External Affairs rather than the Minister of Railways would have been the appropriate channel of approach in a matter of this kind, and when I mentioned that Mr. Pirow was also Minister of Defence he smilingly admitted that he did not know that.'[21] Although Bodenstein told Liesching a couple of days later that his anxieties had been 'inspired by the prospects of questions in the Union House of Assembly' (not actually in session at the time) Bodenstein in fact seems only to have raised the matter with the two British officials to make a point. As Liesching wrote to the Secretary of State while Evans was away in Serowe suspending Tshekedi, 'These conversations . . . appear to me to illustrate so well the customary readiness of this self-conscious Government to co-operate in a practical matter of this kind, coupled with their inveterate disposition to try to discover and exploit any opportunity of saying their autonomy had been infringed. On this occasion they fell into the error of betraying their suspicions before verifying their facts.'[22] There the matter rested, with Hertzog having indicated from the beginning that he was quite satisfied with the explanation of what had happened.[23]

If nothing else, then, Evans had succeeded in raising the delicate matter of the sovereignty of South Africa, which of all the Dominions was the most sensitive on the issue.

The man whose fortunes suffered most as a result of the fiasco over the 'flogging' of Phinehas McIntosh was Rey himself. As one of his officials later wrote, 'Rey's career was wrecked'[24] by it, though Rey never admitted this even in his diaries, which continued to record his victories in pushing through his beloved Proclamations. In truth, although they were finally promulgated a year and three months after Tshekedi's suspension, it was an uphill battle all the way to get them approved by the High Commissioner and the Dominions Office, and an even greater one to get them into effective operation, especially in Gamangwato.

Tshekedi returned from his short exile as determined as ever to prevent the passage of Rey's Proclamations. His offensive consisted of a lengthy petition against the Proclamations addressed to the High Commissioner, Sir Herbert Stanley, followed up by a request that he and two fellow Chiefs visit him to explain in detail their objections to the impending administrative reforms. When finally these were promulgated on 4 January 1935, Tshekedi tried to lobby the new High Commissioner, Sir William Clark, whom he found as unsympathetic as his predecessor. Undaunted, he drew up a Petition against the Proclamations which he sent to the King in May. Meanwhile he resolutely refused to implement the Proclamations in his own territory.

In August Tshekedi was informed that his Petition had been disallowed and that he would now have to comply with the Proclamations and name members of his Council. He delayed doing so until it became clear that if he did not he would be deposed. And then when he did supply the list of his councillors it was one which, as Colonel Rey put it, 'left out most of the important men and put in mostly duds'.[25]

As a final delaying tactic, at the end of November Tshekedi took the High Commissioner to court on the grounds that the Proclamations did not respect Native Law and Custom. This effectively put the Proclamations into abeyance until judgement was delivered almost exactly twelve months later at the end of November 1936. Personally, Rey was nervous about the verdict because the judge seemed 'to favour the view that our Proclamations do not respect native law and custom and that they ought to.'[26]

The outcome of the case turned not on this issue but on whether the Crown under the Foreign Jurisdiction Act of 1890 had 'unfettered and unlimited power to legislate for the government of and administration of justice among the native tribes in the Bechuanaland Protectorate and [whether] this power is not limited by Treaty or Agreement.' The judge referred this issue for a ruling to the Dominions Secretary in London—now Malcolm MacDonald—who confirmed that the British Government did indeed have unlimited power.[27] On that basis Tshekedi and Bathoen lost their case, though in awarding costs against them the judge did exempt them from the costs of the days the Administration spent trying to prove that the Proclamations were not contrary to Native Law and Custom. Judge Watermeyer clearly agreed with Tshekedi and Bathoen that they were.[28]

For Rey this was 'my greatest triumph! The Judge has delivered his judgement in the Tshekedi case, and *we win on all points, with costs*. I am immensely bucked and everyone is fearfully pleased and excited. The papers have great headlines.

'What a fight—nearly six years of argument, and now I am justified. My Proclamations stand, and Tshekedi is defeated.'[29]

But the triumph was a very hollow one. Rey left Mafeking on retirement seven months later without having seen Tshekedi implement his Proclamations in anything but name. Rey had made the mistake of letting his personal feelings about Tshekedi intervene in his official dealings with him. As Mr Justice Isaacs recalled, when he was acting as junior counsel for the Government in Tshekedi's case against the High Commissioner, it was clear that Rey hated Tshekedi, while the young Chief barely concealed his contempt for Rey.[30] Charles Arden-Clarke, who succeeded Rey as Resident Commissioner, recognised not only that the Proclamations were unworkable but that much of Rey's troubles had come from his poor personal relations with the Chiefs, in particular Tshekedi.

Arden-Clarke, who had Nigerian experience, set about revising the Proclamations. Instead of imposing them on Tshekedi and his fellow chiefs from above, he co-opted them into helping him draft them. Tshekedi himself was to play a leading role in the discussions of the new Proclamations, which retained the *kgotla* as the central feature of the system of 'native' administration and was shorn of all the objectionable features of the Rey Proclamations. As Tshekedi told the audience assembled in 1943 to celebrate the new Proclamations, 'This may not be the proper place for doing it, but I wish to express our gratitude for the Proclamations recently promulgated. I still dislike the Proclamations promulgated in 1934, but in the case of these new Proclamations even if others oppose them, I will fight those people tooth and nail in the same manner in which I fought Government regarding the Proclamations of 1934.'[31]

Rey left Mafeking on Tuesday, 15 June to settle among 'the Dutch in the Cape Colony' rather than in a Britain which he felt had failed to recognise the worth of his services and had blocked so many of his initiatives.[32] Though he professed to shun honours, he was bitter that he had not been awarded a knighthood or given any other recognition of his seven hard years as Resident Commissioner.[33] Eventually he was made a mere Knight Bachelor six months after he had left his territory, rather than being awarded the more customary and more prestigious Knight Commander of the Order of St. Michael and St. George, which had been given to several of his predecessors as Resident Commissioner.[34] He himself counted his tour of service a success and quoted in his diary a letter from the man who appointed him Resident Commissioner, Leopold Amery: 'You have done a very fine piece of work, under very adverse conditions, which should have a permanent effect not only on the Bechuanas but also on the general problem of native policy in South Africa.'[35] Indeed, Rey, for all his idiosyncrasies and his difficult relations with the Chiefs of the Bechuanaland Protectorate, will be remembered as the only Resident Commissioner who really did anything to promote its internal development.

But the Johannesburg *Star* was probably more accurate in its assessment of his tenure of office when at the time of Tshekedi's case against the High Commissioner it wrote: 'It is possible to argue with some force that Tshekedi is becoming too fond of litigation. On the other hand he has had a very unfortunate experience of what British Administration can mean. It speaks volumes for his distrust of the Union and for his loyalty to the Throne that, in spite of all that he has suffered, he should still be anxious to remain under direct British protection.

'After the fiasco of Tshekedi's deposition and reinstatement, many South African observers assumed that, after a decent interval, the authorities concerned would transfer the present Resident Commissioner. He has had a distinguished career in Abyssinia and elsewhere, and there is no suggestion that he is incapable, but it is clear that between him and the head of the Bamangwato people exists an incompatibility of temperament such as would, in most countries, be adequate grounds for a divorce. As Tshekedi and his people cannot very well be moved, it seems not unreasonable to suggest a change of Resident Commissioners would improve the situation. The impression which one has is that a state of exasperation exists in official quarters as far as Tshekedi is concerned, and yet he is doing no more than defend what he conceives to be the long-standing rights of his people and of his young ward. The whole situation in the Bechuanaland Protectorate would be improved if it were possible to appoint a Resident Commissioner in whom both Tshekedi and the Union had confidence. I repeat that this is in no way a reflection on the present Resident Commissioner, who would doubtless do excellent service in another area where there was no heritage of past prejudice to contend with.'[36]

What is clear from the struggle between Tshekedi and Rey over the Proclamations is that Tshekedi continued to call the tune. Indeed, throughout the whole McIntosh saga and its aftermath it was around Tshekedi that events revolved, and for much of the time it was he who determined their direction. That he was able to do this was in part due to his resilience and fearlessness. In part it was due to his deep resentment of the way he had been treated by the Administration which drove him to defeat Rey at all costs. But above all it was due to his knowledge of the workings of Britain's imperial system. The reasons for this lie largely in his own intellect. Although he had had to leave Fort Hare before he had matriculated, his education did not end there. He read deeply—if not widely—on matters to do with his office as a Chief under Indirect Rule. Fortunately much of his personal library survives to this day, as well as copies of his orders to booksellers. When Margery Perham visited him in Serowe in 1929, she was impressed by 'his considerable library. He has a good collection of *Africana,* including the blue-books and official reports which he needs so much if he is to understand the complex dangers which threaten the status of his country.'[37] Tshekedi bought anything he could to do with the history and culture of the peoples of Africa. He knew more about the doctrines of Indirect Rule than either Rey or Sir Herbert Stanley and used this knowledge as a weapon against them in his struggle over the Proclamations. In January 1934 he sent the High Commissioner a twelve-page document comparing the Proclamations section by section with the South African Native Administration Proclamation No. 38 of 1927 and the prescriptions of the high priests of Indirect Rule, Lugard and Cameron. By a carefully selective use of the works of these two proconsuls, he made out a strong case that Rey's Proclamations were almost the same as those of South Africa and deviated in important ways from Indirect Rule as practised in other British African territories.[38]

Indeed, so involved did Tshekedi become in the current debate about Indirect Rule that in 1936 he made his own contribution to it in the *Journal of the Royal African Society* in a reply to an article by Professor Victor Murray.[39] Showing an impressive familiarity with the literature on Indirect Rule, Tshekedi defended the institution of African chieftaincy, attacked the system of legislation by Proclamation in which the black community had no say, and criticized 'the tendency for the protecting power to gradually assume the responsibility for the administration of the protected territory not only externally but internally as well, until the Native community in the end finds that even the internal administration is carried on not in its name but in that of the protecting power. It is difficult to convince an African that this is in effect a strengthening of his political freedom.'[40] The burden of his article was a thinly veiled critique of the relationship between the Administration of the Bechuanaland Protectorate and the Chiefs through whom it sought to rule. The underlying refrain was that no finality was ever reached in the solving of administrative problems concerning Africans, because—in the words of Robert Russa Moton, whom he quoted—'the chief factor in the problem—the Negro himself—has had no place at the council table when adjustments were made.'[41]

The article in the *Journal of the Royal African Society* was not only unique as a scholarly contribution by an African chief to the on-going discussions about the principles of 'native' administration led by such luminaries as Margery Perham, W. M. Macmillan and Leonard Barnes, it also demonstrates Tshekedi's powerful though narrowly focussed intellect which sadly was deprived of the full university education he was determined his ward, Seretse, should have. Tshekedi coupled this intellect with a dynamic personality and very considerable charm. Those who became his friends seem to have succumbed completely to his winning smile, his articulate conversation, and his intense, almost manic, enthusiasm for whatever he was doing. He may have had prejudices about inter-racial sexual relations, but he had no other reservations about friendships with whites, and among his closest and most trusted friends were his lawyer, Buchanan, and his missionary, Jennings. Among the Bangwato, only Peter Sebina, his secretary, enjoyed a similar relationship with him.

Tshekedi was at ease in a European world; he had the education, culture and position of authority to deal on equal terms with white men of whatever class. He lived in a European-style house which was more elegantly furnished that most of those lived in by the local white residents. Apart from the doctor's house, only his had running water for the lavatory and bath.

But Tshekedi was in no way a man divorced from his own culture. This is clear from the fact that during the crisis he was ultimately secure amongst his own people and was able to manipulate and control his own turbulent polity. Here he had an initial advantage. By the law of primogeniture he was the rightful occupant of the Regency until Seretse came of age. Only in the most dire circumstances would the people try to rid themselves of him. When he was under threat from the British Administration, even his erstwhile enemies rallied round him. Thus Simon Ratshosa supported him during the McIntosh crisis, though he did have a special interest in doing so: he needed Tshekedi's consent if ever he were to succeed in an appeal to the Administration to be allowed to return to Serowe.[42] Support for

16. General view of Serowe, showing Tshekedi's house on the right (*Illustrated London News*).

Tshekedi in his time of crisis might be the occasion for reconciliation. But that support earned him no pardon. Tshekedi himself was sceptical about the sincerity of Simon's sudden conversion. As he wrote to him in November in reply to his earlier letter of support,[43] 'Now nephew, I believe in talking out my mind when I do talk, and I should like to take this opportunity to express to you that you yourself and some others have been greatly instrumental in driving the Administration to propose legislation upon the status of the Protectorate on the lines they have done. There is a firm belief in the minds of our officials that the young Chiefs of today have enormous autocratic powers which they use to better themselves and not their Tribes. I know how this belief gained currency. . . .' Tshekedi then went on to attack Simon for the way in which he had advised the Ballingers and which had resulted in 'the serious errors which they make in their publications.'[44]

Tshekedi was correct in his assessment of his nephew's sincerity. Only a few days before the 'flogging', Simon had written to Rey reporting a 'secret' meeting between Tshekedi and other Chiefs in which an attempt had been made to organise a common front againt the Proclamations.[45] And less than three weeks after Tshekedi's reinstatement Simon wrote a long letter to the Government Secretary trying to explain away the telegram of support he sent to Tshekedi during the crisis.[46] Then after Tshekedi's 'defeat' in his case against the High Commissioner, Simon wrote Rey a letter of congratulation. In it he welcomed 'the beginning of a new era in Native Administration.' Had the Councils and the Tribunals been abolished, it would have given 'Tshekedi what he wants to act alone with favourites he chooses and will have to go so far to bluff the Administration and jeopardise the very fabric of your great thoughts and intentions aiming to restore order and peace which is the life and standards of native people concerned. I make bold to say during your five years of administration you have no comparable rival among your predecessors to understand the native question.'[47]

Another subject exiled by Tshekedi, Moanaphuti Segolodi, like Simon wrote to congratulate Tshekedi on his restoration and assured him that he would be there to 'defend him if the need arises'.[48] Yet only a month before, Moanaphuti had written to Miss Hodgson that as a result of his suspension from office and exile to Francistown Tshekedi was 'now living to learn humility.'[49] But this was not a lesson Tshekedi learnt, and once he was back in power, resentment of his high-handed ways by the élite and faction fighting within the royal family resumed as though nothing had been changed by the recent crisis.

As far as the British Administration was concerned, Tshekedi co-operated happily with them once Rey had left. He got on famously with Charles Arden-Clarke, Rey's successor as Resident Commissioner, who treated him as an equal, and consulted him closely about all major issues affecting Tshekedi's Reserve and the Protectorate as a whole. But as far as his experiences in 1933 were concerned,

Tshekedi 'never forgot or forgave Rey and Potts and in fact the B.P. Administration for the the humiliation of expulsion and banishment. Those were bitter days for him.'[50] It was a bitterness that lingered on. When Tshekedi read the highly tendentious account of his suspension and reinstatement published in 1946 in the autobiography of Admiral Evans—by then Lord Mountevans—he wanted to take legal proceedings against him. In the end he contented himself with bringing to the attention of the High Commissioner his complaints against what he considered a 'travesty of the facts'.[51] Tshekedi remained unrepentant about his trial of McIntosh. In his account Evans had asserted that Tshekedi had declared that 'he realised that he had no right to order a white man to be flogged.' On the contrary, Tshekedi insisted, the 'Chief had every right and never declared that he had no such right.'[52] Four years later Tshekedi had been so incensed by a related article in the *Empire News* that he considered suing its publishers, Kemsley Newspapers. He was advised against this by Dingle Foot, the distinguished British lawyer and champion of colonial peoples, who considered that it would create 'an unfavourable impression in the public mind'[53] at a juncture when Tshekedi, himself now in exile as a result of the Seretse marriage crisis, needed all the support he could get in Britain.[54] In accepting Foot's advice Tshekedi informed his London solicitor, Graham Page, that he intended attacking Evans 'at some future date when I write my experiences of British Administration in Bechuanaland'.[55] Tshekedi was a man who never forgot an injury, and rarely forgave those he considered had turned against him.

This unattractive side of his character was nowhere more forcefully brought out than in the victimisation of Mahloane, who had interpreted Admiral Evans's speech on the occasion of Tshekedi's suspension. Tshekedi denied that he had been responsible for withdrawing the interpreter's rights to graze cattle in the Reserve and ordering him to make arrangements for his own ploughing on the grounds that he was not a Mongwato. But the denial seems a little hollow in that Tshekedi kept a close watch on all that took place in his capital, and Thankane, the secretary, who gave the instructions, would hardly have dared do so without his Chief's sanction. The Administration was convinced the interpreter was being subjected to disabilities because he had been a party to Tshekedi's humiliation, although he was merely fulfilling his duties as an employee of the Protectorate Administration. Potts considered 'these actions are not those of a chief but a petty tyrant'.[56] The problem was settled by Mahloane's transfer to Mafeking.

That Tshekedi's bitterness was directed specifically against the local British Administration and its representatives was made clear by his reception of H. R. H. Prince George, Duke of Kent, who visited the Bechuanaland Protectorate seven months after his reinstatement. Frew, the Reuter's correspondent who had done so much to publicise Tshekedi's plight over the 'flogging' of McIntosh to the outside world, accompanied Prince George on his tour of Africa, about which he wrote a book. Nothing, he noted, could 'have been more exactly correct than Tshekedi Khama's demeanour in the presence of the Prince, and his well-expressed affirmation of loyalty.' Frew believed that a better atmosphere prevailed in relations between Chiefs and Administration at the time of the Prince's visit, and that Tshekedi was 'anxious to show once more to the best of his ability his never doubted and unswerving loyalty to the Throne.' At the reception for the Prince at Gaberones, Tshekedi, dressed in a dark grey suit, white shirt and light-grey hat, made an address to the Prince in which he alluded to the earlier visit of his elder brother, the Prince of Wales. He told him that these visits of the the great grandsons of 'the never-to-be-forgotten Queen Victoria' were greatly appreciated. Never one to miss the political opportunity provided by the presence of the press corps, he then asked that the arrangements the Queen had made with his father and other chiefs for British Protection should be prolonged.[57] Despite all his difficulties with the British Administration, continuation of British Protection was infinitely preferable to incorporation in South Africa. Tshekedi then presented the Prince with karosses and a skin inscribed with an appliqued loyal message.[58] In 1936, just

17. Tshekedi (left) holds up his loyal address to the Duke of Kent (BBC Hulton Picture Library).

after he had initiated his action against the High Commissioner, Tshekedi was married in a ceremony conducted before a huge Union Jack at his own 'special request'.[59]

However ambivalent Tshekedi's relationship as between British Crown and British Administration may have been, during his crisis with the latter he certainly succeeded triumphantly in achieving his goal of bringing the Bechuanaland Protectorate into the limelight. For a good month after the news of the 'flogging' was broken to the press, his country was headline news in British and South African papers. Large numbers of editorials were written about the administration of the Protectorate, letters were sent to the editors of papers and magazines in support— though sometimes critical—of Tshekedi. One of the most obscure corners of the British Empire was brought into the homes of Britons and South Africans who normally did not concern themselves with events in their colonial dependencies or neighbouring African territories. No other colonial 'event' in the 1930s gained such attention as did the expedition by Evans into the Kalahari. The whole episode was of the stuff on which journalists thrive.

Not all the news published in the British and South African press was sensational—though much of it did focus on flogging, inter-racial sexual relations and

18. The huge Union Jack used at Tshekedi's wedding (*Illustrated London News*).

martial movements in the desert. A good deal of the newspaper comment was thoughtful, raising issues that were to become the currency of the colonial debate after the Second World War. Readers were invited to consider the justice of accusing, trying and condemning an educated African Chief who was denied counsel but nevertheless defended himself with skill and vigour. British readers were made aware that even the South African press, not normally sympathetic to 'native' causes, had almost unanimously condemned the British Administration for failing to accord Tshekedi 'due process' of law. Though, as Sir Alan Pim wrote to his brother Howard in South Africa, 'it would be interesting to know what the Dutch [Afrikaans] papers would have said if nothing at all had been done. The method actually adopted gives anyone an occasion to blaspheme'.[60] Readers had been presented with the spectacle of a senior British officer sending a substantial and expensive naval expedition a thousand miles into the interior of Africa to suppress a non-existent revolt led by a Chief who throughout the affair comported himself with dignity and discretion. As they read their papers at the breakfast table, on the train or in their sitting rooms, they were forced to consider questions of racial prejudice, racial justice, and racial equality. The missionary propagandists like Chirgwin made sure that the image of Tshekedi projected on the pages of their newspapers was not that perceived by Simon Ratshosa or K. T. Motsete, but of a modest, hard-working Christian Chief, who had nothing but the interests of his people at heart. In this context his removal from office appeared all the more unjust. And in a Britain which still disapproved of extra-marital sexual relationships, let alone with people of other races, many readers agreed that Tshekedi gave McIntosh no more than he deserved. William Lunn, MP, summed up their attitude in a speech to the Labour Conference in October. After praising Tshekedi—'A more intelligent man I have never met'—he told delegates: 'We are supposed to be a Christian country. It is a native who has had to tell us how to apply Christianity in dealing with two Christians who are white men, not, perhaps, as severely as some of us would have dealt with them.'[61]

Naturally the whole episode appealed to the prurient interests of both British and South African readers, and the popular press spared few details about the exploits of McIntosh and McNamee, reproducing photographs of the hut in which they carried on their affairs. In some sense the incident had the same press appeal as cases in the 1980s where British nurses are sentenced to flogging in a Saudi court or a British drug peddler is to be executed in a Malaysian jail. White people seem to be more horrified at the idea of physical violence administered on their own people by other races than by their own kind.

Most important of all, the incident raised the whole question of the colonial relationship in the British press, Parliament, and public opinion. In the Britain of the 1930s there was growing lack of confidence in the imperial mission, an increasing questioning of its purpose and achievements. The Bechuanaland Protectorate projected on to the pages of the press in the months of September and October 1933 presented a picture of sorry neglect, lack of development, poverty and incompetence. This image was not just one of sensationalism but had recently been brought to the attention of Parliament[62] by the scholarly report on the Bechuanaland Protectorate by Sir Alan Pim.[63] In it he drew a grim picture of a disastrous economic situation in which water shortage was chronic, much of the population was disease ridden, locked in poverty, and in many places half-starved, with the most able-bodied leaving to seek work in the Union. The territory was bankrupt, and both blacks and whites shared in the 'common calamity'. Among Pim's recommendations was a restructuring of native administration in the Protectorate; reflecting Rey's views, he believed that the Chiefs were too powerful and resistant to the reforms that were necessary to development. But if his report was antipathetic to Tshekedi's position, it was a devastating indictment of the British Government for its neglect of the Protectorate.

While the 'flogging' incident had also succeeed in drawing the attention of the British public and Parliament to what Tshekedi saw as the dreadful state of affairs in the Protectorate, on the vital issue of the Proclamations he did not have the running all the time. Experts on colonial affairs like Margery Perham, the Ballingers, Lionel Curtis, Leonard Barnes and W. M. Macmillan all had their say. If they were critical of the relationship that had existed between the Administration and Tshekedi, like Pim they nearly all advocated reform of the system of Indirect Rule in the direction of reducing the powers of the Chiefs and introducing a more democratic element into 'native' administration. They tended to accept that Tshekedi was indeed autocratic in his behaviour, and it took a great deal of effort by his supporters in the Anti-Slavery Society and the LMS to put his side of the case that the 'democratic' institution that did exist in the Tswana states—the *kgotla*—was the one that was in jeopardy from Rey's Proclamations. Certainly the whole Bechuanaland affair spurred the debate about Indirect Rule as the most appropriate means of administration in Africa.

A number of writers believed, like J. H. Driberg, that 'one of the grave dangers of what is known as "indirect rule" ' was that the 'salutary checks on autocracy which all native constitutions imposed have been largely abrogated.'[64] This increasingly became the focus of criticism of Indirect Rule by both educated Africans and British liberals over the next decade. But even a radical critic like Leonard Barnes believed in the long-term desirability of African development on the basis of the 'native' authorities, and he expressed the hope that Rey's Proclamations would not stifle the growth of native institutions 'beneath the weight of white officialdom.'[65] A more radical view, which became more fashionable in the 1960s, was expressed by Professor Victor Murray, who believed that the 'Bechuanaland incident has shown that indirect rule is simply direct rule with a temporary delegation of powers to the native authority. Those powers can apparently be resumed by the suzerain without any formal declaration at all and without even the sanction of the authorities in London. . . . It is all very well so long as the native ruler has no opinions of his own which conflict with those of the man on the spot and as long as he collects the taxes without obvious corruption and spends his allotted share of the revenue in ways which the suzerain power approves.'[66]

Perhaps the most original contribution to the debate—but one which was completely ignored because it was too unorthodox—was that of Tshekedi himself whereby he advocated the establishment of a formal contractual relationship between the protecting power and those protected.[67] The whole crisis over the 'flogging' of Phinehas McIntosh would have been avoided if there really had been a Treaty between the Bangwato and the British in which the respective powers, duties and obligations of each party were clearly spelt out. Even if Tshekedi did not have formal jurisdiction in his court over white men, in practice he and his father had settled cases in which whites were involved, as the Rev. Haydon Lewis recalled. Certainly such anomalies as that cited so tellingly by Norman Leys, the Kenyan doctor and colonial critic, would not have occurred if there had been a formal contractual relationship between ruler and ruled: while, Leys noted sourly, the British at the League of Nations in Geneva could contrast the Nazi racial thesis with 'the British principle of equality of rights before the law for men and women of every race, creed and colour', the 'same voice' tells us that Tshekedi had 'apologised for having allowed a white man to be tried in a black man's court.'[68]

The debate was carried on not just in the press and in the pages of learned journals. The assiduous Buchanan used every connexion he had with the British establishment to plead Tshekedi's cause. Through a friend at the University of Cape Town he obtained an introduction to Reginald Coupland, the Beit Professor of Colonial History at Oxford. Through Professor Manning of the London School of Economics, Buchanan arranged to spend a weekend in Oxford, where he was entertained by the Warden of All Souls, the Principal of St Edmund's Hall and the Dean of University College. Among those he met and with whom he discussed Tshekedi's case were W. M. Macmillan, Arthur Goodhart, and Professor Coupland himself. The last was about to leave for Nigeria to stay with the Governor, Sir Donald Cameron, and intended 'together with him to go fully into the question of Indirect Rule in the Protectorates under the Sovereignty of Great Britain.'[69]

In the groves of academe at Oxford, conversation turned on the administrative and constitutional aspects of Tshekedi's case. But in South Africa the racial implications of the Bechuanaland crisis were all the more relevant in the context of recent political developments in the country. The formation by Hertzog of the Fusion Government with Smuts was to give him at long last the necessary majority in Parliament to enable him to remove the few blacks in the Cape Province who did have the vote from the common roll. In a society in which the majority of white inhabitants believed in the social segregation of the races, McIntosh's 'crime' was a shocking one. Against this had to be balanced the 'crime' of Tshekedi, a black, albeit a Chief, taking the law into his own hands and trying and sentencing a white man in his court. Although McIntosh's 'crime' was more heinous than Tshekedi's, those who did condone Tshekedi's action did so as an expedient rather than on principle. It was certainly not an act they would tolerate on the part of a Chief within their own borders. Furthermore, the Protectorate was seen as a future part of the Union, so that there was no way in which South Africa would have tolerated the independence of spirit and action of a Tshekedi in one of their Chiefs, a fact he well appreciated. Nevertheless, the reaction of the South African press to the means by which the British sought to bring Tshekedi to heel was almost universally critical. Of course, while some of this was inspired by righteous indignation, a strong element of crowing informed it. The incompetence of the British in Bechuanaland was yet another argument for a South African takeover of its administration.

What was perhaps most surprising about the whole affair was the way it brought together a group of white 'liberals' in southern Africa and Britain to fight Tshekedi's cause. For some, like Eleanor Hull, it was 'the most disgraceful case I have heard of since the treatment of the Irish Chiefs in the 15–16 centuries, and is on all fours with that.'[70] While few were quite so melodramatic in their perception of the events of 1933, such accounts did produce a wave of sympathy among whites for this 'persecuted' African chief that was unique in the annals of British colonialism in Africa in the 1930s. As far as these 'liberals' were concerned, their enthusiasm owed as much to the personality and inspiration of the man on whose behalf they were campaigning as to the cause they were fighting. It was a signal achievement of Tshekedi that he was able to enlist so fervent a group of supporters not only on this occasion but also in the succeeding years in his fight against incorporation, in his struggle to prevent Smuts making South West Africa a fifth province of the Union, and, after his exile in the aftermath of the crisis, over Seretse's marriage, in his efforts to return to Gamangwato and have his political rights restored.

For many in the wider black community Tshekedi became a symbol of the black man fighting successfully against colonial injustice. In Gamangwato, as we have seen, his people backed him in his hour of need. In the Bechuanaland Protectorate itself he emerged from the struggle as the single most important black political figure, around whom the other Chiefs rallied in any future struggle with the British Administration. Beyond its borders in South Africa, where room for political manoeuvre was becoming progressively narrower for blacks, he was a symbol of what a fellow black could achieve in a confrontation with the white man. Thus a body calling itself the Independent African National Congress in Cape Town sent a memorial to Tshekedi accusing Evans of being 'ruled by emotions of colour prejudice' and expressing admiration for Tshekedi's action.[71] In Cape Town six hundred Coloureds packed the City Hall to demonstrate their disapproval of Britain's action against Tshekedi. 'Heated speeches were made by coloured orators, who contended that there was one law for the black, and another for the white in South Africa.' Tshekedi himself was in Cape Town at the time of the demonstration but went to considerable pains to disclaim any knowledge of it.[72] Earlier Buchanan had gone out of his way to ensure that the High Commissioner realised that Tshekedi would not be 'a party to any public meeting or demonstration in Cape Town'.[73] While Tshekedi was sympathetic with the aims of black nationalists in South Africa, he steered clear of any direct political involvement with them, fearing that such involvement would openly provoke the South Africans into demanding the takeover of his territory. Thus it was his lawyer, Buchanan, not the High Commission, who initiated the idea that Tshekedi should be taken off the train at Bellville to avoid involvement in any demonstration on his behalf when he arrived in Cape Town to discuss his reinstatement with Evans.[74] Tshekedi received a number of letters of support from black South Africans as well as Batswana working in South Africa. One group of Bangwato labourers on the Randfontein Estates in the Transvaal collected £2 as a donation for the Chief to enable him to buy water containers to use while he was in exile.[75]

For the League of Coloured People in London Tshekedi became a symbol in the struggle against racial injustice. As its President, Harold Moody, told the annual meeting of the LMS and Colonial Missionary Society at Nottingham, 'The intelligentsia of my race are watching the affair very keenly. Among the members of the League are men who are going to be chiefs and princes in their own country.'[76] Earlier Moody had written to Tshekedi on behalf of the League to say that they felt he had added 'lusture [sic] to our race' and to say that should he come to London the League would welcome him at a public dinner in his honour.[77]

Five years later, on a visit to South Africa, Eslanda Goode Robeson, wife of the great singer, found that the events of 1933 were still vividly remembered by black friends with whom she stayed. Tshekedi's actions then, and his subsequent suit against the High Commissioner, had made him 'a legend among Negroes who know about him'.[78]

Surprisingly, Tshekedi's suspension and reinstatement evoked almost no comment from the vigorous black-owned press in West Africa. Those papers that did carry news about the 'flogging' and its aftermath relied on Reuter despatches, while their editorials at the time were concerned with purely domestic issues.[79] This lack of interest from the most active group of African politicians of the day was more than compensated for by the wide range of sympathy and support Tshekedi gained from people, white and black, in other countries—Canada, Northern Rhodesia, Southern Rhodesia, South Africa, Ireland and far-off Australia, from where the Rev. S. C. Wiserman of Bingara wrote to him: 'All Christian people rejoice at the stand you took about McIntosh. We sorrowed at the foolishness of Evans, so like the English, they bully us Australians too.'[80]

But the situation, as we have seen, was much more complex than the view from Bingara. While some Englishmen bullied Tshekedi, many more came to his aid. Although the blacks of Gamangwato were technically junior partners in the imperial enterprise, they not only manipulated whites to their advantage but also, in the case of Tshekedi himself, managed to dominate them and have a dominant influence on the outcome of events. In his famous *Analysis of a Social Situation in Modern Zululand*,[81] written about the ceremonies surrounding the opening of a new bridge in the Mahlabatani District, Max Gluckman insisted that the existence of a single black-white community in Zululand should be the starting point for his analysis.[82] So, too, has it been in this study of the crisis of 1933 in Gamangwato, with the difference that, unlike Zululand, there was not a schism between the two colour groups. In Serowe, whites lived next door to blacks, at times attended the same church services, depended on the Chief for their livelihood, and in many cases had sexual relationships with Bangwato women, which, though frowned on, were much more commonplace and sometimes open than the cases of McIntosh and McNamee taken in isolation would suggest. Their children sometimes attended the same school as the Bangwato. So, for the short period he attended Mrs Clark's private school, Tshekedi sat in a classroom next to the one in which a young white boy called Phinehas McIntosh was studying.[83] The white residents of Serowe had social relations with the Chief and some of the more important headmen, even if these were limited and very formal. Thus Mrs Pretorius and her husband, a blacksmith, were used to being visited socially by Sekgoma II. Tshekedi by contrast did not visit them very often and then mainly on business. But Mrs Pretorius got to know his family well, and Tshekedi's sister, Bonyerile, would come and visit her when she was ill; to this day she treasures a vase Bonyerile later gave her. Mrs Pretorius recalls with pride that she made the wedding dress for Tshekedi's first wife and helped at funerals for which she made the wreaths.[84]

Gluckman's assessment of the relationship between black and white in Zululand, therefore, did not obtain in Gamangwato. He concluded that in Zululand 'the dominant form of the [social] structure is the existence within a single community of two co-operating colour-groups which are differentiated by a large number of criteria so as to stand as opposed and even hostile to one another. The White group is dominant over the Zulu group in all the activities in which they co-operate, and this dominance is expressed in some social institutions, while all institutions are affected by it.'[85] On no occasion was the difference between Gamangwato and Zululand in the matter of relations between the two communities more dramatically demonstrated than when the white community went to commiserate with 'their Chief' over what their white officials had done by suspending him from office. In seating the white community at the ceremonial suspension, Rey and the Resident Magistrate had tried to emphasize the separation of the two communities; the whites by their action breached this divide to express the real nature of relations between black and white in Gamangwato.

The whole episode surrounding the 'flogging' of Phinehas was full of such ironies and ambiguities, which are the more important since they concern a central event in Botswana's history. The main myth, echoed often to this day, is that the Bangwato themselves had to dig Admiral Evans's guns out of the sand. It gained currency almost from the day of the 'invasion'. Lord Lugard had heard the rumour as early as November 1933. He wrote to Colonel Rey in reply to his letter soliciting his support that 'it looked as though Admiral Evans's escort was, to say the least, unnecessarily large, and the fact that the guns etc. stuck in the sand and had to be dragged by the very people against whom they were supposed to be taken gave an appearance of farce.'[86] Rey vigorously denied the rumour: 'The guns did *not* stick in the sand and they were *not* dragged out by the people. I do not know who was responsible for this grotesque travesty of the facts but they certainly ought to be pilloried for it.'[87] None of the reporters present on the day of the suspension seems to have recorded what would have been so delicious an item for the consumption of their readers. Neither Tshekedi nor Buchanan made use of it, which they surely would if it had indeed happened. And yet the rumour can be picked up as far away as Australia, and some of the marines who settled in Cape Town after their tour of duty in Simonstown regaled one official of the Bechuanaland Protectorate service with it. For them it was fact, not fiction.[88] True or false, it is only one of the myths that have grown up in Gamangwato about the day the Navy arrived in Serowe. Some believe that, but for Tshekedi, war would have broken out between the Bangwato and British.[89] One old man recalls that 'some of us wanted war with the whites who were heavily armed with cannons. Although we were bound to be defeated, we could still have inflicted serious casualties on their part.'[90] The event is recalled with contempt for the British, who 'ended by being a laughing stock in the public eye, even in the international community.'[91] For Mr Tomeltso Tom Kgosi, a teacher in Serowe at the time of Tshekedi's deposition, the comforting aspect of the case was that it 'was encouraging on our part to hear white settlers living in Serowe and Palapye ridiculing the Queen's government with the utmost contempt it deserved.'[92]

But perhaps the greatest ambiguity of the whole affair centred on the 'flogging' of Phinehas McIntosh. Though the Commission of Enquiry at Palapye Road held unequivocally that McIntosh had been flogged, the circumstances surrounding his trial and punishment subsequently became increasingly confused as far as the Administration was concerned. When, in February 1934, Sir Herbert Stanley was trying to persuade Tshekedi to accept the replacement of his *kgotla* by a Tribunal which would keep written records of all cases before it, he told him: 'I think you must have something a little more regular than a lot of people coming together and everybody talking at random. There must be some means of a thing being tried properly. There is a dispute now as to whether McIntosh was sentenced or not. Some people say he was sentenced to a flogging, and other people say someone got up in the Court and said he ought to be flogged, and thereupon he was flogged, and no-one knows what happened. There should be no question as to whether a man was sentenced or not sentenced, and no-one seems to know. That kind of procedure must be altered.'

To this Tshekedi replied: 'Mistakes have happened in our Magistrate's Courts.' Stanley rejoined: 'There may have been a miscarriage of justice but there should be no question as to whether a man has been sentenced or not. Any tribunal can make mistakes, but now no-one knows whether a sentence was passed or not. We believe and assume that McIntosh had been sentenced, and some people say that he was sentenced. There ought to be no possibility of doubt. I do not want to discuss the right or wrong of the case, but there seems to be some doubt as to what happened.'

As so often before, Tshekedi had the last word on the matter: 'We are not pleased by the way the Special Court carried on the Enquiry. Had it really conducted the Enquiry as it should, the truth would have come out. I was not given the opportunity of defending myself, and of leading evidence as to what happened. It is for that reason that there is confusion. There should not have been confusion.'[93]

ABBREVIATIONS

BNA	Botswana National Archives
S	Secretariat
DCS	District Commissioner's Office Serowe
DCF	District Commissioner's Office Francistown
BNB	Botswana National Book Collection
BT Adm	Bamangwato Tribal Administration
PRO	Public Record Office, Kew
CO	Colonial Office
DO	Dominions Office
CAB	Cabinet
CWM	Council of World Missions Archives, School of Oriental and African Studies, London
LMS	London Missionary Society
NAZ	National Archives of Zimbabwe
TKP	Tshekedi Khama Papers, Pilikwe
RHL	Rhodes House Library

NOTES

PROLOGUE: REY VERSUS TSHEKEDI

1. TKP, Pilikwe, 72, 'Statement of Rasetompi', in typed document entitled 'The assault [or] a series of assaults which brought matters to a crisis'. This undated document, which includes a number of other statements by Bangwato concerning the activities of Phinehas McIntosh, was clearly one of the many Tshekedi gathered in early October to justify retrospectively his sentence of McIntosh to a flogging. See below, chapter IX.
2. BNA, Gaborone, BNB 174–8, Dominions Office, Printed Papers, 1933: (b), 'Suspension and Reinstatement of Tshekedi Khama, Acting Chief of the Bamangwato', p. 155. Statement taken and sworn before J. D. A. Germond, J.P., 7 September 1933. These papers are also in the PRO, Kew, in the DO 35 452/20283 series. This reference, for instance, is to DO 35 452/20283/74. Enclosure in Despatch No 109, High Commissioner to Dominions Office, 12 September 1933. In this Prologue references are to the Printed Correspondence, as it is easier to follow the sequence of events than in the separate Dominions Office files. Elsewhere in the book reference is made not to the Printed Correspondence but to the relevant Dominions Office file in the PRO.
3. *Ibid.*
4. TKP 72, statement of Ramananeng confirmed by Aleck Jamieson and Mokwati, in 'The assault [or] a series of assaults which brought the matter to a crisis'.
5. *Ibid.*, statement of Kelebetse.
6. *Ibid.*, 'Remarks'.
7. Lt Col. Sir Charles Rey, *'Monarch of all I survey': Bechuanaland Diaries, 1929–37*, ed. Neil Parsons and Michael Crowder (Gaborone: Botswana Society and London: James Currey, 1987) hereinafter Rey, *Diaries*. Entry for Sunday, 20 October to Sunday, 17 November 1929.
8. L. S. Amery, *My Political Life: 'War and Peace' 1914–29* (London: Hutchinson, 1953), p. 415. Whipsnade is a well-known zoological park in England.
9. See Jack Parson, *Botswana: Liberal Democracy and Labour Reserve in Southern Africa* (London: Gower, 1984), pp. 21–26, 33–34.
10. Ronald Hyam, *The Failure of South African Expansion 1908–48* (London: Macmillan, 1972), p. 20.

11. *Ibid.*, p. 109, citing CO 417/705/60080, Secretary of State to High Commissioner. Telegram. 19 January 1925.
12. Cited in Anthony Sillery, *Botswana: A Short Political History* (London: Methuen, 1974), p. 109.
13. See Hyam, *The Failure of South African Expansion,* in particular pp. 119–20
14. Neil Parsons and Michael Crowder, preface to Rey, *Diaries.*
15. José Harris, *William Beveridge: A Biography* (Oxford: Clarendon Press, 1977), p. 156. I am grateful to Roy Hay for drawing my attention to this reference.
16. Cited in *ibid,* p. 188.
17. Parsons and Crowder, introduction to Rey, *Diaries.*
18. Charles F. Rey, *Unconquered Abyssinia as It Is To-day* (London: Seeley, Service & Co., 1923).
19. Charles F. Rey, *In the Country of the Blue Nile* (London: Duckworth, 1927).
20. Indeed, while he was in Mafeking, Rey prepared a new edition of *Unconquered Abyssinia,* which was reissued in 1935 as *The Real Abyssinia* (London: Seeley, Service & Co.).
21. C. F. Rey, *The Romance of the Portuguese in Abyssinia* (London: H. and G. Witherby, 1929).
22. Rey, *In the Country of the Blue Nile,* p. 233.
23. Hyam, *The Failure of South African Expansion,* p. 122.
24. Amery, *My Political Life,* p. 409.
25. Rey, *Diaries.* Entry for Sunday, 20 October to Sunday, 17 November 1929.
26. *Ibid.* Entry for Saturday, 29 and Sunday, 30 November 1929.
27. *Ibid.* Entry for Sunday, 20 October to Sunday, 17 November 1929.
28. *Ibid.*
29. Neil Parsons, 'The Economic History of Khama's Country in Botswana, 1844–1930', in Robin Palmer and Neil Parsons, eds., *The Roots of Rural Poverty in Central and Southern Africa* (London: Heinemann Educational Books, 1977), p. 133.
30. Q. N. Parsons, '"Khama & Co." and the Jousse Trouble, 1910–1916', *Journal of African History,* 16:3 (1975): 338. See also CWM LMS Q 26. Letter from Rev. R. Haydon Lewis, LMS missionary in Serowe until 1929, to Mr David Chamberlain, Livingstone House, Broadway, London SW1, 22, September 1933. Lewis recalled one case which 'occurred while I was in Serowe involving a Whiteman, whose right to collect money for medicines he had provided to Natives was disputed.' Khama's decision was accepted, and the matter did not come before the Magistrate's Court. It was one among numerous such cases.
31. I. Schapera, *A Handbook of Tswana Law and Custom* (London: International Institute of African Languages and Cultures and Oxford University Press, 1938), p. 61.
32. BNA DCS 1/15, Tshekedi to Resident Magistrate, 29 November 1929.
33. This is a reference to the exiling of important royal headmen to Rhodesia by Khama III at the end of the nineteenth century. Among these headmen was Phethu's own father. Thus, in asking the Resident Commissioner to banish Phethu, Sekgoma II requested him to 'take Phehtu away to his father's place in Rhodesia.' BNA S 3/6, 'Notes of an Interview between the Acting Resident Commissioner and Chief Sekgoma on 17th November 1923'.
34. The above account is based on Michael Crowder, 'The Succession Crisis over the Illness and Death of Sekgoma II of the Bangwato', in Jack Parson, ed., *Succession to High Office in Botswana* (Athens: Ohio University Press, forthcoming).
35. BNA S 266/2, 'Tshekedi—Relations with Government'. Statement by Resident Commissioner J. Ellenberger, 19 November 1927.
36. See Michael Crowder, 'Tshekedi Khama and Opposition to the British Administration of the Bechuanaland Protectorate, 1926–1936', *Journal of African History,* 26 (1985): 193–214.
37. BNA S 358/6, 'Draft Proclamations'. Tshekedi Khama to High Commissioner, 13 January 1934.
38. Sekgoma II Papers, Pilikwe. Letter book. Tshekedi to Messrs Juta and Co. Ltd., Cape Town. Tshekedi was not the only Chief to appreciate the value of law books. Much earlier Sebele I of the Bakwena had ordered a collection of legal texts for the Bakwena National Office from the African Book Company, Grahamstown (Sebele I, out correspondence, 1904–08). Reference kindly supplied by Jeff Ramsay.

39. Schapera, *Handbook*, pp 61–2.
40. Privy Council Appeal No 41 of 1930. Judgment delivered on 10 January 1931 by Sir Lancelot Sanderson, p. 9.
41. BNA 43/7, High Commissioner to Secretary of State, 13 August 1933.
42. Suzanne Miers and Michael Crowder, 'The Politics of Slavery in Bechuanaland: Power Struggles and The Plight of the Basarwa in the Bamangwato Reserve, 1926–40', in Suzanne Miers and Richard Roberts, eds., *The End of Slavery in Africa* (Madison: University of Wisconsin Press, forthcoming).
43. Rey, *Diaries*. Entry for Friday, 7 February to Sunday, 16 February 1930.
44. PRO DO 116/3, Secretary of State to High Commissioner, 9 November 1927. See also Michael Crowder, 'Tshekedi Khama and Opposition to Mining in Botswana, 1926–59', in Alan Mabin, ed., *Organization and Economic Change. Southern African Studies* Vol. 5 (Johannesburg: Ravan Press, forthcoming), for a detailed discussion of the way in which the British Administration concealed from Tshekedi the fact that he could legally cancel the Concession by giving notice.
45. *Ibid*. Athlone to Secretary of State, 22 March 1929.
46. BNA DCS 10/18, Nettelton to Government Secretary, 8 February 1930.
47. BNA S 63/9, 'Transcripts of Tshekedi Khama's Interviews with Lord Passfield, Dominions Secretary, London April 1930'.
48. PRO DO 35/339/10141, E. J. Harding, minute of 12 February 1930 to Secretary of State and Mr Lunn.
49. BNA DCS 10/10, Nettelton to Government Secretary, 27 May 1930.
50. Rey, *Diaries*. Entry for Tuesday, 26 to Thursday, 28 January 1932.
51. *Ibid*. Entry for Friday, 28 November 1930, after visit to 'Modder B' Mine on the Rand.
52. BNA S 63/9, 'Transcripts of Tshekedi Khama's Interviews . . .'.
53. Ethelreda Lewis, *Wild Deer* (London: Faber and Faber, 1933). New edition with introduction by Tim Couzens (Johannesburg and Cape Town: David Philip, 1983), pp. 166–7 and 'Introduction', pp. xxi–xxii.
54. See Titus Ka Mbuya, 'Legitimacy and Succession in Tswana States: The Case of Bakwena, 1930–56', B.A. history diss. University of Botswana, 1984.
55. Minutes of the Fourteenth Session of the Native Advisory Council, March 1932, p. 28.
56. *Ibid*. p. 29.
57. *Ibid*. p. 31.
58. *Ibid*. p. 32.
59. BNA S 323/2, 'Tshekedi Chief:- Interview—His Honour at Serowe 26. 6. 33'.
60. Rey, *Diaries*. Entry for Monday, 26 June 1933.
61. BNA S 323/2, 'Interview of 26.6.33'.
62. Minutes of the Fifteenth Session of the Native Advisory Council, 1932, p. 19.
63. *Ibid*., p. 28.
64. *Ibid*., p. 29.
65. *Ibid*., p. 33.
66. Rey, *Diaries*. Entry for Thursday, 13 July 1933.
67. *Ibid*. Entry for Friday, 14 and Saturday, 15 July 1933.
68. *Ibid*. Entry for Friday, 1 to Thursday, 7 September 1933.
69. PRO DO 35 386/10817/22, Eales to Tait, 25 August 1933.
70. *Ibid*.
71. CWM LMS, Africa Odds Box 23. Tshekedi Khama and Bathoen II to Administrative Secretary, High Commissioner's Office, 23 August 1933, enclosing telegram for despatch to Sir Herbert Stanley.
72. See BNA S 429/10, 'Complaints by Resident Commissioner regarding Ag. Chief Tshekedi writing direct to High Commissioner, 1931–1946'.
73. PRO DO 35 386/10817/21, Rey to Eales, 12 August 1933.
74. PRO DO 35 386/10817/22, Eales to Tait, 23 August 1933.

75. *Ibid.*, Rey to Eales, 25 August 1933.
76. *Ibid.*, Rey to Tshekedi and Bathoen, 25 August 1933; Tshekedi to Rey, 30 August 1933.
77. *Ibid.*, Evans to Rey, 4 September 1933.
78. Rey, *Diaries*. Entry for Friday, 1 to Thursday, 7 September 1933.
79. *Star,* Johannesburg, 15 September 1933.
80. *Ibid.*
81. Cmd. 4368, *Financial and Economic Position of the Bechuanaland Protectorate. Report of the Commission appointed by the Secretary of State for Dominion Affairs, March, 1933* (London: H.M.S.O., 1933), p. 157.
82. NAZ BU 1/1/3, Burns Papers. Rev. J. H. L. Burns to Fergie (Rev. A. F. Simpson, Edinburgh), 23 January 1933.
83. TKP 22, 'Blackbeards'. Samuel Blackbeard to Semane Khama, 8 March 1933.
84. *Ibid.*, Tshekedi to Blackbeard Bros., 7 August 1933, in reply to theirs of 5 August 1933.
85. BNA S 338/3, Potts to Resident Commissioner, 28 June 1933.
86. See correspondence in *ibid.*
87. BNA S 263/3, 'Tshekedi, Ag. Chief. Report by Capt. Potts on'.
88. From notes made in 1959 for Mary Benson by a member of the Administration, who was closely involved in these events but asked to remain anonymous. I am grateful to Mary Benson for giving me access to these notes.
89. TKP 70, Tshekedi to Mr A. Kerr, Fort Hare, 31 August 1933.
90. Quoted by Jeff Ramsay in 'Resistance from Subordinate Groups: BaBirwa, BaKgatla Mmanaana and Bakalanga Nswaszwi', in R. F. Morton and Jeff Ramsay, eds., *Birth of a Nation: The Making of Botswana* (Gaborone: Longman, forthcoming).

CHAPTER I: THE FLOGGING OF PHINEHAS MCINTOSH

1. See above, p. 75.
2. CWM LMS Archives Africa Odds Box 39, Tshekedi 1933/36. Wilkie to Oldham, 27 September 1933.
3. BNA DCS 11/4, Nettelton to Secretary, Chamber of Commerce, 6 October 1927.
4. National Museum, Gaborone, Minutes of the Serowe Chamber of Commerce, Special Meeting of Thursday, 13 October 1927.
5. BNA DCS 11/4, Nettelton to Government Secretary, 6 September 1929.
6. *Ibid.* See Interpreter to Resident Magistrate, 24 July 1929, and Tshekedi to Nettelton, 6 September 1929.
7. *Ibid.*, Nettelton to Government Secretary, 6 September 1929.
8. *Ibid.*, Tshekedi to Nettelton, 6 September 1929.
9. *Ibid.*, Nettelton to Government Secretary, 6 September 1929.
10. BNB 174–8, p. 190, telegram from Resident Commissioner to High Commissioner, 24 September 1933.
11. BNA S 182–10, Nettelton to Government Secretary, 9 December 1930.
12. *Ibid.*
13. *Ibid.*, Government Secretary to Nettelton, 23 December 1930.
14. *Ibid.*, Nettelton to Government Secretary, 30 December 1930.
15. *Ibid.*
16. Madge Page-Wood was a formidable woman who ran a boarding house for visiting whites and supplied the South African press with news items about affairs in Gamangwato from the 1930s to the 1950s.
17. BNA S 182/10, Nettelton to Government Secretary, 30 December 1933.
18. *Ibid.*
19. BNA DCS 11/4, Nettelton to Tshekedi, 14 January 1931.

20. TKP 72, 'The assault or series of assaults. . .', p. 3.
21. TKP 72, Statement of Matome, a member of the Bamangwato Tribal Police, taken and sworn before R. P. Garrett, J. P., at Palapye Road, 7 October 1933.
22. BNA 182/10, Government Secretary to Nettelton, 8 January 1931.
23. BNB 174–8, p. 147, telegram from High Commissioner to Dominions Office, 25 September 1933.
24. *Ibid*, p. 178, Potts to Resident Commissioner, 8 October 1931.
25. *Ibid.*
26. *Ibid.*, p. 167, despatch from High Commissioner to Dominions Office, 26 September 1933.
27. *Ibid.*, p. 178, Potts to Resident Commissioner, 8 October 1931.
28. *Ibid.*, p. 147, telegram from High Commissioner to Dominions Office, 25 September 1933.
29. TKP 72, Rex versus H. McNamee and P. McIntosh. In the Court of the Resident Magistrate for the Ngwato District of the Bechuanaland Protectorate, 9 December 1931.
30. BNB 174–8, p. 147, High Commissioner to Dominions Office, 25 September 1933.
31. BNA S 261–5 Nettelton to Government Secretary, 30 April 1932.
32. BNB 174–8, p. 179, Annexure F, Nettelton to Government Secretary, 28 April 1932.
33. *Ibid.*
34. *Ibid.*
35. *Ibid.*, p. 180, Government Secretary to Nettelton, 9 May 1933.
36. *Ibid.*, p. 167, High Commissioner to Dominions Office, 26 September 1933.
37. *Ibid.*
38. *Ibid.*, p. 157, enclosure in Despatch No 109 from High Commissioner to Dominions Office, 12 September 1933, Booker to Resident Magistrate, 27 March 1933.
39. *Ibid.*, Potts to Tshekedi, 29 March 1933.
40. *Ibid.*, Tshekedi to Potts, 7 April 1933.
41. *Ibid.*, p. 171, enclosure in Despatch No 118 from High Commissioner to Dominions Office. 'Enquiry by the Resident Commissioner and Mr. Liesching into alleged failure of the Resident Magistrate, Serowe, to take action with regard to complaints lodged by Chief Tshekedi as to conduct of certain European residents of Serowe, Wednesday, 13th September, 1933.'
42. *Ibid.*, p. 158, enclosure in Despatch No 109, Potts to Tshekedi, 15 April 1933.
43. *Ibid.*, Tshekedi to Potts, 18 April 1933.
44. Mary Benson Personal Papers. Letter from the contemporary witness of these events who wished to remain anonymous.
45. What follows is based on the accounts given by Tshekedi and Phinehas. Only discrepancies in their testimonies and other sources are noted.
46. TKP 72, 'Statement of Matome'. There is a note in the margin of the signed statement made by Tshekedi: 'Evidence given in the kgotla during the hearing of McIntosh's case.'
47. TKP 72, statement signed and sworn by S. G. Seretse before R. P. Garrett, J. P., Palapye Road, 7 October 1933.
48. *Ibid.*, statement of Disang Raditladi sworn before R. P. Garett, J.P., 7 August 1933.
49. BNA S 349/3, Tshekedi to Acting Resident Magistrate, by whom he meant Germond, since on several occasions later he refers to this letter as the one he wrote to Germond. The contents of the letter suggest that it was written specifically to Germond rather than Potts. 6 September 1933.
50. BNA S 349/3, message from Potts to Tshekedi, 6 September 1933.
51. *Ibid.*, Tshekedi to Ag Resident Magistrate, 6 September 1933.
52. *Ibid.*
53. BNA DCS 19/5, Germond to Potts, 12 September 1933.
54. BNA S349/7, 'Proceedings of an Enquiry held at Palapye Road on the 13th September, 1923, under High Commissioner's Notice No. 145.A. of 1933.' Evidence of Peter Sebina. The signed original was handed in by Sebina at the Enquiry and is now in BNA S 349/3.
55. BNA S 349/3, Tshekedi to the European Residents of Serowe, 6 September, 1933.
56. TKP 72, Tshekedi to Potts, carbon copy dated 8 September 1933.

57. See note 2 above.
58. TKP No. 72, Tshekedi to Potts, 8 September 1933.
59. Rey, *Diaries*. Entry for Friday, 1 to Thursday, 7 September 1933.
60. BNB 174–8, p. 152, Rey to Evans, 8 September 1933.
61. Sir Edwin Arrowsmith, in an interview with me, London, 28 May 1986.

CHAPTER 2: SEND IN THE MARINES

1. Rey, *Diaries*. Entry for Friday, 1 to Thursday, 7 September 1933.
2. BNA DCS 18/5, telegram Rey to Potts, 7 September 1933.
3. BNA DCS 19/5, telegram Potts to Rey, 7 September 1933. Also PRO DO 20283/74, Potts to Rey, 7 September 1933, enc. in Evans to D.O., 12 September 1933.
4. BNA DCS 19/5, telegram Rey to Pot′ , 7 September 1933.
5. *Ibid.*, statement of Phineas William McIntosh signed and sworn before A. Germond, Justice of the Peace, 7 September 1933.
6. *Ibid.*, Potts to Government Secretary, 7 September 1933.
7. Rey, *Diaries*. Entry for Friday 8, to Wednesday, 13 September 1933.
8. BNA S 349/3, Rey to Evans, 8 September 1933.
9. PRO DO 35 452/20283/38, Eales to Harding, Dominions Office, telegram, 8 September 1933.
10. *Ibid.*
11. *Ibid.*, Whiskard to Eales, 8 September 1933.
12. *Ibid.*, Whiskard to Secretary of State, 8 September 1933.
13. BNA DCS 19/5, Rey to Potts, 8 September 1933.
14. BNA S 349/4, Certificate of Medical Examination: Phineas McIntosh.
15. TKP 72, Statement of Ketshuhile of Maboledi village signed and sworn before R. P. Garrett, Justice of the Peace, Palapye Road, 7 October 1933.
16. BNA S 349/3, Potts to Government Secretary, 7 September 1933.
17. Bechuanaland Protectorate, Proclamation of 10 June 1891, Section 10, modified by Proclamation No 17 of 1922.
18. BNA S 349/3, Rey to High Commissioner, 8 September 1933.
19. Rey, *Diaries*. Entry for Friday, 8 to Wednesday, 13 September 1933.
20. *Ibid.*
21. PRO DO 35 452/20283/74, Evans to Secretary of State, Dominions Office. Despatch dated 12 September 1933.
22. *Ibid.*
23. PRO DO 35 452/20283/98, Liesching to Secretary of State, 16 September 1933. Received 9 October 1933.
24. BNA S350/3, Navycom, Pretoria, to Britannic, Simonstown, 9 September 1933
25. PRO DO 35 452/20283/97, Evans to Thomas, Personal and Private 25 September 1933. See also 20283/98, Liesching to Secretary of State, 16 September 1933.
26. The news of the flogging was first published in the British and South African press on Monday, 11 September 1933.
27. Reginald Pound, *Evans of the Broke. A Biography of Admiral Lord Mountevans, K.C.B., D.S.O., LL.D.* (London: Oxford University Press, 1963), p. 219.
28. *Ibid.*
29. PRO DO 20283/97, Evans to Thomas, Personal and Private, 25 September 1933
30. Admiral Lord Mountevans, *Adventurous Life* (London: Hutchinson, 1946), p. 194.
31. BNA S 350/3, Navycom, Pretoria, to Britannic, Simonstown, telegram, 9 September 1933.
32. BNA DCS 19/5, Assistant Resident Commissioner to Potts, 9 September 1933.
33. *Ibid.*, Government Secretary to Potts, 9 September 1933.
34. *Ibid.*, Potts to McIntosh, 9 September 1933.

35. BNA S 349/4, Potts to Government Secretary, 9 September 1933.
36. Leslie Blackwell, *Blackwell Remembers* (Cape Town: Howard Timmins, 1971), p. 115.
37. RHL MSS Afr. s. 1514, Mary Benson Papers. Notes from Leslie Blackwell, March 1961, fol. 128.
38. PRO DO 35 452/20283/97, Evans to Thomas, Personal and Private, 25 September 1933.
39. BNA S 349/3, Assistant Resident Commissioner to Resident Commissioner, 10 September 1933.
40. I have no clear evidence that Blackwell did secure this concession, but it was not until the Sunday morning conference that the matter was raised. Of course Rey was only too well aware of Tshekedi's litigious nature and probably also thought it wisest to anticipate him by agreeing to assist him in seeking legal advice.
41. PRO DO 35 452/20283/39, Evans to Secretary of State, 10 September 1933.
42. *Ibid.*
43. TKP 72, 'Message sent by the Chief Tshekedi to the Resident Magistrate per Disang Raditladi on September 10th, 1933'.
44. *Ibid.* Potts is referring here to *bolaya,* which in Setswana means, both figuratively and literally, 'to kill'.
45. BNA DCS 19/5, Rey to Potts, 10 September 1933.
46. BNA S 349/7, Evans to Tshekedi, dated 10 September 1933.
47. *Ibid.* Rey to Tshekedi, dated 10 September 1933.
48. *Ibid.*
49. These two telegrams are in BNA DCS 19/5.
50. BNA S 349/5, Rey to Potts, 10 September 1933.
51. BNA S 349/3, Assistant Resident Commissioner, Mafeking, to Resident Commissioner, Pretoria, 10 September 1933.
52. Rhodes House Library MSS Afr. s. 1514 (4), Mary Benson Papers. Typescript of the draft biography of Tshekedi by Douglas Buchanan (p. 42) on which Mary Benson in part based her *Tshekedi Khama,* (London: Faber and Faber, 1960). Blackwell was, however, adamant that it was not he who phoned Buchanan and suggested that it must have been Eales who did so. Notes from Leslie Blackwell to Mary Benson in *ibid.,* (2) March 1961.
53. Rey, *Diaries.* Entry for Friday, 8 to Wednesday, 13 September 1933.
54. BNA DCS 19/5, Potts to Commander Fearn, High Commissioner's Office, Pretoria, and to Government Secretary, Mafeking, 11 September 1933.
55. *Ibid.*
56. *Ibid.* Government Secretary to Potts, 11 September 1933.
57. *Ibid.* Potts to Government Secretary, 11 September 1933.
58. *Ibid.*
59. Minutes of the Executive Committee of the South Africa District Committee of the London Missionary Society, Tiger Kloof, September 1933. Cited in Kathleen M. Mulligan, 'Alfred E. Jennings: The Political Activities of the London Missionary Society in Bechuanaland, 1900–1935', Ph.D., diss. St John's University, 1974, p. 441.
60. *Ibid.,* p. 442.
61. CWM LMS Africa Odds Box 39, 'Suspension of Chief Tshekedi from the Chieftainship of the Bamangwato', p. 1.
62. RHL MSS Afr. s. 1514 (2), Mary Benson Papers. Notes by the Rev. J. H. L. Burns.
63. *Ibid.,* Tshekedi to Charles Roden Buxton, 11 September 1933.
64. TKP 72, series of telegrams sent out by Tshekedi, 11 September 1933.
65. *Ibid.*
66. BNA DCS 19/5, 'September 11, 1933 at Magistrate's Office.'
67. *Ibid.,* Potts to Tshekedi, 11 September 1933.
68. BNA S 349/5, Potts to Resident Commissioner, 11 September 1933.
69. BNA S 350/3, Rey to Neale, 11 September 1933.
70. BNA S 350/3, Evans to Resident Commissioner et al., 11 September 1933.

71. Buchanan's draft biography of Tshekedi, p. 43.
72. *Ibid.*, p. 43.
73. *Ibid.*, p. 44.
74. Jennings to Chirgwin, 4 October 1933, cited in Mulligan, 'Jennings', p. 453.
75. PRO DO 35 452/20283/39, Secretary of State to Prime Minister, 11 September 1933.
76. *Ibid.*, Thomas to Eyres-Monsell.
77. J. H. Thomas, *My Story* (London: Hutchinson, 1937), pp. 82–83.
78. PRO DO 35 452/20283/39, Thomas to Evans, 11 September 1933.
79. *Mafeking Mail*, 13 September 1933
80. Rey, *Diaries*. Entry for Friday, 8 to Wednesday, 13 September 1933.
81. *Natal Mercury*, 12 September 1933.
82. *Daily Mail*, 12 September 1933.
83. The *Times*, 12 September 1933.
84. *Rand Daily Mail*, 12 September 1933.
85. CWM LMS Africa Odds Box 39, Tshekedi to Buxton, 12 September 1933.
86. TKP 72, Simon Ratshosa to Tshekedi, 12 September 1933.
87. CWM LMS Africa Odds Box 39, 'Suspension of Chief Tshekedi'.
88. PRO DO 35 452/20283/44, Evans to DO, 12 September 1933.
89. *Ibid.*
90. PRO DO 35 452/20283/39, Eyres-Monsell to Thomas, 12 September 1933.
91. PRO DO 35 452/20283/44, Thomas to Evans, 12 September 1933.
92. *Ibid.*, Evans to Thomas, 12 September 1933.
93. PRO DO 35 452/20283/39, minute by Whiskard, 12 September 1933.
94. BNA S 349/7, Evans to Rey, 12 September 1933.
95. Evans, *My Adventurous Life*, p. 196.
96. *Die Vaderland*, 13 September 1933.
97. *Natal Mercury*, 13 September 1933.
98. *Ibid.*

CHAPTER 3: KANGAROO COURT

1. *Natal Mercury*, 13 September 1933.
2. BNA DCS 19/6, message from Tshekedi to Potts 12 September 1933.
3. *Natal Mercury*, 13 September 1933.
4. PRO DO 35 452/20283/41, Evans to Dominions Office, 11 September 1933.
5. University of Witwatersrand, Cullen Library, Ballinger Papers, A 3.1.43. D. G. McLaggan to Howard Pim, 27 September 1933.
6. *Die Burger*, 13 September 1933.
7. *Natal Mercury*, 13 September 1933.
8. Ballinger Papers, McClaggan to Pim, 27 September 1933.
9. *Rand Daily Mail*, 12 September 1933.
10. BNA DCS 19/6, Potts to A. E. Woods, 12 September 1933.
11. *Natal Mercury*, 13 September 1933.
12. *Ibid.*
13. Rey, *Diaries*. Entry for Friday, 8 to Wednesday, 13 September 1933.
14. *Ibid.*
15. Interview with Sir Edwin Arrowsmith, London, 28 May 1986.
16. BNA S 350/14, 'Report on Events in Connection with Tshekedi Affair from Tuesday, the 12th, September to Sunday, the 17th, September.' Draft by C. F. Rey, hereinafter referred to as Rey, 'Report on Events'.
17. Rey, *Diaries*. Entry for Friday, 8 to Wednesday, 13 September 1933.

18. *Natal Mercury,* 13 September 1933.
19. *Daily Herald,* 14 September 1933.
20. RHL MSS Afr. s. 1514 (2), Mary Benson Papers. Notes by the Rev. J. H. L. Burns, fol. 22.
21. This section is based on Buchanan's draft biography of Tshekedi, p. 45, and Burns, 'Suspension of Chief Tshekedi', p. 2.
22. Burns, 'Suspension of Chief Tshekedi', p. 2.
23. *Evening Standard,* 13 September 1933.
24. Rey, *Diaries.* Entry for Friday, 8 to Wednesday, 13 September 1933.
25. *Ibid.*
26. Buchanan, draft biography, p. 45. Where there are discrepancies between the times given in Buchanan's account and that of Rey, I have followed Rey's, as his correspond to the times given in official documents and by press reports. For instance, Buchanan states on several occasions that the Enquiry began at 9:00 A.M. when in fact it began at 10:00 A.M.
27. Rey, *Diaries.* Entry for Friday, 8 to Wednesday, 13 September 1933.
28. Burns, 'Suspension of Chief Tshekedi', p. 2.
29. BNA S 349/3, Resident Commissioner to Potts and Government Secretary, telegram, 10 October 1933.
30. Burns, 'Suspension of Chief Tshekedi', p. 2.
31. Mulligan, 'Jennings', p. 445, citing 'Notes taken on visitation from Jennings on his Return from Serowe', 17 September 1933.
32. BNA S 349/7, High Commissioner to Tshekedi Khama, Acting Chief of the Bamangwato, 10 September 1933. Note on file copy by Potts, dated 13 September 1933.
33. BNA S 349/8, Resident Commissioner to Tshekedi Khama residing in the Bamangwato Reserve, 10 September 1933. In BNA S 349/5 it is specified that this order was to be handed to Tshekedi on the morning of the Enquiry.
34. *Natal Mercury,* 14 September 1933.
35. Rey, 'Report on Events'.
36. CWM LMS Africa Odds Box 39, Tshekedi to Charles Roden Buxton.
37. BNA S 350/1, Rey to Evans, telegram, 9:30 A.M., 13 September 1933.
38. *Ibid.,* Evans to Rey, 13 September 1933.
39. Photograph, *Rand Daily Mail,* 15 September 1933.
40. The above account is based on reports in the *Evening News, Evening Standard* and *Daily Herald,* 13 September 1933.
41. BNA S 349/7, Rey to Evans, 13 September 1933.
42. Rey, *Diaries.* Entry for Friday, 8 to Wednesday, 13 September 1933.
43. Unless otherwise noted, all extracts from the Proceedings of the Commission of Enquiry are taken from the copy in BNA BT Adm. 12/1, which was Tshekedi's copy. This is a more clearly typed version than that in the Mafeking Secretariat file S 349/7. The full title is: 'Proceedings of an Enquiry held at Palapye Road on the 13th September, 1933, under High Commissioner's Notice No. 145.A. of 1933'.
44. *Ibid.*
45. This is taken from an insert into the proceedings and was not recorded in this fashion by the official shorthand writer. See the copy in BNA S 349/7. For the correspondence between Buchanan and the High Commissioner's Office on this see below, pp. 130–31.
46. Buchanan, draft biography, p. 47.
47. *Ibid.*
48. BNA BT Adm. 12/1, 'Affidavit of John Whiteside, 7 October 1933'.
49. *Evening Standard,* 13 September 1933.
50. I. Schapera, *A Handbook of Tswana Law and Custom* (London: IAILC and Oxford University Press, 1938), p. 266. In the original, Prof. Schapera wrote *o senyegile,* but he has kindly informed me that it should have been *o sentswe.* Letter to author, 4 February 1987.
51. Buchanan, draft biography, p. 48.

52. Pound, *Evans of the Broke*, p. 225. Rear-Admiral Searle, as he had become by the time Pound interviewed him, also suggested that there were only '50 to 80 natives' present at the Enquiry, 'lounging about outside the perimeter.' This certainly does not correspond with the accounts of either the press or of Rey.
53. BNA S 343/12 contains the original of this letter, which I have used as the basis for this quotation rather than the shorthand writer's version, which differs slightly. High Commissioner to Tshekedi, Confidential, 26 July 1933.
54. TKP 72, handwritten notes by Tshekedi outlining his line of defence at the Enquiry in English and Setswana. In these notes he listed nine girls alleged to have had relations with McIntosh, some of whom were 'available' as witnesses. He also listed eleven instances of assault by McIntosh on Bangwato. I am grateful to Glorious Gumbo for translating the Setswana sections of these notes for me.
55. Mary Benson Personal Papers. Anonymous official's report.
56. See Prologue, p. 24 above.
57. *Daily Herald*, 14 September 1933.
58. *Natal Mercury*, 14 September 1933.
59. BNA S 349/12, 'Enquiry into alleged non-action of Resident Magistrate'.
60. Rey, *Diaries*. Entry for Friday, 8 to Wednesday, 13 September 1933.
61. BNA S 350/14, 'Report on Events'. Rey had originally written 'ordered' for 'directed'.
62. RHL MSS Afr. s. 1514 (2), Mary Benson Papers. Notes by the Rev. J. H. L. Burns, fol. 24.
63. *Natal Mercury*, 14 September 1933
64. *Ibid.*
65. *Ibid.*
66. PRO DO 35 452/20283/46, Sir Clive Wigram at Balmoral to Sir Harry Batterbee, 13 September, 1933.

CHAPTER 4: AN AFRICAN DREYFUS?

1. Burns, 'Suspension of Chief Tshekedi', p. 5.
2. RHL MSS Afr. s. 1514 (2), Mary Benson Papers. Rev. J. H. L. Burns to Mary Benson, 30 March 1960.
3. *Ibid.*, p. 5.
4. TKP 72, Serogola Seretse to Tshekedi, n.d., trans. from the Setswana by Glorious Gumbo. Though there is no date on the letter, from its position in Tshekedi's file and in the context of subsequent events it was either delivered that night or early on Thursday morning.
5. BNA S 349/7, Neale and Liesching to High Commissioner, 13 September 1933.
6. Rey, 'Report on Events.'
7. PRO DO 35 452/20283/54, Evans to Dominions Office, telegram, 17 September 1933.
8. Rey, *Diaries*. Entry for Friday, 8 to Wednesday, 13 September 1933.
9. *Ibid.* Entry for Thursday, 14 September 1933.
10. *Cape Argus*, 14 September 1933.
11. The *Star*, 14 September 1933.
12. *Daily Telegraph*, 15 September 1933.
13. *Evening News*, 14 September 1933.
14. *Rand Daily Maij*, 15 September 1933.
15. *Bulawayo Chronicle*, 15 September 1933.
16. *Rand Daily Mail*, 15 September 1933.
17. Buchanan, draft biography, pp. 49–50
18. *Ibid.*, p. 50.
19. *Daily Herald*, 15 September 1933.
20. *Natal Mercury*, 15 September 1933.

21. NAZ, Burns Papers, Bu 5/2/2. Burns to Helen, 17 September 1933
22. Rey, *Diaries*. Entry for Thursday, 14 September 1933.
23. Rey, 'Report on Events', p. 4.
24. *Daily Herald,* 15 September 1933.
25. *Daily Telegraph,* 15 September 1933.
26. Both the British and South African press gave extensive photographic coverage to the suspension of Tshekedi.
27. *Natal Mercury,* 15 September 1933.
28. Rey, *Diaries*. Entry for Thursday, 14 September 1933.
29. Buchanan, draft biography, p. 50.
30. Rey, *Diaries*. Entry for Thursday, 14 September 1933.
31. Buchanan, draft biography, p. 50.
32. *Daily Telegraph,* 15 September 1933.
33. BNA S 350/7, 'Decision by His Excellency the High Commissioner announced at Serowe, Thursday, 14th September 1933.'
34. *Natal Mercury,* 15 September 1933.
35. *Manchester Guardian,* 15 September 1933.
36. I have been unable to find a written letter of apology from Tshekedi to Evans or Rey for writing direct to Stanley, or at least one that could in any way be described in these terms.
37. RHL MSS Afr. s. 1514 (2), Mary Benson Papers. Notes by the Rev. J. H. L. Burns, fol. 23.
38. *Daily Herald,* 16 September 1933.
39. *Daily Telegraph,* 15 September 1933.
40. *Ibid.*
41. Rey, *Diaries*. Entry for Thursday, 14 September 1933.
42. Buchanan, draft biography, p. 51.
43. Burns, 'Suspension of Chief Tshekedi', p. 4.
44. *Daily Herald,* 16 September 1933.
45. *Star,* 15 September 1933. In fact the *Star* describes its despatch as 'From our representative', but it appears in other papers as from 'Reuter'.
46. Ballinger Papers, A. 3.1.43. D. G. McLaggan to Howard Pim, 27 September 1933.
47. 'A Native View of the Bamangwato Affair', cited in Mulligan, *Jennings,* p. 449.
48. *News Chronicle,* 15 September 1933.
49. Rey, *Diaries*. Entry for Thursday, 14 September 1933.

CHAPTER 5: 'THE ROAD TO RHODESIA'

1. See Prologue, p. 13.
2. Rey, 'Report on Events', Appendix A.
3. *Ibid.*
4. *Ibid.*
5. *Ibid.*
6. Buchanan, draft biography, p. 52.
7. BNA DCS 19/6, Potts to the Mohumagadi Semane Kgama, 16 September 1933.
8. Buchanan's account, written some twenty years later, is not always reliable. He records that he personally handed Semane's petition to Rey that afternoon, but the administrative record shows otherwise. It seems clear that Rey did not receive it until the 16th, and then it was sent to him by Potts. See Rey, 'Report on Events'.
9. BNA S 350/2, petition of Queen Semane, 14 September 1933.
10. Buchanan, draft biography, p. 53.
11. *Cape Times,* 16 September 1933.
12. Burns, 'Suspension of Chief Tshekedi', p. 4–5.

13. *Daily Herald,* 16 September 1933.
14. Rey, *Diaries.* Entry for Friday, 15 September 1933.
15. *Ibid.*
16. Rey, 'Report on Events'.
17. BNA S 349/8, order dated 14 September 1933 and signed by Evans.
18. BNA DCS 19/6, orders dated 14 September 1933 and signed by Rey.
19. BNA S 349/9, Resident Magistrate to Resident Commissioner, 15 September 1933.
20. Buchanan, draft biography, p. 53. Buchanan's chronology of events with regard to the 'election' of an Acting Chief is again confusing. He appears to conflate events of the Thursday, Friday and Saturday. In particular he suggests that the *kgotla* took place on the Thursday, when the administrative record shows clearly that it took place early on Friday morning, which would have been the normal time to hold a *kgotla* meeting.
21. BNA DCS 19/4, 'Notes taken at the Magistrate's Office 15th. Sept. 1933.'
22. See Genealogy, pp. 10–11 above.
23. BNA DCS 19/6, notes on telephone message from Sergeant Dixon, n.d., but clearly from its context and place in the Resident Magistrate's file it was on the morning of the 15th.
24. *Ibid.*
25. TKP 72, pencilled notes by Tshekedi, n.d., but probably 15 September 1933.
26. *Rand Daily Mail,* 15 September 1933.
27. The *Star,* 15 September 1933.
28. *Cape Times,* 15 September 1933.
29. *Times,* 16 September 1933.
30. *Die Burger,* 15 September 1933, trans. Jane Starfield. Also the *News Chronicle.*
31. Reuter despatch, Palapye Road, 15 September 1933.
32. Rey, *Diaries.* Entry for Friday 15 September 1933.
33. BNA DCS 19/4, notes by Resident Commissioner, 15 September 1933.
34. Rey, 'Report on Events'.
35. *Cape Times,* 16 September 1933.
36. *Natal Mercury,* 15 September 1933.
37. BNA S 349/10, Lt. Lawrenson to Government Secretary, Mafeking, 18 September 1933.
38. Buchanan, draft biography, p. 55.
39. *Cape Times,* 16 September 1933.
40. *Ibid.*
41. The above is based on the report by Lt. Lawrenson in BNA S 349/8.
42. BNA S 349/8, order dated 14 September 1933 and signed by Rey.
43. See correspondence in BNA DCF 4/4.
44. BNA S 349/10, Ag Resident Magistrate, Francistown, to Assistant Resident Commissioner, 16 September 1933.
45. Rey, *Diaries.* Entry for Saturday, 16 September 1933.
46. BNA S 350/1, telephone message received by Sgt Dixon from Capt. Potts, 10:00 A.M., 16 September 1933.
47. BNA S 350/1, Rey to Evans, telegram, 'Urgent Clear the Line', 16 September 1933.
48. Field notes made by I. Schapera, January 1935: Gabolebye Dinti Marobela, informant. I am deeply grateful to Prof. Schapera for this information.
49. Mulligan, 'Jennings', p. 449.
50. NAZ Bu/5/2/2, Burns to Jennings, 16 September 1933.
51. Neil Parsons, 'Seretse Khama and the Bangwato Succession Crisis, 1948–1953', in Jack Parson, ed., *Succession to High Office in Botswana.*
52. See Titus Mnamana-ka-Mbuya, 'Legitimacy and Succession in Tswana States: The Case of the Bakwena, 1930–33', B.A. history diss., University of Botswana, 1984.
53. See Michael Crowder, Jack Parson and Neil Parsons, introduction to Parson, *Succession to High Office in Botswana.*

54. Rey, 'Report on Events', Appendix A.
55. BNA S 350/1, genealogy showing order of succession to the Ngwato throne.
56. NAZ Bu 5/2/2, Burns to Jennings, 16 September 1933.
57. BNA S 349/7, Rey to Evans, 16 September 1933.
58. BNA S 349/12, Rey to Evans, 16 September 1933.
59. *Ibid.*, 17 September 1933.
60. *Daily Express*, 15 September 1933.
61. *Manchester Guardian*, 15 September 1933.
62. *Daily Herald*, 16 September 1933.
63. *Ibid.*, 15 September 1933.
64. *Daily Express*, 14 September 1933.
65. *Cape Times*, 16 September 1933.
66. Vice Admiral E. R. G. R. Evans, *The Ghostly Galleon* (London: John Lane, 1933), pp. 117, 126.
67. Quoted in the *Star*, 16 September 1933.
68. *Daily Worker*, 16 September 1933.
69. Thomas, *My Story*, p. 82.
70. PRO DO 35 452/20283/46, Thomas to Evans, telegram, 15 September 1933.
71. See the very cautious responses by Thomas in his interview with the *News Chronicle*, 16 September 1933.
72. PRO DO 35 452/20283/46, Sir H. Batterbee to Sir Clive Wigram, 15 September 1933.
73. *Ibid.*, Secretary of State to Prime Minister, 15 September 1933.
74. *Ibid.*, minute by Whiskard to Secretary of State, 14 September 1933.
75. Thomas, *My Story*, p. 81.
76. *News Chronicle*, 16 September 1933.
77. *Diamond Fields Advertiser*, 16 September 1933.
78. *Natal Mercury*, 16 September 1933.
79. Rey, *Diaries*. Entry for Thursday, 14 September 1933.
80. CWM LMS Africa Odds Box 39, Papers on Tshekedi 1933/36, Snelling to Chirgwin, 16 September 1933.

CHAPTER 6: 'FLATTENED OUT FOR ALL TIME'?

1. *Sunday Times*, 17 September 1933.
2. *Star*, 15 September 1933.
3. *Cape Times*, 20 September 1933.
4. *Cape Argus*, 20 September 1933.
5. *Ibid.*
6. BNA DCF 4/4, Tati Company to Resident Magistrate, 22 September 1933.
7. BNA BTA C/4/635, Buchanan and Jennings to Tshekedi, 17 September 1933. On the train en route to Cape Town.
8. *Ibid.*, Buchanan to Tshekedi, 17 September 1933.
9. *Ibid.*, Buchanan to Tshekedi, 19 September 1933.
10. University of Witwatersrand, Cullen Library, South African Institute of Race Relations Papers, AD 843 B 84.1, 'The Case of Chief Tshekedi'.
11. TKP 72, Simon Ratshosa to Margaret Hodgson, 16 September 1933.
12. Simon Ratshosa indicates that this letter appeared in the *Manchester Guardian* of 18 June 1931. His own quotation from the letter differs. I have used the original here.
13. TKP 72, Simon Ratshosa, 'A Native view on Bamangwato affair'.
14. TKP 73, Tshekedi to Simon Ratshosa, 15 November 1933.
15. TKP 72, Serogola Seretse, n.d., trans. Glorious Gumbo. Judging from the contents, it seems to have been sent to Tshekedi early on in his exile.

16. NAZ Bu 5/2/2, Jennings to Burns, 16 September 1933.

17. BNA S 350/14.

18. *Ibid.*, pencilled note attached to report.

19. *Ibid.*

20. *Ibid.*, Appendix A.

21. *Ibid.*, Apendix C.

22. *Ibid.*, Appendix D. See also Q. N. Parsons, ' "Khama & Co." and the Jousse Trouble', *Journal of African History* 16, 3 (1975):383–408.

23. *Review of Reviews*, October 1933. Elsewhere he is quoted as saying: 'You can criticize the handling of a ship, but it is the captain who is responsible.' The quote used in the text seems the more likely version.

24. *Sunday Times*, 17 September 1933.

25. PRO DO 35 452/20283/52,54,55,56, 17 September 1933.

26. *Ibid.*, 20285/55, Whiskard to Secretary of State, 18 September 1933.

27. *Ibid.*, Thomas to Evans, 18 September 1933.

28. RHL Anti-Slavery Society Papers, Charles Roden Buxton, telegram to Jennings, 21 September 1933.

29. BNA DCF 4/4, Ag Resident Magistrate to Tshekedi, 18 September 1933. I am grateful to Jeff Ramsay for the information about Sebele's surveillance by the Special Branch.

30. *Ibid.*

31. PRO DO 35 452/20283/55, Evans to Thomas, 17 September 1933.

32. BNA C/4/635, Kieser to Tshekedi, 19 September 1933.

33. CWM LMS Africa Odds Box 39, Papers on Tshekedi 1933/36, Tshekedi, telegram to Charles Roden Buxton, 18 September 1933.

34. BNA BTA C/4/636, Tshekedi to Buchanan, 18 September 1933.

35. TKP 72, Bathoen II, telegram to Tshekedi, 19 September 1933.

36. *Daily Telegraph*, 19 September 1933.

37. University of the Witwatersrand, Cullen Library, South African Institute of Race Relations Papers, AD 843 B 84.1, Rheinhallt Jones to Lord Sanderson, n.d., but probably 18 September 1933.

38. *Rand Daily Mail*, 18 September 1933, and *Die Vaderland*, 20 September 1933. I am grateful to Alan Mabin for arranging the translation of the latter editorial.

39. *Die Burger*, 18 September 1933.

40. NAZ Bu 5/2/2, Burns to Jennings, 18 September 1933.

41. BNA DCS 19/6, Serogola to Potts, 19 September 1933 and reply from Sgt Dixon of same date.

42. TKP 72, copies of above correspondence in Tshekedi's personal papers on the McIntosh affair.

43. BNA DCS 19/6, Serogola to Potts, 19 September 1933.

44. *Ibid.*, Potts to Serogola, 19 September 1933.

45. CWM LMS Africa Odds Box 1, Chirgwin to Jennings, 19 September 1933.

46. RHL Anti-Slavery Society Papers G 149–51, Harris to Tshekedi, 21 September 1933.

47. For example, the *British Weekly*, 'Chief Tshekedi as I know him', 21 September 1933.

48. *Cape Times*, 15 September 1933.

49. *Daily Herald*, 19 September 1933.

50. *Evening Standard*, 21 September 1933.

51. *Daily Mail* (London), 19 September 1933.

52. *Manchester Guardian*, 20 September 1933.

53. *New Britain*, 20 September 1933.

54. RHL Anti-Slavery Society Papers G 149–51, Harris to Thomas, 19 September 1933.

55. *Ibid.*, Harris to Berry, 20 September 1933.

56. BNA S 350/10, Harold Moody to Thomas, 15 September 1933.

57. *Star*, 19 September 1933.

58. PRO DO 35 452/20283/55, Thomas to Evans, 19 September 1933.

59. PRO DO 35 452/20283/59, Whiskard to Eales, 20 September 1933.
60. PRO DO 35 452/20283/59, Eales to Whiskard, 20 September 1933.
61. PRO CAB 23, 77 of 20 September 1933.
62. PRO CAB Conclusions 51(33), 20 September 1933.
63. PRO DO 35 452/20283/59, Whiskard to Eales, 20 September 1933.
64. PRO DO 35 452/20283/62, Evans to Thomas, 20 September 1933.
65. BNA S 350/5, Evans to Rey, Secret, 21 September 1933.
66. BNA BTA C/4/635, Buchanan to Tshekedi, 10:00 P.M., 19 September 1933.
67. BNA DCF 4/4, Ag Resident Magistrate to Resident Commissioner, 21 September 1933. The original letter from Tshekedi Khama of that date is in the same file.
68. Rey, *Diaries*. Entry for Monday, 18 September to Sunday, 24 September 1933.

CHAPTER 7: A TACTICAL RETREAT

1. BNA DCS 19/4, Rey to Resident Magistrate, telegram, 30 September 1933.
2. Rey, *Diaries*. Entry for Monday, 18 to Sunday, 24 September 1933.
3. Interview with former Chief Bathoen II, Friday, 19 April 1985.
4. BNA S 349/11, Buchanan to High Commissioner, 23 September 1933.
5. PRO DO 35 452/20283/55, Thomas to Evans, 19 September 1933.
6. BNA DCF 4/4, Ag Resident Magistrate to Tshekedi, 23 September 1933.
7. BNA S 349/7, Neale to Eales, 19 September 1933.
8. TKP 72. Contains a line-by-line comparison of the two versions in Annexure F, 'Amendments to Proceedings of an Enquiry held at Palapye Road, 13 September 1933.'
9. PRO DO 35 452/20283/66, Evans to Thomas, 22 September 1933.
10. PRO DO 35 452/20283/66, minute by Whiskard, 22 September 1933.
11. *Ibid.*
12. *Ibid.*
13. PRO DO 35 452/20283, files 85–87 all 'Destroyed under Statute'.
14. PRO DO 35 452/20283/68, Thomas to Evans, telegram, 22 September 1933.
15. PRO DO 35 452/20283/70, Thomas to Evans, 23 September 1933, despatched at 2:50 P.M.
16. *Ibid.*, Evans to Thomas, 23 September 1933, received at 3:51 P.M.
17. BNA S 350/6, Rey to Evans, 23 September 1933.
18. BNA S 350/6, 'Notes on telephonic conversation between His Excellency the High Commissioner and His Honour the Resident Commissioner, 24.9.33, 11:30 A.M.'
19. PRO DO 35 452/20283/71, Evans to Dominions Office, 25 September 1933.
20. BNA S 350/6, Rey to Evans, 24 September 1933.
21. PRO DO 35 452/20283/63, J. C. Wedgwood, MP, to Secretary of State, 20 September 1933.
22. *Morning Post*, 18 September 1933.
23. *Cape Times*, 20 September 1933.
24. Quoted in *Die Burger*, 22 September 1933.
25. *Cape Argus*, 18 September 1933.
26. *Manchester Guardian*, 23 September 1933.
27. *New Statesman and Nation*, 23 September 1933.
28. *Umsebenzi: The South African Worker*, 23 September 1933. Before 1931 *Umsebenzi* had been an opponent of the *dikgosi* of the Bechuanaland Protectorate, whom it saw as greedy autocrats and agents of British emperialism. It was only when some of their number—Sebele II, Tshekedi, and later Molefi of the Bakgatla—were deposed that they became patriots in the struggle against capitalism. Communication from Jeff Ramsay.
29. G. L. Steer, 'Tshekedi and Mackintosh', The *Spectator*, 23 September 1933.
30. The Rev. A. M. Chirgwin, 'Chief Tshekedi as I know him', The *British Weekly*, 21 September 1933.

31. The *Star,* 20 September 1933.
32. See BNA S 350/10.
33. *Ibid.,* T. M. Stone to Rey, 29 September 1933, enclosing copy of resolution to be forwarded to Thomas.
34. TKP 73, Geraldine Theobalds to Tshekedi, 17 September 1933.
35. Charles Roden Buxton to the editor, The *Friend,* 22 September 1933.
36. PRO DO 35 452/20283/62, Whiskard to Secretary of State, minute on telegram no 106 from High Commissioner to Secretary of State, 20 September 1933.
37. BNA C/4/635, Kieser to Tshekedi 28 September 1933.
38. BNA S 349/14, Liesching to Evans 22 September 1933.
39. South African Institute of Race Relations Papers, AD 843 B 84.1, 'The Case of Chief Tshekedi'.
40. BNA S 349/14, Liesching to Evans, 22 September 1933.
41. BNA S 350/6, 'Notes on Telephonic Conversation between His Excellency the High Commissioner and His Honour the Resident Commissioner on 24th September, 1933, at 5:45 P.M.'
42. BNA S 349/12, Liesching: 'May I suggest that if the Acting Chief's memory is not good enough to remember conversations then it is not good enough to lodge complaints of inability.'
43. BNA S 350/6, Notes on telephone conversation.
44. PRO DO 35 452/20283/72, minute by Whiskard to Secretary of State, 25 September 1933.
45. BNA S 349/11, Resident Commissioner to Ag Resident Magistrate, Francistown, 23 September 1933.
46. BNA DCF 4/4, Ag Resident Magistrate to Tshekedi, 23 September 1933.
47. *Ibid.,* Tshekedi to Resident Magistrate, Francistown, 26 September 1933. In this letter he refers to the request he made the day before to go to Mafeking.
48. *Ibid.,* Tshekedi to Resident Magistrate, 26 September 1933, second letter of this day's date.
49. *Ibid.,* Ag Resident Magistrate to Government Secretary, 27 September 1933.
50. BNA BT Adm. C/4/635, notes on a telephone conversation between Eales and Buchanan made by Buchanan, 25 September 1933.
51. PRO DO 35 452/20283/76, Evans to Thomas, 26 September 1933.
52. PRO DO 35 452/20283/73, minute by Tait, 25 September 1933.
53. PRO DO 35 452/20283/76, Thomas to Evans, 26 September 1933.
54. BNA S 349/11, Evans to Rey, 27 September 1933.
55. PRO DO 35 452/20283/78, Evans to Thomas, 27 September 1933, received 9:46 P.M.

CHAPTER 8: OUT OF EXILE

1. Ballinger Papers, A 3.1.43. D. G. McLaggan to Howard Pim, 27 September 1933.
2. BNA S 350/13, 'Petition to Right Honourable J. H. Thomas, Secretary of State for the Colonies', dated 25 September 1933 but not dispatched to London until 3 October 1933.
3. Ballinger Papers, McLaggan to Howard Pim, 27 September 1933.
4. *Ibid.,* McLaggan to Pim, 28 September 1933.
5. *Ibid.,* McLaggan to Pim, 27 September 1933.
6. *Ibid.,* A 3.1. 39, K. T. Motsete to Margaret Hodgson, 23 September 1933.
7. *Ibid.,* Simon Ratshosa to Margaret Hodgson, 25 September 1933, unsigned copy but from the context clearly from Simon.
8. *Ibid.,* A 3.1.41, 'Wait and See', by Simon Ratshosa.
9. *Ibid.*
10. See p. 130–31 above.
11. BNA BTA C/4/635, Kieser to Tshekedi, 28 September 1933.
12. *Ibid.*
13. TKP 72, Kieser & McLaren, Attorneys, to Acting Chief Serogola, 28 September 1933.
14. TKP 72, 'Draft of Petition to His Excellency the acting High Commissioner'.

15. *News Chronicle,* 30 September 1933. There is some confusion as to whether Buchanan did in fact get through to Tshekedi at Vryburg. While the Cape Town correspondent of the *News Chronicle* is clear that he did, the *Cape Argus* of the previous afternoon states that he failed to. It is almost certain that Tshekedi would have heard the news one way or other on the train before he arrived at Cape Town, since all the local papers were full of it.
16. PRO DO 35 452/20283/84, 'Press Notice issued by the Dominions Office, 28th September, 1933'.
17. BNA S 350/4, Rey to Evans, 17 September 1933.
18. *Ibid.,* Rey to Evans, 22 September 1933.
19. *Ibid.,* Evans to Rey, 22 September 1933.
20. DO 35/452/20283/74, minutes of September 1933, cited in Mulligan, 'Jennings', p. 455.
21. See *Cape Times,* 2 October 1933.
22. *Manchester Guardian,* 29 September 1933.
23. *Times,* 29 September 1933.
24. *Star,* 28 September 1933.
25. *Daily Herald,* 29 September 1933.
26. *Cape Times,* 29 September 1933.
27. *Cape Argus,* 29 September 1933.
28. BNA BT Adm. C/4/635, notes made by Buchanan on his meeting with Shirley Eales, 28 September 1933.
29. *Ibid.,* 'Resumé of a conversation held between Mr. Eales and Mr. Buchanan, 29th September 1933'.
30. *Ibid.*
31. *Star,* 27 September 1933.
32. BNA S 350/9, Evans to Tshekedi, 28 September 1933.
33. *Ibid.,* Tshekedi to Evans, 29 September 1933.
34. *Cape Argus,* 29 September 1933.
35. CWM LMS Africa Odds Box 39, cable to Reuters and LMS.
36. Buchanan, draft biography, p. 57.
37. BNA BTA C/4/635, 'Notes of Interview between Vice-Admiral E. R. G. R. Evans, Acting High Commissioner, and Tshekedi Khama, Acting Chief of the Bamangwato on board "The Dorset"', September 30th, 1933'. This is the only copy I have found of this interview. It bears two corrections in Tshekedi's handwriting. It is not clear whether the record was made by the Administration or by Tshekedi, who sometimes made transcripts of his interviews. It is difficult to tell from the style and format who might have made it. It is unlikely that Tshekedi would have described himself as *Acting* Chief. Occasional phrases suggest that it probably was not made by the High Commissioner's Office, which did produce a terser memorandum on the discussions between Evans and Tshekedi (see BNA S 349/11). It is quite possible that Peter Sebina wrote it.
38. Benson, *Tshekedi Khama,* p. 107.
39. Buchanan, draft biography, p. 58.
40. BNA DCS 19/4, Rey to Potts, telegram, 30 September 1933.
41. *Ibid.,* for sequence of telegrams, etc., relating to these preparations.
42. *Ibid.,* Potts to Serogola, 30 September 1933.
43. Pound, *Evans of the Broke,* p. 228.
44. *Cape Argus,* 2 October 1933.
45. *Rand Daily Mail,* 5 October 1933.
46. BNA S350/9, Rey to Evans, coded telegram, 29 September 1933. See p. 132 above, with reference to the Dominions Office and Evans's statement.
47. BNA DCS 19/4, text of address by High Commissioner, Serowe, 4 October 1933.
48. *Rand Daily Mail,* 5 October 1933.
49. See Benson, *Tshekedi Khama,* p. 109, and Mary Benson Personal Papers. The eyewitness concerned was the official who asked to remain anonymous.

50. RHL MSS, s. 1514 (2), Mary Benson Papers, Burns to Benson, 4 July 1960.
51. *Ibid.*
52. BNA DCS 19/4, handwritten transcript of statement by Serogola and other headmen made by Potts, n.d.
53. *Ibid.*, Potts, telegram to Rey at Palapye Road, 4 October 1933.

CHAPTER 9: TSHEKEDI'S VICTORY?

1. BNA DCF 4/4, H. B. Neale, Ag Resident Commissioner to all Resident Magistrates in the B.P., 10 October 1933.
2. BNA S 170/1/4, Group of Heads of the Tribe to District Commissioner, Serowe, 18 July 1949. The title of Resident Magistrate was changed to District Commissioner in 1936.
3. TKP 72, Tshekedi to Bathoen II, 6 October 1933. Letter translated from the Setswana by Glorious Gumbo. Although it is written as from Tshekedi, the carbon copy bears the typed title of the writer as 'The Secretary to Chief Tshekedi' ['Mokwaledi oa Kgosi Tshekedi'].
4. University of Cape Town Library, MSS Collection, W. G. Ballinger Papers, BC 347 G.2 I 5, Moanaphuti Segolodi to Miss M. L. Hodgson, 6 October 1933.
5. BNA DCS 19/6, Ag Government Secretary to Resident Magistrate, Serowe, 20 November 1933.
6. *Natal Mercury*, 3 October 1933, editorial: 'The Serowe Rebuff'.
7. TKP 72, Tshekedi to R. P. Garrett, 7 October 1933.
8. BNA DCF 4/4, Ag Government Secretary to Resident Magistrate, Francistown, 27 September 1933, referring to Tshekedi's request of 19 September 1933.
9. TKP 72, statement signed by Baikgantshi and sworn before R. P. Garrett, J.P., 22 September 1933.
10. BNA S 349/3, Tshekedi to Germond, 6 September 1933.
11. TKP 72, statement signed by Baikgantshi.
12. TKP 72, testimony of E. P. Cavanagh (junior), signed and sworn before Garrett, 7 October 1933.
13. *Ibid.*, statement of F. J. Mollentze, signed and sworn before Garrett, 7 October 1933.
14. Rey, *Diaries*. Entry for Sunday, 1 October to Sunday, 8 October 1933.
15. *Ibid.*, introduction by Neil Parsons.
16. PRO DO 35 386/10817/25, High Commissioner to Secretary of State, 5 October 1933.
17. BNA DCS 19/4, Potts to Tshekedi, 9 October 1933, communicating contents of telegram just received from Resident Commissioner.
18. PRO DO 35 386/10817/25, minute by Whiskard, 5 October 1933.
19. PRO DO 35 386/10817/28, Dominions Office to High Commissioner, telegram, 11 October 1933.
20. TKP 72, Tshekedi to the European Residents in the Bamangwato Country, 9 October 1933.
21. BNA BT Adm. 12/1, 'The Petition of Tshekedi Chief of the Bamangwato Tribe of the Bechuanaland Protectorate'.
22. *Ibid.*, p. 2.
23. *Ibid.*, p. 3.
24. *Ibid.*
25. *Ibid.*
26. *Ibid.*, p. 5.
27. *Ibid.*, p. 6.
28. *Ibid.*
29. *Ibid.*, p. 7.
30. *Ibid.*, p. 8.
31. BNA S 182/10, statement of Alfred Mahloane sworn before J. D. A. Germond, J.P., 2 October 1933.
32. *Ibid.*, Potts to Rey, 6 October 1933.

33 BNA S 349/14, Evans to Thomas, 10 October 1933.

34. *Ibid.*, Rey to Evans, 19 October 1933.

35. Lord Lugard was former Governor-General of Nigeria, a member of the League of Nations Permanent Mandates Commission and father of 'Indirect Rule'. Sir Alan Pim was an expert on colonial finance and had recently completed a survey of the economic problems of the Bechuanaland Protectorate, during the course of which he had met Rey; Viscount Wolmer was heir to the Earl of Selborne, former British High Commissioner in South Africa. Wolmer himself was MP for the Aldershot Division of Hampshire. The Earl of Buxton was a former Governor-General of South Africa. Mr. (later Sir Percy) Pybus was Minister of Transport from 1931–33 and probably knew Rey when he was a civil servant in the Home Government.

36. BNA S 350/11, Rey to Lugard and others, 17 October 1933.

37. BNA S 350/11, Rey, 'Notes on the Serowe Incident'. This is printed as an appendix in Rey, *Diaries.*

38. TKP 73, Oliver Whiting to Tshekedi, 22 September 1933.

39. See the article by Jeff Ramsay on the visit to Botswana of King Moshoeshoe of Lesotho in *Mmegi Wa Dikgang,* 4, 19, 23 May 1987, p. 7.

40. *Manchester Guardian,* 29 September 1933.

41. Leonard Barnes, 'The Bechuanaland Crisis', *Time and Tide,* 7 October 1933.

42. *Time and Tide,* 7 October 1933. Letter from 'Imperialist', Hull, E. Yorks.

43. *Daily Telegraph,* 29 September 1933.

44. *Time and Tide,* 14 October 1933.

45. J. Wentworth Day, 'Tshekedi—the Price of Shame: The Treachery of the Premier and Mr. J. H. Thomas', the *Saturday Review,* 7 October 1933.

46. *Hansard,* 5th series, Parliamentary Debates, House of Commons, vol. 284, 1933–34 Session, December 11th–December 21st, column 182, 12 December 1933.

47. *Ibid.*

48. *Ibid.*

49. BNA BT Adm. 11/13, Tshekedi to Jennings and Buchanan, 26 December 1933.

50. *Hansard,* 1933–34, column 183, 12 December 1933.

51. *Ibid.,* column 183.

52. *Ibid.,* column 200.

53. *Ibid.,* column 201.

54. *Ibid.,* column 364, 13 December 1933. Mr. Rhys Davies (for Mr. Morgan Jones).

55. *Ibid.,* column 371. Mr. Rhys Davies (for Mr. Morgan Jones).

56. *Ibid.,* column 730, series of questions by Mr. Lunn.

57. *Ibid.,* columns 730–1.

58. *Hansard,* 5th series, Parliamentary Debates, House of Lords, vol. 90, 1933–1934 session, November 21st–March 1st, column 466, 13 December 1933.

59. *Ibid.,* column 467.

60. *Ibid.,* column 475.

61. *Ibid.,* column 476.

62. *Ibid.,* column 490.

63. *Ibid.,* column 493.

64. RHL Anti Slavery Papers MSS Brit. Emp. 522 Box G 149–51, Tshekedi to Sir John Harris, 4 November 1933.

65. CWM LMS Africa Odds Box 1, Chirgwin to Jennings, 3 October 1933.

66. *Northampton Evening Telegraph,* 7 October 1933.

67. TKP 73, letters of support.

68. *Ibid.,* Mrs. Catherine Wright to Tshekedi, 9 October 1933.

69. *Ibid.,* Nurse Anne Murphy to Tshekedi, 11 October 1933.

70. *Ibid.,* J. Bryant Lindley to Tshekedi, 24 September 1933.

71. *Ibid.,* Willie P. de Koek (Ramosa), Randfontein, to Tshekedi, 8 October 1933.

72. *Ibid.*, 26 January 1934.
73. *Ibid.*, Tshekedi to Oliver Whiting, 4 November 1933.
74. *Ibid.*, Tshekedi to Edward Little, Yorks, 4 November 1933.
75. *Ibid.*, Tshekedi to the Rev. John Whiteside, 1 November 1933.
76. PRO DO 35 452/20283/48, Sir John Harris to Secretary of State for the Dominions, 15 September 1933.
77. *Ibid.*, 20283/75, letters of 22 and 30 September 1933.
78. *Ibid.*, notes taken by Treasury note-taker of reception of deputation from members of the African Group by the Secretary of State, 14 November 1933. See W. M. Macmillan, *Africa Emergent* (London: Pelican, 1938), and Mona Macmillan, *Champion of Africa. W. M. Macmillan: The Second Phase* (Long Wittenam: Mona Macmillan, 1985), pp. 33–35, 88.
79. BNA BT Adm. 11/13, Jennings and Buchanan to Tshekedi, 7 November 1933.
80. *Ibid.*, 'Rough Draft Treaty'.
81. *Ibid.*, 'Report of Interview with Mr. Bushe, Legal Advisor to Dom. and Col. Off., Friday Dec 1st 1933'. Bushe in fact quickly saw that the implications of the draft 'Treaty' were that 'the Chiefs would regain their sovereignty and thus be in a position to negotiate their own future.' See Mulligan, *Jennings,* p. 476.
82. *Ibid.*, Sir E. J. Harding to Buchahan, Personal, 12 December 1933.
83. *Ibid.*, Buchanan to Harding, 19 December 1933. Buchanan's letter was in fact signed for him by Jennings, and the officials at the Dominions office believed that it had been written by Jennings and considered taking legal action on some of the statements. Mulligan, 'Jennings', p. 480.
84. BNA BT Adm. 11/13, Harding to Buchanan, 11 January 1933.
85. PRO DO 35 386/10817/38, Malcolm MacDonald, minute of 15 October 1933 on interview with Buchanan.
86. BNA BT Adm. 11/13, Tshekedi to Jennings and Buchanan, 20 November 1933.
87. *Ibid.*, Tshekedi to Jennings, 13 January 1934.
88. PRO DO 35 386/10817/37, unsigned brief for Secretary of State.
89. BNA BT Adm 11/13, 'Notes of a Deputation to the Secretary of State for the Dominions from the Anti-Slavery and Aborigines Protection Society, Tuesday, 16th January, 1934. Notes taken by Treasury Reporter.'
90. BNA BT Adm. 11/13, Harding to Harris, 1 February 1933. Also reprinted in the *Anti Slavery Reporter,* April 1934.
91. BNA BT Adm. 11/13, Jennings and Buchanan to Tshekedi, 17 January 1933.

EPILOGUE: MYTHS AND AMBIGUITIES

1. BNA BT Adm. 12/1, Proceedings of the Commission of Enquiry at Palapye Road, 13 September 1933.
2. TKP 72, evidence of Matome, sworn before R. P. Garrett, J.P., at Palapye Road, 7 October 1933.
3. NAZ Bu 5/2/2, Burns to Helen (his daughter), 17 September 1933.
4. University of Witwatersrand, Ballinger Papers A.3.1.4.4., D. G. McLaggan to Howard Pim, 28 September 1933.
5. BNA S 349/9 European residents of Lobatsi to Resident Commissioner, n.d., but circa late September/early October 1933.
6. *Ibid.*, C. Ledeboer, Resident Magistrate, Lobatsi, to Government Secretary, 16 October 1933.
7. *Ibid.*, Nettelton to Government Secretary, 2 January 1933.
8. Interview with Mr P. W. McIntosh, 12 September 1983.
9. Ballinger Papers A.3.1.39, Simon Ratshosa to Miss M. Hodgson, 25 September 1933.
10. Personal communication from Jeff Ramsay, 7 June 1987.
11. BNA S 365/10, Potts to Neale, Personal, 19 December 1933.

12. BNA/BNB, *Hansard,* House of Commons, Supply Committee, 5 March 1934, columns 1559–68.
13. *Ibid.,* column 1552.
14. *Ibid.,* column 1556.
15. *Ibid.,* column 1561.
16. *Ibid.,* column 1568.
17. *Evans, Adventurous Life,* p. 196.
18. *Ibid.*
19. *Natal Mercury,* 12 September 1933.
20. The *Friend,* Bloemfontein, 12 September 1933.
21. PRO DO 35 452/106391, notes by Shirley Eales on conversation with Dr Bodenstein, 12 September 1933.
22. *Ibid.,* Liesching to Secretary of State, 16 September 1933.
23. *Ibid.,* notes by Eales.
24. Mary Benson Personal Papers, notes from the official who wished to remain anonymous.
25. Rey, *Diaries,* p. 246. Entry for Wednesday, 12 December 1935.
26. *Ibid.,* p. 267. Entry for Monday, 13 to Saturday, 18 July 1936.
27. 'Tshekedi Khama and Another v. the High Commissioner', *The High Commission Territories Law Reports: 'Decisions of the High Court and Special Courts of Basutoland, the Bechuanaland Protectorate and Swaziland, 1926–1953',* ed. Sir Harold William, C.M.G. (Maseru: 1935), p. 31.
28. The above is in part based on Crowder, 'Tshekedi Khama's Opposition to British Rule', pp. 208–12.
29. Rey, *Diaries,* p. 278. Entry for Monday, 23 to Sunday, 29 November 1935.
30. Interview with Mr Justice Isaacs, Lobatse, 3 April 1933.
31. BNA S 363/6/3, Chief Tshekedi at an informal meeting held by the High Commissioner with Chiefs at Gaborone on 14 October 1943.
32. Rey, *Diaries.* Entry for Tuesday, 15 June 1937.
33. *Ibid.* Entry for Friday, 23 April 1937.
34. Parsons, conclusion in Rey, *Diaries.*
35. Rey, *Diaries.* Entry for Tuesday, 15 June 1937.
36. The *Star,* Johannesburg, 23 September 1933.
37. Margery Perham, *African Apprenticeship: An Autobiographical Journey* (London: Faber and Faber, 1974), pp. 206–7. The orders for his books are to be found scattered in files in his papers at Pilikwe, which are kept with his library. It is not clear how many of his books were lost when his house in Serowe was burnt in 1951.
38. BNA S 358/6, Tshekedi to Sir Herbert Stanley, 13 January 1934, with enclosure.
39. Tshekedi Khama, 'Chieftainship under Indirect Rule', *Journal of the Royal African Society,* 140 (July 1936): 251–61. It was written in reply to an article published in the same journal the previous year by Victor Murray entitled 'Education under Indirect Rule'.
40. *Ibid.,* p. 255.
41. *Ibid.,* p. 253, quoting Moton, *What the Negro Thinks.*
42. See PRO DO 35 386/10817/21, Rey to Eales, enclosing extract from letter from Resident Magistrate, Lobatsi, to Resident Commissioner, 11 August 1933.
43. See 116 above.
44. TKP 73, Tshekedi to Simon Ratshosa, 15 November 1933.
45. BNA S 352/8, Simon Ratshosa to Rey, 1 September 1933.
46. BNA S 352/7, Simon Ratshosa to Government Secretary, 23 October 1933.
47. BNA S 422/7/1, Simon Ratshosa to Rey, 21 December 1936.
48. TKP 73, Moanaphuti Segolodi to Tshekedi, 3 November 1933. Trans. Glorious Gumbo.
49. University of Cape Town Library MSS Collection, W. G. Ballinger Papers, BC 347 G2 I 5, Moanaphuti to Miss M. L. Hodgson, 6 October 1933.
50. Mary Benson Personal Papers. Notes supplied by the official who requested anonymity.

51. Draft of the letter to the High Commissioner from Tshekedi made by Douglas Buchanan. Photocopy kindly supplied by Neil Parsons, who obtained it from Mary Benson.

52. *Ibid.*

53. TKP 55, opinion by Dingle Foot, 21 January 1952.

54. See Michael Crowder, 'Professor Macmillan goes on Safari: The British Government Observer Team and the Crisis over the Seretse Khama Marriage', in Shula Marks and Hugh Macmillan (eds), *Africa and Empire. W. M. Macmillan, Historian and Social Critic.* (London: Institute of Commonwealth Studies, forthcoming).

55. TKP 55, Tshekedi, writing from exile in Rametsana to his lawyer in London, Graham Page, 18 February 1952. In his letter Tshekedi refers to Evans as Lord Mountbaton.

56. PRO DO 35 452/20283/114, Potts to Government Secretary, 21 November 1933. See also 20283/121.

57. A. A. Frew, *Prince George's African Tour* (London: Blackie and Son Ltd., 1934) ch. 21, 'Chief Tshekedi Khama'.

58. F. Leslie Burch, *With Prince George through South Africa* (London: Macmillan, 1934), p. 73.

59. *Illustrated London News,* 29 February 1936.

60. University of the Witwatersrand, Cullen Library, J. Howard Pim Papers, Ba 9/1. Sir Alan Pim to Howard Pim, 4 October 1933.

61. *Cape Times,* 7 October 1933.

62. *Hansard,* 5th series, Parliamentary Debates, House of Lords, vol. 88, 1932–1933 Session, 26 July 1933. Debate on 'Conditions in South African Protectorates', columns 1121–30.

63. Cmd. 4368.

64. J. H. Driberg, 'Khama's Country', *New Statesman,* 6 January 1934.

65. Leonard Barnes, 'The Bechuanaland Crisis', *Time and Tide,* 7 October 1933.

66. A. Victor Murray to the editor of the *Manchester Guardian,* 27 September 1933.

67. See his article in the *Journal of the Royal African Society.*

68. Norman Leys letter to the editor, *Time and Tide,* 14 October 1933.

69. BNA BT Adm. 11/3, 'Mr Buchanan's Visit to Oxford'.

70. Rhodes University Library, Grahamstown, PR 3348, Eleanor Hull to Bishop Ferguson Davie, i/c Anglican Hostel, Fort Hare.

71. TKP 73, 'The Big Six'—Independent African National Congress, Cape Town, to Tshekedi, 22 September 1933.

72. *Daily Mail,* 13 October 1933.

73. BNA BT Adm. C/4/635, Buchanan to High Commissioner, 26 September 1933.

74. *Ibid.*

75. TKP 70, letter dated 19 December 1933. The amount contributed by each of the thirty-two subscribers is listed by his name. The covering letter acknowledges that events have overtaken them, but that they send Tshekedi the money anyway. The reason for the delay was that the man in charge of the money was sent to hospital. Trans. Glorious Gumbo.

76. *Northampton Evening Telegraph,* 7 October 1933.

77. TKP 73, Harold Moody to Tshekedi, 30 September 1933.

78. Eslanda Goode Robeson, *African Journey* (New York: John Day & Co., 1945), p. 64. I am grateful to Andrew Roberts for this reference.

79. For instance *Sierra Leone Daily Mail,* Nigerian *Daily Times, Lagos Weekly Record, Gold Coast Independent.*

80. TKP 73, the Rev. S. C. Wiserman to Tshekedi, 25 November 1933.

81. Max Gluckman, *Analysis of a Social Situation in Modern Zululand.* (Manchester: Manchester University Press, for the Rhodes Livingstone Institute, 2nd. imp., 1968).

82. *Ibid.,* p. 10.

83. Interview with Mr Phinehas McIntosh, Serowe, 12 October 1984.

84. Interview with Mrs Pretorius, aged about 79 (who came to Serowe in 1923), 12 October 1984.

85. Gluckman, *Analysis of a Social Situation,* pp. 25–26.

86. BNA S 350/11, Lugard to Rey, 16 November 1933.
87. *Ibid.*, Rey to Lugard, 6 December 1933.
88. This information was given to me by Mr Dennis Atkins, a former officer of the Bechuanaland Protectorate Administration, December 1986.
89. Interviews Serowe conducted in Setswana and transcribed into English by Odirile Gabasiane, December 1983/January 1984. Mr Radisego Diseko, Mokoshwane Ward, Serowe. Born 1903.
90. *Ibid.* Mr Motsolathebe Dipatane, Konyana Ward, Mahalapye. Born 1905.
91. *Ibid.*, Mr Ranko Monnaesi, Maboledi ward, Pilikwe. Born 1895.
92. *Ibid.*, Mr Tomeletso Tom Kgosi, Mowane Ward, Serowe. Born 1901.
93. BNA DCS 16/9, 'Interview between High Commissioner, Tshekedi Khama, Bathoen II, etc. Cape Town, 23–24 February 1934'.

GLOSSARY

NGWATO:	the eponymous founder of the Ngwato state.
MONGWATO:	an individual member of the Ngwato state.
BANGWATO:	more than one member of the Ngwato state, or the population as a whole. Can be used adjectivally, as in Bangwato women and children.
SENGWATO:	the dialect of Setswana spoken by the people of the Ngwato state.
GAMANGWATO:	the territory of the Ngwato state.

COLONIAL VARIANTS

BAMANGWATO, MANGWATO:	Bangwato.
MASARWA:	Basarwa (Bushmen).
BECHUANA:	Batswana, i.e., the Tswana peoples. Hence Motswana, an individual Tswana, and Setswana, the language of the Tswana peoples.
BECHUANALAND:	Botswana or the Tswana 'together'.

GENERAL

KGOTLA:	as a place, the forum in which the Chief dispensed justice and made political and administrative decisions, in consultation with his headmen and royal uncles and the adult male members of the 'Tribe'; as an institution, a court rather like the Icelandic 'Thing'.
MORAFE:	the nation or community. This was translated by the colonial rulers as the 'Tribe'. Accordingly, under colonial rule the eight Tswana *morafe* that were incorporated by the British into the Bechuanaland Pro-

tectorate were called Tribes, hence the Bamangwato Tribe. Though in other colonial territories the word *tribe* was resented as a denigratory colonial appellation, it was freely adopted by the Batswana themselves and is used in post-colonial Botswana. Thus, in deference to nationalist sentiments in other parts of Africa about this term, the Native Authority appointed by the British to replace the exiled Regent Tshekedi Khama and the exiled Chief Seretse Khama, was designated 'African Authority' rather than 'Tribal Authority', the title used by the present representative of Seretse's son and successor as Kgosi, Chief Seretse Khama Ian Khama.

KGOSI: the title by which Tswana rulers were designated, translated in pre-colonial times as 'King'. Thus Tshekedi's father, Khama III, was known as King Khama III or 'the Great' by the British before his state was incorporated into the Bechuanaland Protectorate in 1885. Thereafter he was known as Chief Khama. The term *kgosi* is given as of right both to the hereditary Chief and to the Regent acting for a minor or incapacitated Chief. It would be used as a matter of courtesy for a royal headman acting for a Chief or his Regent.

BIBLIOGRAPHY

Because the issues Tshekedi raised during the crisis of 1933 were so fundamental to the colonial relationship, and because the occasion for his raising them—the 'flogging' of a white man—was so sensational in the context of the colonial order of the day, the events that took place in an otherwise obscure backwater of the British Empire in the months of September and October 1933 became headline news in Britain and South Africa and were the subject of numerous editorials, leading articles and letters to the editor. The issues involved in the crisis were debated in both Houses of Parliament. The files of the Dominions Office were thick with telegrams, despatches and letters concerning these events. Humanitarian lobbyists had a field day. Several of the participants wrote their own accounts of what took place. Most exciting of all for the researcher, the black voice, so often mute in such situations, either because the participants were illiterate, or were diffident about putting pen to paper, comes through loud and clear in the Bechuanaland of the 1930s.

The young Regent of the Bangwato was educated and had a lawyer's approach to his task, putting everything on paper and carefully preserving his records. The British Administration, staffed mainly by former police officers rather than regular colonial officials, inherited one virtue from their erstwhile profession—at least as far as the historian is concerned: they took down evidence, much of it verbatim. The records of the Bechuanaland Protectorate Administration are full of 'statements' by blacks made at interviews, meetings or sometimes just casually. The members of the Bamangwato Tribal Administration learnt something of this habit from their British administrators, and as a result black attitudes to the events of 1933 are richly documented. The historian is thus able to provide a 'thick description' of the colonial relationship between British and Bangwato, such as Max Gluckman did in his famous *Analysis of a Social Situation in Modern Zululand* (Manchester: Manchester University Press for the Rhodes-Livingstone Institute, 2nd imp., 1968). Using evidence gathered as a participant observer, Gluckman sought to unravel social and political relationships in Zululand in terms of the ceremonies that surrounded the opening of a new bridge in Mahlabitini District by the Chief Native Commissioner for

Zululand in the presence of the Regent of the Zulu. Gluckman's study, as well as Shula Marks's recent work, *The Ambiguities of Dependence in South Africa: Class, Nationalism, and the State in Twentieth Century Natal* (Johannesburg: Ravan Press, 1986) have been points of departure for the present book. The conclusions reached, however, are somewhat different.

Like any other student of the Batswana, I have been heavily dependent on the works of Isaac Schapera, of which only the principal ones are listed here. There is a full bibliography of his publications on the Batswana in *The Tswana* (London: International African Institute, 1976). See in particular his *Handbook of Tswana Law and Custom* (London: International Institute of African Languages and Culture, 1938), *Married Life in an African Tribe* (London: Faber and Faber, 1940), 'The Political Organization of the Ngwato in the Bechuanaland Protectorate' in M. Fortes and E. E. Evans Pritchard (eds), *African Political Systems* (London: International Institute of African Languages and Cultures, 1940), *Tribal Legislation among the Tswana of the Bechuanaland Protectorate* (London: London School of Economics, Monographs on Social Anthropology, No. 9, 1943) and *Tribal Innovators: Tswana Chiefs and Social Change, 1795–1940* (London: Athlone Press, 1970).

PRINCIPAL BOOKS AND ARTICLES CONSULTED

Amery, L.S. *My Political Life: 'War and Peace' 1914–29*. London: Hutchinson, 1953.

Benson, Mary. *Tshekedi Khama*. London: Faber and Faber, 1960.

Blackwell, Leslie. *Blackwell Remembers*. Cape Town: Howard Timmins, 1971.

Burch, F. Leslie. *With Prince George through South Africa*. London: Macmillan, 1934.

Crowder, Michael. 'Tshekedi Khama and Opposition to the British Administration of the Bechuanaland Protectorate, 1926–1936'. *Journal of African History* 26 (1985).

Frew, A. A. *Prince George's African Tour*. London: Blackie and Son, 1934.

Harris, José. *William Beveridge: A Biography*. Oxford: Clarendon Press, 1977.

Hyam, Ronald. *The Failure of South African Expansion, 1908–1948*, London: Macmillan, 1972.

Khama, Tshekedi. 'Chieftainship under Indirect Rule'. *Journal of the Royal African Society* 140 (July 1936).

Lewis, Ethelreda. *Wild Deer*. London: Faber and Faber, 1933. New edition edited by Tim Couzens, Cape Town: David Philip, 1938.

Mountevans, Admiral Lord. *Adventurous Life*. London: Hutchinson, 1946.

Mulligan, Kathleen. 'Alfred E. Jennings: The Political Activities of the London Missionary Society in Bechuanaland, 1900–1935'. Unpublished Ph.D. diss. St John's University, 1974.

Macmillan, W. M. *Africa Emergent*. London: Pelican, 1938.

Parsons, Neil. 'The Economic History of Khama's Country in Botswana, 1844–1930', in Robin Palmer and Neil Parsons (eds), *The Roots of Rural Poverty in Central and Southern Africa*. London: Heinemann Educational Books, 1977.

Parsons, Q. N. ' "Khama and Co." and the Jousse Trouble, 1910–1916'. *Journal of African History* 16:3 (1975).

Perham, Margery. *African Apprenticeship: An Autobiographical Journey*. London: Faber and Faber, 1974.

Pound, Renginald. *Evans of the Broke, A Biography of Admiral Lord Mountevans*. London: Oxford University Press, 1963.

Ramsay, Jeff. 'Resistance from Subordinate Groups: BaBirwa, Bakgatla Mmanaana and Bakalanga Nswaszwi', in R. F. Morton and Jeff Ramsay (eds), *Birth of a Nation: The Making of Botswana*. Gaborone: Longman, 1987.
Sillery, Anthony. *Botswana: A Short Political History*. London: Methuen, 1974.

PRIMARY SOURCES

Botswana National Archives
Papers of the Bechuanaland Protectorate Administration, Secretariat, Mafeking.
Papers of the Resident Magistrate's Office, Serowe.
Papers of the Bamangwato Tribal Administration, Serowe.

Tshekedi Khama Papers, Pilikwe
Some of the files are in the personal care of Leapeetswe Khama and are indicated as such in the notes.

Public Records Office, London
Papers of the Dominions Office.

University of the Witwatersrand Library
Ballinger Papers (W. G. Ballinger and Margaret Hodson)
Howard Pim Papers
Institute of Race Relations Papers

University of Cape Town
W. G. Ballinger Papers
Z. K. Matthews Papers

Rhodes University, Grahamstown
Fort Hare University College Papers
Lovedale Papers

British Library Colindale
Newspapers

ACKNOWLEDGMENTS

It was in the course of conducting research for a new biography of Tshekedi that I began to realise the central role that his 'flogging' of the young white man played not only in his career but also in the colonial history of Botswana. The rich documentation of the events following on the 'flogging' offered unique insights into relationships between African and European, and analysis of them would heighten understanding of the nature of the colonial situation. Though I had toyed idly with the idea of a separate essay on the crisis of 1933, it was only after discussing it with John Middleton on a visit to Yale in December 1985 that the idea of writing a book about it crystallised. He was so excited by the possibilities of a full monograph on the subject that he arranged a meeting for me with Ellen Graham of Yale University Press the next day. There, accompanied by Mary Smith, author of that splendid account of the life of Baba of Karo,[1] I told the story with apparently as much enthusiasm as I had the night before, and I was asked to submit a synopsis. The result was that two months later I was under contract to produce the book presented here.

That I was able to finish the book within a year of being commissioned to write it is due above all to Deakin University, where I was appointed Gordon Fellow from August to October 1986. This Fellowship, which I held in the School of Social Sciences, allowed me to carry on with a piece of current research or writing unencumbered by teaching. To the Vice Chancellor of Deakin University, Professor Malcolm Skilbeck, and to Jim Polhemus, Dean of the School of Social Sciences, who first encouraged me to apply for the Fellowship, I am especially grateful for the hospitality they and their colleagues showed me while I was at their university. In the School of Social Sciences, I received help and advice from a number of quarters. I am particularly grateful to John Perry, anthropologist and student of the Basotho, for his perceptive and encouraging comments on my study of a related people, the Batswana. Roy Hay read the nine chapters I had written while I was at the School from

1. Mary Smith, *Baba of Karo: A Woman of the Moslem Hausa* (London: Faber and Faber, 1954).

the point of view of the non-Africanist historian and saved me from many instances of the vice of over-specialisation. He, together with John Craig, initiated me into the mysteries of the Mackintosh computer and on several occasions saved text I thought lost for ever. I am particularly grateful to Professor Francis West for his friendship and for comments on my ideas in discussion, as I am to Magnus Clarke, Ian Cowman, Bill Rubinstein, Belinda Yuille, Aynsley Kellow, the very helpful Sub-Dean of the School, and Michael Muetzelfeldt of Melbourne University, who like me was also a Visiting Fellow in the School. Above all I owe a great debt to Jim Polhemus, who shares the same pleasurable affliction that many of us who have worked on Botswana do: Botswanaphilia.

The research on the life of Tshekedi Khama, out of which this book grew, began, properly, in Botswana. I am particularly grateful to the University of Botswana, which made me two research grants to undertake a study of the Native Proclamations 34 and 35 of 1934, which were central to the struggle between Tshekedi and the British Administration that culminated in the crisis of 1933. It was as a result of my research on these two Proclamations that I decided to write a biography of Tshekedi and, much later, this book.

I am especially indebted to Leapeetswe and Sekgoma Khama, Tshekedi's elder sons, who gave me unrestricted permission to consult their late father's papers in Pilikwe, and to Leapeetswe for letting me see some of the files in his personal care in Gaborone. These include the file on Tshekedi's suspension in 1933 and the letters of support which were catalogued by Mary Benson as nos 72 and 73 respectively. These files were, as the endnotes show, vital to the realisation of this present book. I also owe a particular debt to Leapeetswe and his wife, Siode, for making me feel part of their family while I was working on Tshekedi's papers, and to Tshekedi's widow, the Mohumagadi Ella Khama, who gave me hospitality on my visits to her home in Pilikwe where the bulk of Tshekedi's papers are stored.

The Director and Staff of the Botswana National Archives were most generous with their time and in giving permission to photostat documents. This meant that in the midst of a busy schedule as Professor and Head of the Department of History at the University of Botswana I was able to go through a much wider range of files related to the biography (and incidentally this book) than would otherwise have been possible. In this connexion I would like to express my warm thanks to Mr Gilbert N. Mpolokeng. I was given considerable help by the Library of the University of Botswana and in particular its Librarian, Mrs Kay Raseroka, and the Curator of its excellent Botswana Collection, Ms Karla Jones.

In Botswana I was given generous support by the University's Research and Publication Committee, as well as two grants for local research by the Shell Company of Botswana, to whose Managing Director, Mr Philip Steenkamp, I should like here to express my thanks. I should also like to acknowledge the support of the Ford Foundation, the Anglo-American/DeBeers Chairman's Fund and the Nuffield Foundation, which made me grants for researching and writing the biography of Tshekedi out of which this present study arose.

I completed the writing up of this book while at the Institute of Commonwealth Studies of the University of London. My late friend James Pope-Hennessy once wrote that 'writing is a lonely business'.[2] I am especially grateful to the Director of the Institute, Professor Shula Marks, for offering me an 'academic home' in London, and to her staff for making me

2. 'Writing, like living, is a lonely business'. James Pope-Hennessy to Diana Crawford in *A Lonely Business. A Self-Portrait of James Pope-Hennessy,* ed. Peter Quennell (London: Weidenfield and Nicholson, 1981), frontispiece.

feel so welcome. It certainly made my task a less solitary one. I was very fortunate to have a month-long residency at the Rockefeller Center at Bellagio, where in a most beautiful setting on the banks of Lake Como I was able to finalise the manuscript for press. I am deeply grateful to my literary agent, Andrew Best, for encouragement and advice, to Jackie Hunt for help in finalising the manuscript for publication, and to Jackie Guy for assistance with research for the illustrations.

During my work on papers connected with Tshekedi's life at the Rhodes House Library, Oxford, I was offered hospitality by the Warden and Fellows of St Antony's, where I was appointed Senior Associate Fellow for the Hilary and Trinity terms of 1986. I should like to express especial thanks to Mr A. H. M. Kirk-Greene of St Antony's and Mr Alan Bell of the Rhodes House Library for their assistance to me while I was in Oxford.

I should also like to acknowledge the assistance of the Public Records Office, and especially my old friend Robert Smith, who lives within walking distance of the Kew depository, and while I was in Botswana kindly looked up files for me and made notes and photostats from them.

Mary Benson, who wrote the first full-length biography of Tshekedi, has been most generous with her papers, most of which are deposited in Rhodes House. She very kindly let me see some of the documents and letters she had retained for her continued use: several of these proved vital to my understanding of this story, which she first told in detail in her chapter 'The Navy on Dry Land' in *Tshekedi Khama*,[3] and have since been deposited in the Rhodes House Library. All scholars of the colonial period of Botswana's history owe Mary Benson a great debt not only for cataloguing Tshekedi's personal papers but making her own papers available to them.

I first tried out the ideas that inform this study at consecutive seminars at the University of Edinburgh's Centre for African Studies and the St Antony's African Studies Seminar. I am grateful to Dr Ian Duffield and Professor Kenneth Kirkwood respectively for providing me with the opportunity to discuss my ideas before I began writing the book. In Australia, I was able to discuss these ideas in the context of writing the book itself at seminars at Deakin University, arranged by Bill Rubinstein; at La Trobe, arranged by David Dorward; at Sydney, arranged by Derek Schreuder; and Western Australia, arranged by Pen Hetherington. To them all I should like to express my thanks for the lively comments I received in discussion.

No book on colonial Botswana can be published without the appropriate acknowledgement of the monumental contribution to our understanding of Tswana society under colonial rule provided by the work of Professor Isaac Schapera.[4] I have been privileged to discuss some of my ideas with him and to have benefited from his generosity with his own papers and notes. If I have any understanding of Tswana society, it is to him and to my friend Neil Parsons that I owe my greatest debt. If my understanding is faulty it is because of my failure to listen to them carefully enough or read what they have written with sufficient attention. To Neil my debt is incalculable. Author of a superb study of Tshekedi's father, Khama III,[5] and a forthcoming biography of Seretse Khama, his nephew and ward, Neil offered me his

3. Mary Benson, *Tshekedi Khama* (London: Faber and Faber, 1960).

4. For the principal works on the Batswana by Isaac Schapera see the Bibliography, p. 237 above.

5. Q. N. Parsons, 'Khama III, the Bamangwato and the British, 1895–1923', Ph.D. diss., University of Edinburgh, 1973.

generous friendship and hours of his time, some of it happily spent together in Serowe and Pilikwe, during which even my most naive questions were answered with Neil's unfailing charm and unrivalled knowledge of colonial Gamangwato.

Other colleagues at the University of Botswana who helped me directly or indirectly in my search for understanding of Tswana society are Professor Thomas Tlou, the Vice-Chancellor, who is currently working on the early life of Sir Seretse Khama; the former Vice-Chancellor, Professor J. M. Turner; Professor Leonard Ngcongco, who succeeded me as Professor of History; David Kiyaga-Mulindwa, who gave me so much friendship and help during my stay in Botswana, as did Fred Morton, Brian Mokopakgosi, Part Mgadla, Kevin Shillington, now in London where he made very helpful comments on the Prologue, and Athaliah Molokomme. Jeff Ramsay, a visiting research student whose work on the Bakwena and the Bangwaketse promises to make a major contribution to southern African history, offered me many valuable insights into the colonial situation in Botswana while I was in Gaborone and made helpful and trenchant comments on the manuscript.

I owe a special debt to the students in the Department of History research seminar from whom I learnt an immense amount about their country and its history. I can only mention here those who conducted fieldwork for me or translated letters used in this book: Odirile Gabasiane, Theophilus Mooko, Keene Boikhutso and Glorious Gumbo.

For the translation of material from Afrikaans into English I am grateful to Alan Mabin and Jane Starfield.

I have benefited considerably from many conversations about my ongoing work with my neighbour, Professor Jean LaFontaine, who often brought me up sharp when my ideas were running away with themselves or, as more often was the case, were sticking in a rut. I am also grateful to her daughter, Amanda Sackur, who gave me help in locating documents and information that I needed before leaving for Australia. Professor Leonard Thompson, who read the manuscript for Yale University Press, agreed to shed the customary anonymity of the publisher's reader, and I am much indebted to him for his helpful suggestions for revision, as I am to Charles Grench, my editor at the Press, and to Otto Bohlmann, who did as fine a job of manuscript editing as I have yet seen and also made some very helpful suggestions as to how the organization of the Prologue might be improved. Roland Brown made many perceptive comments on the wider implications of the 'story', which I have done my best to take into account.

Finally, I would like to thank Lady Khama, Jackie Khama and Major General Ian Khama, present *kgosi* of the Bangwato, who recommended me to his deputy in Serowe, for their kindness to me throughout my stay in Gaborone and on visits since.

INDEX

References to Tshekedi Khama and Charles Rey have not been included as they are cited throughout the text.